With my songs the evening spread echoing
And the early dawn emerged with a good sound.
The firm mountains stood echoing therewith
And the trees stood deep rooted.

Singing for Power: The Song Magic of the
Papago Indians of Southern Arizona,
Mary Murray Underhill

The Rhetoric Society of America—Organized in 1968 for the advancement of the study of rhetoric, "The purpose of this Society shall be to gather from all relevant fields of study, and to disseminate among its members, current knowledge of rhetoric, broadly construed; to identify new areas within the subject of rhetoric in which research is especially needed, and to stimulate such research; to encourage experimentation in the teaching of rhetoric; to facilitate professional cooperation among its members; to organize meetings at which members may exchange findings and ideas; and to sponsor the publication of newsletters and reports concerning all aspects of rhetoric."

—RSA Constitution

Making
and
Unmaking
the Prospects for Rhetoric

Selected Papers from the 1996
Rhetoric Society of America Conference

Editor

Theresa Enos
University of Arizona

Associate Editor

Richard McNabb
University of Arizona

Consulting Editors

Roxanne Mountford
University of Arizona
Carolyn Miller
North Carolina State University

 LAWRENCE ERLBAUM ASSOCIATES, PUBLISHERS
1997   Mahwah, New Jersey

Lawrence Erlbaum Associates, Inc., Publishers
10 Industrial Avenue
Mahwah, New Jersey 07430

Library of Congress Cataloging-in-Publication Data

Rhetoric Society of America. Conference (7th : 1996 : Tucson, Ariz.)
    Making and unmaking the prospects for rhetoric : selected papers
from the 1996 Rhetoric Society of America Conference / editor,
Theresa Enos : associate editor, Richard McNabb : consulting
editors, Roxanne Mountford, Carolyn Miller.
        p. cm.
    Selected papers from the seventh biennial Rhetoric Society of
America, held May 30-June 1, 1996 in Tucson, Arizona.
    Includes bibliographical references and index.
    ISBN 0-8058-2014-0 (c : alk. paper). -- ISBN 0-8058-2015-9 (p :
alk. paper)
    1. Rhetoric--Congresses. I. Enos, Theresa. II. McNabb, Richard.
III. Title.
P301.R4714 1996
808--dc21   96-45595
                                                    CIP

Books published by Lawrence Erlbaum Associates are printed
on acid-free paper, and their bindings are chosen
for strength and durability.

Printed in the United States of America

10 9 8 7 6 5 4 3 2 1

Contents

Preface

The seventh biennial Rhetoric Society of America conference came to Tucson, Arizona—"*les esperamos en Tucson.*" Held in the heart-of-the-desert Doubletree Hotel May 30-June 1 1996, the conference attracted some 325 participants at 83 panels. The twenty-fifth anniversary of Lloyd Bitzer and Edwin Black's *The Prospect of Rhetoric* gave scholars and teachers in various disciplines from all over the country the opportunity to talk about new prospects for rhetoric.

The 1996 conference was chaired by RSA president, Carolyn R. Miller from North Carolina State University, assisted by the Program Committee: Gregory Clark from Brigham Young University, Susan Jarratt from Miami University, Edward Schiappa from the University of Minnesota, and Marie Secor from Penn State University. Local arrangements was my purlieu, and I gratefully acknowledge support from the Department of English and the College of the Humanities at the University of Arizona, the able assistance from Melody Bowdon, and the professionalism and grace of the Tucson Doubletree Hotel staff. I thank Roxanne Mountford and Carolyn Miller for peer reviewing the seventy submitted conference papers that prospected the past in order to gain new perspectives for rhetoric and from them selecting the twenty-four presented in this volume, and I am grateful to Bill Endres for coming up with a title that reflects the vision and content of the published conference proceedings. I especially thank Richard McNabb, associate editor of this volume, for his painstaking preparation of manuscripts for printing. Introducing you to the selected papers from the 1996 RSA conference is Roxanne Mountford's own essay, "Making and Unmaking the Prospects for Rhetoric."

Theresa Enos
University of Arizona

ROXANNE MOUNTFORD

University of Arizona

Making and Unmaking the Prospects for Rhetoric

"We have rights over the words that make and unmake the world."
—Guillaume Apollinaire

If this book were to be dedicated to a god, that god would be Janus, the god of gates and passages who looks forward and back. Commemorating the twenty-fifth anniversary of *The Prospect of Rhetoric*'s publication, the essays in this volume, originally presented at the 1996 Meeting of the Rhetoric Society of America, illustrate a discipline at odds over the future. Like the participants of the January 1970 Wingspread Conference and May 1970 National Conference on Rhetoric that produced *The Prospect of Rhetoric*, 1996 RSA conferees were asked to present their vision of rhetoric studies or to demonstrate what rhetoric studies could be by example. Perhaps the most surprising event of the conference was the first plenary session, in which Lloyd F. Bitzer and Edwin Black withdrew aspects of the revolution they began in 1971.

These proceedings occur at a watershed moment for rhetoric. Other fields, motivated by questions of self-representation and the status of knowledge, have discovered rhetorical criticism and begun to study rhetoric through fresh disciplinary perspectives. The new anthology on rhetoric, *Rhetoric: Concepts, Definitions, Boundaries* by William A. Covino and David A. Jolliffe, illustrates this trend. Included in the volume are essays written by and for scholars in other disciplines but which Covino and Jolliffe classify within rhetoric studies (e.g., bell hooks, "Culture to Culture: Ethnography and Cultural Studies as Critical Intervention"). Another anthology that shows the inroads of rhetoric into other disciplines is Bender and Wellbery's *The Ends of Rhetoric: History, Theory, and Practice*, based on a Stanford University Comparative Literature conference in 1987. The collection treats rhetoric as "a universal of literary production and reception" that allows comparative literature scholars to link their work, through rhetoric, to an "interdisciplinary matrix that touches on such fields as philosophy, linguistics, communication studies, psychoanalysis, cognitive science, sociology, anthropology, and political theory" (vii-viii). Rhetorical theory and criticism is now a substantive part of the work of such varied scholars as Emily Martin (medical anthropologist) and James Clifford (historian), prominent scholars in their disciplines.

This trend was welcomed by authors of the 1971 "Report of the Committee on the Scope of Rhetoric and the Place of Rhetorical Studies in Higher Education" in *The Prospect of Rhetoric*. Concerned that "communication problems to some degree underlie racial conflict, antiwar protest, alienation of the young, attempts to suppress free speech, campus disruptions, and inattention to differing views," they recommended that "although the primary responsibility for the study of language and symbols may rest with one or two groups of teachers (commonly called "departments"), a concern for how language in particular and symbols in general affect their creators and audience should not be narrowly confined, but shared by scholars in whatever fields of learning symbols are prominently employed" (209, 213). Defining rhetorical study as a concern with "the process by which symbols and systems of symbols have influence upon beliefs, values, attitudes, and actions" and the methodologies for rhetorical study as "philosophical, historical, critical, empirical, creative, or pedagogical," the authors of this report, as well as the authors of many essays in *The Prospect of Rhetoric*, showed an evangelical belief in a future with rhetoric at the heart of the curriculum (208).

At the time of these reports, higher education was undergoing tremendous expansion. Just three years before the Wingspread Conference, a small college in northeastern Ohio hired my father, with only a master's degree, from a high-school band program in Kansas City, Kansas. A scholar I met recently told me that department heads offered him jobs in the elevators at the 1971 MLA meeting. He came home from that conference with ten offers. Those of us who prepare graduate students for the present job market or have been recently looking for jobs ourselves know those days are gone. Graduate students come to us wondering what kinds of projects will make them attractive to other institutions and get them published. They look at job lists and ask us what it means to be a rhetorician in English or in speech communication: Does it come down to whether one is trained to teach composition versus public speaking? Is it acceptable to do cultural studies-type projects as a rhetorician, *really*?

In this economic climate, the tremendous optimism in interdisciplinarity expressed at the Wingspread Conference and in *The Prospect of Rhetoric* seems muted by a concern over the boundaries of our disciplines. As James Porter puts it,

> We . . . need to map out a general field of concern to call "rhetoric."
> If we become too diffuse, if we overlap too many other areas, we
> risk losing our identity. If rhetoric tries to encompass everything, it
> becomes nothing; rhetoric as a field disappears. On the other
> extreme, if we insist on too rigid boundaries, then we risk
> irrelevance, we risk becoming overspecialized, arcane. We risk
> isolating ourselves from knowledge, from information, from the

substance of discourse—and return to a view of rhetoric as
"technical." (213)

And yet, for the younger generation of scholars, the vision of Wingspread was
prophetic: Dame Rhetoric will not be wedded to English or speech
communication; she believes in free love.

In their keynote addresses, Lloyd F. Bitzer and Edwin Black look back on
the Wingspread Conference and *The Prospect of Rhetoric* and attempt to
unmake the interdisciplinary vision presented there. Bitzer uses the following
story to illustrate how unrestricted participants at Wingspread were in their
discussions of rhetoric's scope and definition:

> After a morning session at which the notion of "rhetorical
> phenomena" had been considerably expanded, [Larry] Rosenfeld in
> the afternoon conference returned to that expansive notion and
> remarked, with seeming exasperation, "So far as I can tell, the
> notion of rhetorical phenomena includes everything but tidal
> waves." McKeon's immediate quip was: "Why not tidal waves?"
> (19-20)

Bitzer goes on to attack the "Report of the Committee on the Scope of Rhetoric
and the Place of Rhetorical Studies in Higher Education," noting that given
their definition of rhetoric, "I find it difficult to find instances of nonrhetorical
human interactions" (20). Instead, Bitzer calls for an end to universal theories
of rhetoric: "The time has come to narrow rhetoric's scope—to narrow its
territory—and to restore invention to its old position of authority and
centrality" (19).

Edwin Black also turns to McKeon as his example of what was wrong with
The Prospect of Rhetoric, noting, in retrospect, that McKeon's essay is
"abstract," "omnivorous," and "flaccid"—not unlike the rest of the volume.
McKeon's declaration of rhetoric as "an architectonic art, 'an art of structuring
all principles and products of knowing, doing, and making'" has not, in Black's
view, done anything for the field (22, 23). Nor has *The Prospect of Rhetoric*.
Black writes,

> The meaning of *rhetoric*, as a discipline, is to be found in concrete
> performances of scholarship, in engagements with specific
> discourses, in substantive acts of criticism, of analysis, of historical
> reconstruction. In the absence of such particulars, discussions of
> *rhetoric* float toward an academic version of the condition that the
> notable orator, Warren G. Harding, called "bloviation." (23)

Turning to the social upheaval that surrounded Wingspread, Black focuses on the rhetoric of the "flower children," demonstrating how he would have rhetoric study "phenomena." Focusing on a phrase that Crowley names a "common topic" of our times—"the personal is the political" (53)—Black suggests that the ideology of the cultural revolution throws into jeopardy "the continued existence of rhetoric as a discipline" (24). He warns us that viewing rhetoric as "instinctive, spontaneous, uncrafted and uncontrived" would take us away from rhetoric as it has been defined since its inception (24). And thus, by clever demonstration, he brings us back around to his original objection with McKeon's definition of rhetoric: It is *not* "everything." And with that, he reasserts a more traditional model for rhetoric as persuasion.

In contrast, the plenary addresses that follow begin with and extend the interdisciplinary view of rhetoric that Carole Blair calls rhetoric in the "post-Wingspread" world (34). While some find problems with some aspects of the book, none suggest that the wide net cast by McKeon should be reeled in. Addressing the fate of rhetoric study in speech departments after Wingspread (or "Hotel California," in her extended Eagles metaphor), Carole Blair concurs with Bitzer and Black's assessment that "unproblematically equating rhetoric with symbolicity and marking theory contribution as the unquestioned goal of rhetorical studies . . . assigned rhetorical practice and its effectivity—its political capacity to do things in the world—to disciplinary oblivion" (32). She finds it ironic that cultural studies—"an upstart, interdisciplinary group"—would begin occupying this abandoned territory and studying rhetorical practice with such "great productivity" (34). However, she does not believe that a retreat from Wingspread is possible; rather, she suggests that we take the scope and definition of rhetoric offered there and go forth to study rhetorical practice from within it.

Similarly, Patricia Bizzell and Mary Garrett begin with an interdisciplinary perspective of rhetoric and expand it, refining some issues along the way. Bizzell addresses the problem of agency, suggesting that for all their postmodern leanings, the authors of *The Prospect of Rhetoric* assume a view of the author as "unified" and "rational" that "seems most distant from our concerns" (37). She goes on to develop a new definition of rhetorical agency that takes into consideration postmodern theories of the subject in a way that does not lose sight of the exigencies of civic participation. Mary Garrett suggests that "the original conferees [of Wingspread] would be surprised, and then proud, to see how far we've come" (43). She praises the call for study of contemporary movements in *The Prospect of Rhetoric* and notes that that call has benefited the field many times over, with study of women's movements giving rise to feminist critiques of rhetorical theory, study of black power movements giving rise to critiques of rhetoric's ethnocentrism, and so forth (44). Garrett argues that the study of rhetoric in a global context is the next step. By locating ourselves in the world community, we are in a better position to evaluate who benefits from trends in rhetoric, such as study of the World Wide Web (when such a tiny percentage of the world is online) (47).

Steve Mailloux offers the most expansive and challenging interpretation of *The Prospect of Rhetoric*. In his view the humanities are the place within the university where "cultural literacy" or "cultural rhetoric" are studied. That is to say, in his view, the vision for rhetoric suggested by Wingspread could become the organizing principle for schools of humanities. He writes, "In the future rhetorical study will help organize and reconceptualize the humanities and the interpretive social sciences, meeting the intellectual and political challenges of its historical moment, as it did twenty-five years ago" (51). However, Mailloux suggests that postmodernism has fundamentally changed the terms under which the next twenty-five years will be lived, and therefore, rhetoric will have a different look. In particular, Mailloux notes that contemporary critical theorists who prefigure postmodernism embraced sophistic rhetoric, and so must we. Pointing to the work of Susan Jarratt and Victor Vitanza, Mailloux suggests that rhetoric has a philosophical perspective to offer in this postmodern moment in history, a perspective that could revitalize both the university and the community at large. Perhaps the furthest away from Edwin Black in perspective, Mailloux puts emphasis on the theoretical opportunities for rhetoric if the vision of Wingspread is extended.

Rhetoric and Community

A prominent theme in *The Prospect of Rhetoric* is the need for taking the study of rhetoric into national civic life. With the turmoil of the 1960s and early 1970s serving as a noisy backdrop to Wingspread, authors expressed hope that greater education in rhetoric would bring understanding—if not civility—to violent public debates. The question of how we define our constituents is a strong theme in this volume. Mary Garrett, in particular, extends the Wingspread call for scholarship and education on public discourse to the global community, suggesting that comparative rhetoric could enlighten our international policies and enhance public appreciation for other cultures.

However, as Bizzell argues in her keynote address, the nature of community—our theoretical understanding of what community is, and how we can come to know it—is impacted by postmodern definitions of the self. For Bizzell, postmodern notions of self do not allow us unified definitions of individual citizens—and, by extension, the idea of "community" is also thrown into question. Quoting Faigley, Bizzell argues that working with groups of students in our classrooms as though they are "communities" is hopelessly idealistic. In fact, recently, the notion of rhetoric as a "cure" for democratic process has been extended (Clark) and critiqued both from an experiential base (Mountford) and from a theoretical one (Davis).[1]

The authors of Part II address the connection of rhetoric, community, and social action. The first two papers concern the nature of our profession as a community. Henry W. Johnstone, Jr.'s essay is a personal reflection on how our profession is created in and by the pages of *Philosophy and Rhetoric*, the journal he edited from 1968 to 1976, and from 1987 to the present. Leah Ceccarelli also focuses on our profession, identifying three competing conceptions of rhetoric that have dominated our field since 1970. Arguing for an appreciation of our scholarship as plural and our perspective multiple, she suggests that there can be no reconciliation—and therefore no unified scholarly objectives—over the ends of rhetoric as they are currently conceived.

James F. Klumpp returns to the Wingspread hope that rhetoric could be the "key to *communities* successfully negotiating times of change" (80). Working with modern definitions of rhetoric that emphasize "the building of communities as a central rhetorical task," he suggests that traditional concepts of rhetoric as persuasion are not capable of resolving current social crises (78). Charles Bazerman and David Sebberson take up Carolyn Miller's theory of genre as social action to reposition rhetorical theory as an agent of democratic process. Bazerman's essay is a bibliographic history of the ways that attention to genre has moved the social sciences to take up rhetorical concerns. Bazerman suggests that viewing genre as social action offers us a way to "take up the tools and knowledge of the social sciences" and vice versa, enriching our understanding of rhetorical situations (83). Both Bazerman and Sebberson hope that the interdisciplinary study of rhetoric will help us understand the role of language in human life. Sebberson recuperates Plato and Habermas, two philosophers whose statements against rhetoric are widely understood as "antirhetorical, antidemocratic, or both" (93) but whom he sees as helpful for creating a critical rhetorical perspective that could resolve current identity and power issues in national life.

The last essay in this section, by Martha Cooper, promotes the contributions made by feminist rhetoricians to the issue of rhetoric's place in community. Her words are especially timely. Michael Leff, when asked what it would take to get a feminist essay into the pages of *Rhetorica*, said, "When I see a good one, and if my readers will tolerate it, I'll be happy to publish it." Given this response, it is not surprising that the first essay on feminism ever to be published in *Rhetorica* (Ede, Glenn, and Lunsford) came out in 1995.[2] Why has it taken so long for one of the best journals in our field to publish a feminist essay? Johnstone writes, "I don't think we [*Philosophy and Rhetoric*] have a reputation for treating feminists badly. If we had, we might have expected a torrent of contributions in protest. I do not think, on the other hand, that we are guilty of having treated feminism too well" (59).

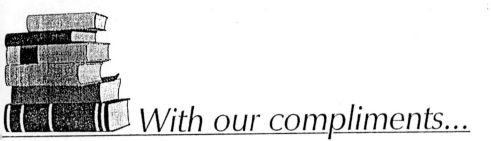
With our compliments...

Women were not included in the all-male world of Wingspread and *The Prospect of Rhetoric*, and feminists continue to sit at the borderlands of our profession's consciousness. For instance, although both feminist and African-American activists have long combined academic and social service, their work is often invisible when the field evaluates its contributions to society.[3] Martha Cooper writes,

> I was surprised to read a recent extension of the notion of critical rhetoric that lamented "while scholars sympathetic to the project of critical rhetoric have made significant theoretical advances, they still have not examined a practical application of the theory, i.e., a critical rhetor addressing an audience" (Clark 112). It seems to me that one quite viable face for the critical rhetorician is that of the feminist communication scholar who engages in ongoing struggle either to critique the grand narrative of patriarchy or to expose the operation of power in those smaller discourses that promise freedom. (102)

"Let us occupy ourselves with phenomena," Black says emphatically at the end of his keynote address (27). What practices count in Black's world view? For Cooper, the work of feminists from before Wingspread and beyond offers us a model for "how to create a new discursive space that allows for both diversity and community" (104-05). She suggests that "feminist scholarship reminds us that rhetoric can be both critical and creative, both suspicious and affirming, both resistant and renewing"—if only we all were reading it (105).

The Prospect for Rhetoric: New Perspectives

Perhaps the prospect for rhetoric is nowhere better illustrated than in the work of the scholars who are presented in the final section of these proceedings. There is little question that the work of graduate students and recent graduates can tell us much about the future of our profession (Miller 70). New scholars who were trained by the children of Wingspread begin with an interdisciplinary vision, showing us both the possibilities and potential limitations of the Wingspread vision.

The luminaries in this volume have taken to listing trends, so to introduce this section, I will follow their lead.

(1) **Cultural Histories**. In his survey of rhetoric curricula across the United States, Thomas P. Miller found that many graduate instructors are turning away from the history-survey approach to teaching rhetoric and are opting to teach more depth in their courses, including "developments in literacy, education, politics, and the pragmatics of discourse" in historical periods

alongside canonical texts (76). However, to know more about the context in which rhetorics were written and taught, we need new archival research, research that uncovers both texts and cultural histories of those texts. Susan Kates presents both kinds of history in her essay on Mary Augusta Jordan's rhetoric. In her study of the ways women, African-Americans, and laborers were educated in rhetoric between 1889 and 1937, Kates uncovered what she calls "activist writing and speaking instruction" and the textbook of one such activist instructor (109). By studying the courses that she gave in her 37-year career at Smith as well as her textbook, Kates makes the case that Jordan "enacted a pedagogy on the borderlands of more traditional institutions that allowed women to see the importance of rhetoric for reading and revising the world" (113).

(2) **Comparative Rhetorics**. With Mary Garrett's essay serving as an introduction, the essays of Hui Wu, Scott Lyons, and Rex Veeder seem a natural extension and explication of an overall interest in comparative rhetorics. Wu works within an Aristotelian definition of rhetoric, contrasting the Chinese and Western ways of reasoning and styles of argument. Noting that "Chinese argumentative mode[s] . . . [are] puzzling and impenetrable to many Western scholars" (119), Wu uses both her own experience and the experience of her Chinese students to show how the ethymeme is at issue in most Chinese/Western misunderstandings.

Scott Lyons and Rex Veeder take up cross-cultural communication issues within the United States. Lyons takes up the question of Native-American rhetorics of separatism and essentialism, noting that there exists a "dissent in the woods propagated by mixed-bloods who occupy multiple spheres in a post-AIM, post-*Pocahontas* world" (125). According to Lyons, these "postmodern Indians," whom he studied at an all-Native-American Anishinabe language retreat on the White Earth reservation in Minnesota, were picking their way through traditions, taking up some, and throwing others away. What Lyons found there was a rhetoric of tradition in search of itself, a tradition "oriented toward the future, not the past," and another way to contend with the question of rhetoric and community (129). Lyons suggests that when it comes to Native-American traditions, there is no going home. All traditions are created anew with each generation.

Drawing on the work of Mary Louise Pratt, and three prominent Chicano/as, Rex Veeder argues that one of the goals of our shared work as rhetoricians should be to practice and promote "zone rhetoric," or "a rhetoric that allows people to be bicultural or multicultural" (134). One of the problems with practicing traditional rhetorics or in turning to traditional rhetorics for help with intercultural conflicts, he writes, is that "rhetoricians who settle in one culture or society will exercise the old rhetoric of power and coercion" (135). Like Lyons, Veeder suggests that understanding and promoting the rhetorics of those who exist on the borderlands between cultures has much to offer us in this postmodern moment. The rhetoric of Chicano/as that Veeder has discovered offers ceremony and celebration—"rhetorical tools" he gathered from entering surrounding cultures and learning other ways of practicing rhetoric (138).

(3) **Rhetoric as Hermeneutic**. As one of my graduate students is often reminding me, "There is nothing more annoying than reading rhetoricians who fail to see that their work is rhetorical, too." Such is the view of Richard Johnson-Sheehan and Rolf Norgaard, whose essays focus on the rhetoric of science and the writing-across-the-curriculum movements, respectively. Johnson-Sheehan, working against what he calls the "interaction view of metaphor" in the work of scholars who study the rhetoric of science, suggests that metaphor in writing by scientists is suggestive of the way science is *invented* (141-42). By looking at the ways statements move from the status of metaphors to truth statements, one can see that metaphors serve an interpretive or hermeneutic function. Johnson-Sheehan illustrates the way science is constructed through language.

Rolf Norgaard takes up the question of why writing-across-the-curriculum (WAC) programs have failed to follow the vision of Wingspread and place rhetoric at the center of the curriculum. In Norgaard's view "WAC's inclination is to accommodate disciplinary concepts of expertise and existing curricular structures—an inclination that has allowed WAC to develop, even prosper, over several 'generations'—while [also] diminish[ing] its rhetorical prospects" (149). The twin approaches to WAC that have diminished the intellectual opportunities for reform are the "writing to learn" and "writing in the disciplines" movements, which have had a tendency to "suffer under the tyranny of content" (153). Norgaard writes, "If we are to improve the prospect of rhetoric in writing across the curriculum, if we are to 'rhetoricize WAC,' we ourselves must approach disciplinary expertise, curricular structures, and prevailing institutional arrangements in explicitly rhetorical terms" (156).

(4) **New Vistas for Rhetoric.** In the final five essays of this collection, authors take rhetoric beyond its traditional concerns and into new cultural arenas. While it would be tempting to categorize these essays under an interdisciplinary rubric like "cultural studies," I believe these essays are distinct in their call for rhetoric either to look at traditional concerns from a new vantage point or for traditional theories of rhetoric to be used to analyze new cultural phenomena—from roadmaps to databases.

Janice Norton argues that feminist rhetoricians in the field need to take up concerns forgotten in a phallogocentric world. Working with French feminist Luce Irigaray, she suggests that rhetoricians should take into consideration the body, the operations of binary logic in language, and the problem of sexual difference in developing their theories. To illustrate the problems created by binary logic, Norton interrogates Edwin Black's keynote address and his reassertion of the public/private distinction as necessary for the survival of rhetoric. Norton suggests that the reliance of the field on binaries reinforces one thing only: the dominance of the masculine in the field. She nominates a new vista for rhetoric, one in which scholars—especially those who are prominent—examine "the history of their own theory production," which for her is "the real, rhetorical phenomenon" that should occupy us (163).

Ulrike Zinn Jaeckel looks at another place where rhetoric is complicated: when hecklers break up a public speech. According to traditional rhetorical models, rhetoric is dependent upon docile listeners and a single speaker. Hecklers do not have a prescribed space in rhetoric; their speech acts appear outside the rhetorical situation. Jaeckel wonders why, in rhetoric, "speaking is more powerful than listening" (169). Working her way through several moments in literature and history in which hecklers shout down a speaker, Jaeckel suggests that hecklers illustrate the power of audience members, who can, at any moment, resist their role as listeners.

Working through texts about travel in America from 1800-1950, Greg Clark examines how discourse on travel transformed American identity. As roads made possible national travel, a discourse of regionalism gave way to a discourse of nationalism. Travel literally made possible something like a shared public experience: Landscapes did not exist only for those who lived near them; rather, landscapes became an experience for all. For Clark, this discourse is valuable because it suggests a way that we see ourselves as citizens. He writes,

> If national community is imagined in terms of the common experiences of those individuals who constitute it and if those individuals each draw upon conceptual resources of a shared national imaginary in the process of shaping themselves into an identity as citizens, . . . the perception of a shared landscape afforded them by the experience of autotravel might suggest to them a fluid kind of identity within community, one that requires individuals . . . "to be on the move." (178)

Like Clark, Van E. Hillard looks for a model that might help develop our concept of community. He finds it in another public place: the city. For Hillard, the term *community* is too localized to help explain the nature of public life at the end of the century. Building on the work of Susan Miller and Richard Sennet, Hillard suggests that cities provide a better working model of civic life because they provide multiple contact points for their residents but are neither uniform nor intimate. The problem with using the metaphor of *community* to describe national life is that it does not make visible the kinds of communication problems rhetoric must respond to in the current age.

Dianne L. Juby's essay serves as an example of Bitzer's contention that rhetoric should concern itself with invention. She examines the ways information retrieval specialists working with the World Wide Web are using Aristotelian concepts to organize databases, noting how helpful the *topoi* can be for facilitating online searches. For Juby, being able to study the disputes of other fields through the *topoi* could bring about the interdisciplinary potential of rhetoric. She writes, "The expansion of databases and documents from specialized disciplines available 'freely' on the World Wide Web . . . can force us out of [our] comfortable communities and into a cosmopolis of multidisciplinarity" (195).

An Allegory, a Song, and Conclusions

We end this volume with the Kneupper Memorial Address, given this year by Winifred Horner. It is appropriate that Horner's address, an extended allegory of rhetoric's place in the academy, should have the final word, since its theme of disciplinary kinship patterns illustrates the complexity and irrationality of our field's history. It is followed by the lyrics of the Composition Blues Band (Barry Briggs, guitar; Larry Burkett, guitar; Clyde Moneyhun, guitar; John Warnock, bass; and Marvin Diogenes, lyrics and vocals), who entertained RSA participants at the opening reception. Together, Horner and the Blues Band remind us not to take ourselves too seriously.

The 1996 RSA participants did not sit down together to draft a set of documents outlining the future of rhetoric studies. Had we done so, no doubt the deliberations would have been contentious and exhilarating, just as those that led to the publication of *The Prospect of Rhetoric*. However, the good will present in Tucson, especially after a memorable outdoor fiesta complete with full moon and mariachi band, may well have brought about another revolution (if not another affair for Dame Rhetoric). Instead, we present to you a portion of the fine papers presented there, which together show the continued influence and vitality of other papers, on the same subject, published twenty-five years ago.

Notes

[1] In her paper for the 1996 RSA (forthcoming, online journal *PRE/TEXT: Electra(Lite)*, http://wwwpub.utdallas.edu/~atrue/PRETEXT/PT.html), Diane Davis takes Patricia Bizzell's explorations a step farther. She writes, "If finite beings are not stable individuals but a mass of loose ends, what can it mean to be-with-one-another? This may be *the* question of our time. If what we share is our unsharable loose ends, then what we will necessarily give up in any common work effort or quest for solidarity *is the very possibility for community*" (6).

[2] The first article on a woman rhetor was published in 1991 (Sutherland).

[3] For instance, in his keynote address at the 1994 RSA, Edward Schiappa called on all rhetoricians to become involved in their communities, suggesting that no one had combined community service with academic work. After this oversight was brought to his attention, Schiappa graciously gave credit to

African-American and feminist activists in the revision of that keynote, published in the 1994 Proceedings.

Works Cited

Bender, John, and David E. Wellbery, eds. *The Ends of Rhetoric: History, Theory, and Practice.* Stanford, CA: Stanford UP, 1990.

Clark, Gregory. "Rescuing the Discourse of Community." *College Composition and Communication* 45:1 (1994): 61-74.

Clifford, James. *The Predicament of Culture: Twentieth-Century Ethnography, Literature, and Art.* Cambridge, MA: Harvard UP, 1988.

Covino, William A., and David A. Jolliffe, eds. *Rhetoric: Concepts, Definitions, Boundaries.* Boston: Allyn, 1995.

Crowley, Sharon. *Ancient Rhetorics for Contemporary Students.* New York: MacMillan, 1994.

Davis, Diane. "Laughter." Rhetoric Society of America Conf. Doubletree Hotel, Tucson. 2 June 1996.

Ede, Lisa, Cheryl Glenn, and Andrea Lunsford. "Border Crossings: Intersections of Rhetoric and Feminism." *Rhetorica* 13 (1995): 401-41.

Martin, Emily. *The Woman in the Body: A Cultural Analysis of Reproduction.* Boston: Beacon, 1992.

Miller, Thomas P. "Teaching the Histories of Rhetoric as a Social Praxis." *Rhetoric Review* 12 (1993): 70-82.

Mountford, Roxanne. "Classrooms as Communities: At What Cost? in Things That Go without Saying in the Teaching of Composition: A Colloquy." *Journal of Advanced Composition* 15 (1995): 304-07.

Porter, James E. "Developing a Postmodern Ethics of Rhetoric and Composition." *Defining the New Rhetorics.* Ed. Theresa Enos and Stuart C. Brown. Newbury Park, CA: Sage, 1993. 207-26.

Schiappa, Edward. "Intellectuals and the Place of Cultural Critique." *Rhetoric, Cultural Studies, and Literacy.* Ed. John Frederick Reynolds. Hillsdale, NJ: Erlbaum, 1995. 21-27.

Sutherland, Christine. "Outside the Rhetorical Tradition: Mary Astell's Advice to Women in Seventeenth-Century England." *Rhetorica* 4 (1991): 147-63.

Part I

The Prospect of Rhetoric:
Twenty-Five Years Later

LLOYD F. BITZER

Emeritus, University of Wisconsin

Rhetoric's Prospects: Past and Future

During the past few weeks, I reread *The Prospect of Rhetoric*, and then I opened a box that had been closed for twenty-five years. The files in that box contain hundreds of pages—memos, letters, drafts of proposals, reports, notes, and minutes of meetings, all related to The National Developmental Project on Rhetoric, the project that produced *The Prospect of Rhetoric*. Documents in the files concern planning the Project, funding it, designing the format of its two conferences, selecting participants, planning the book and its title, and the like.

The Prospect of Rhetoric has a history that can be expressed serially, in the fashion of "This is the house that Jack built." Here is the volume. (1) But, in the beginning was a 1968 memo written by Donald C. Bryant, calling for a national interdisciplinary conference on rhetoric. (2) That memo prompted positive action by the Research Board and Administrative Committee of the Speech Communication Association. (3) That favorable action led to formation of a planning committee, of which I was a member and the chair. (4) The committee met, deliberated, and created a proposal submitted by SCA to the National Endowment for the Humanities. (5) As a result of that proposal, NEH provided major funding, supplemented by a grant from the Johnson Foundation of Racine, Wisconsin, and another from the University of Wisconsin, Madison. (6) Because of the grants, the essays that appear in the book were commissioned and two conferences were held—the Wingspread Conference, which convened the authors of the essays, and later the Pheasant Run Conference, which convened twenty-three scholars. (7) Those commissioned essays prompted hours of deliberation at both conferences and influenced the reports and recommendations fashioned at Pheasant Run. (8) Because of those papers, reports, and recommendations, the editors received materials for a volume. (9) The editors did their work. (10) Lastly, in 1971 Prentice-Hall published *The Prospect of Rhetoric: Report of the National Developmental Project*.

This is a proper occasion for a brief expression of gratitude to the persons most responsible for the Project and the volume: Donald C. Bryant, University of Iowa, whose 1968 memo proposed such a project; Jack Matthews, University of Pittsburgh, who as chair of the SCA Research Board requested formation of the planning committee; members of the planning committee—Carroll Arnold, Pennsylvania State, Gerry Miller, Michigan State, and James J. Murphy,

University of California, Davis; SCA Director of Research James E. Roever, who worked with the planning committee from the beginning; SCA Executive Secretary William Work. Thanks also to the Chairman of the National Endowment for the Humanities, Dr. Barnaby Keeney, a classicist who understood rhetoric and its history. Thanks also to Prentice-Hall for publication and distribution of the volume. And thanks to Ed Black, for superbly editing essays and reports.

Obviously, we owe a large debt to the participants in the two conferences. The Wingspread scholars wrote the essays appearing in the volume—Perelman, Johnstone, McKeon, Wallace, Booth, Corbett, Becker, Duncan, Baskerville, Brockriede, and Rosenfield. How could we go wrong if we received several first-rate essays by people of that calibre? At Pheasant Run twenty-three scholars deliberated in general sessions and in three committees—one on rhetorical criticism, chaired by Thomas O. Sloan; a second on rhetorical invention, chaired by Robert L. Scott; and the third on rhetoric's scope and its place in higher education, chaired by Douglas Ehninger. For the reports and recommendations of those committees, we are much indebted to Sloan, Ehninger, Scott, and others.

Carroll Arnold deserves a particular tribute from me. I wrote to him a month ago to tell him I would be speaking at this conference and to ask for his recollection of some aspects of our planning committee's work. I added these lines: "I've reread the volume; and am now going through the 'Project' files that have not been opened in twenty-five years. Browsing those files brings back memories. I am struck again and again by how much you contributed—nominations of participants, prose for the proposal and the final report, editing, format changes, and on and on. I know I said it before—but now again, thanks, thanks, thanks. I and those who have been educated by the project and the book owe you more than can be repaid." Carroll's letter to me a few days ago indicated that he would like to be at this Tucson conference, but he does not travel much any more.

Creating the right title of a book is not easy—it is a rhetorical invention of the first order. In my files I found several pages of letters, notes, and minutes of meetings recording titles—titles nominated, titles suggested, titles crossed out. For example, my August 7, 1970, memo to the planning committee listed twenty or so titles we had ranked after the Pheasant Run conference. I won't burden you with all of them—some were dreary, others pretentious, none of them fetching. Here's a sample:

Rhetoric: The Theory of Human Communication
Rhetoric: An Architectonic Art
Rhetoric: The Future of a Discipline
Dialogues on Rhetoric

> Rhetoric: The Structure of Communication
> Rhetoric and Humane Studies
> Rhetoric in an Age of Change
> The National Project on Rhetoric: Essays on the Nature
>   of Public Discourse

After listing those and other titles, my memo added a question: "Have you any new titles to offer? Do you find one of the above titles compelling? Let me know what two or three titles you would like to use." After receiving answers from committee members, I wrote a note to Ed Black telling him what I knew: There was no unanimity; no one found any proposed title "compelling." Ed solved the problem by creating "The Prospect of Rhetoric"—a stroke of inventive genius, the explanation of which I leave to him.

Reading through the files reminded me of a quite remarkable fact: Each person listed as our first choice for the Wingspread Conference said "yes" when invited to write a major paper and participate in the conference. A bit of strategy no doubt helped. Planning Committee member Carroll Arnold first approached his good friend Henry Johnstone, and Henry said yes. With one aboard, we then invited another, saying "Johnstone has accepted." And, with Johnstone, Perelman, Booth, and Corbett aboard, we could say to Richard McKeon, "Come join your friends."

I must say that my recent voyage through the volume was satisfying. The essays stand up remarkably well—as they should, since they were written by people who took the long view. As well, the reports and recommendations written at Pheasant Run often sparkle with insights and fresh approaches to rhetorical invention and criticism.

In one respect, the essays, reports of committees, and recommendations are dated by the participants' responses to the troubles and pressures of the decade—racial discord, the Vietnam War, the assassinations of John F. Kennedy and Martin Luther King, violence in the streets and on campuses. Professor Phil Tompkins was to have been a participant in the Pheasant Run Conference but, as a note on page vi informs us, he could not take part "because of the tragic events on his campus immediately prior to the conference." Phil was then at Kent State University. Understandably, in the book are numerous references to rhetoric and violence, demonstrations, the New Left, sit-ins, the rhetoric of the streets, and the like.

I do not know how to estimate the long-term effects of the project and the volume. One can count citations in books, essays, dissertations, and reports. But five hundred or five thousand citations may amount to less in the long run than the work of a few scholars for whom the book, or an essay in it, was a decisive influence.

As well, it is hardly possible to separate the influence of *The Prospect of Rhetoric* from the influence of other projects. We should recall that during a dozen years, several initiatives important to rhetorical studies were launched. In the early sixties, a Pennsylvania State University conference of rhetoricians and philosophers recommended what became, in 1968, the journal *Philosophy and Rhetoric*. In the same year, the Rhetoric Society of America commenced publication of its newsletter—now the *Rhetoric Society Quarterly*. In 1968 the National Developmental Project on Rhetoric was initiated, in 1970 it was completed, and in 1971 *The Prospect of Rhetoric* was published. At about the same time—in 1970—The Center for the Study of Democratic Institutions at Santa Barbara sponsored an international symposium on the occasion of the publication in English of Perelman's *The New Rhetoric*. In 1977 the International Society for the History of Rhetoric was born at a conference in Zurich; a few years later the Society's journal, *Rhetorica*, appeared. All these innovations contributed to the vigor of rhetorical studies.

So much for the past. I would make a few observations about rhetoric's future. Two future facts seem quite certain.

First, without doubt rhetoric as practice will thrive. I mean that the basic conditions of human existence will continue to supply the circumstances, motives, and means of rhetorical practice. The work-a-day world will abound with rhetorical situations, and rhetors of all stripes will create countless messages and address them to audiences. Rhetoric as practice will continue to be as necessary to life as will language and thought. Therefore, we students and teachers of rhetoric should be completely confident that rhetorical practice is continuous and secure. But, we must correctly identify it.

Second, doubtless also that same practice will continue to exhibit wide variation in quality. Dismal rhetoric will continue, produced by the usual causes—sham enthymemes, fabrications, vices, mistakes of fact, misreadings of situations, and on and on; but, on the other hand, there will continue to be "good persons speaking well"—abundant instances of exemplary rhetoric. While rhetorical practice is, I think, inevitable, the ratio of dismal to exemplary rhetoric is not inevitable. Education in method makes a difference. Acquiring the art of rhetoric alters the ratio in favor of the exemplary. That is a large part of our rationale for providing instruction. We teachers of rhetoric can be confident that the need for our instruction will continue, and that our teaching will improve practice. But we must teach the art of rhetoric, and not merely some fragment of it.

If we were to convene a new conference charged to set the course of rhetorical studies and teaching for the next twenty-five years, I would nominate three topics, two of which are related to the just-mentioned facts.

First, I would recommend that we take pains to identify and define *rhetorical practice* rather than some "rhetorical phenomenon" such as belief or persuasion or influence or figuration. Rhetorical practice is, I think, the fundamental object of our professional concern, the focus of criticism, and the reality-check for theory construction.

While correctly identifying rhetorical practice might seem an easy task, I need not remind this audience that in rhetoric's history there have been monumental disagreements—and misidentifications. Some rhetoricians have equated rhetorical practice with ornamentation, some with figuration; George Campbell and other "new" rhetoricians took rhetorical practice to be the adaptation to audiences of any and all discourses—including messages literary, scientific, philosophical, even mathematical. Kenneth Burke found rhetorical practice in all the uses of "identification," and Perelman in all argumentations aiming to secure the adherence of audiences to theses.

My second recommendation would be that we consider how we can teach the art of rhetoric to the students who need to acquire it. I think everyone needs it; everyone needs principles and methods of creation and judgment, structure and style, in the preparation and presentation of discourses regarding contingent subjects and problems. Teaching the art to nearly all students will not be easy because there are numerous continuing problems: Instructional budgets are strained; administrators often resist mandating a course; few administrators know anything of substance about rhetoric; of current courses in public speaking and English composition, most contain only parts of the art of rhetoric; and invention, the most important part, is infrequently taught.

Lastly, I would nominate one additional item for discussion at the next conference on rhetoric's future. I think it is time to refurbish the art of rhetoric not by any striking innovation, but by prudent restoration. During the past three centuries, rhetoric has been universalized; concomitantly, rhetoric suffered loss of invention. The time has come to narrow rhetoric's scope—narrow its territory—and to restore invention to its old position of authority and centrality.

The new rhetoricians of the eighteenth century made two monumental changes in the nature and scope of the art. First, they substituted scientific method—inductive logic—in place of the inventional methods, topics, and lines of argument taught by classical authors. Second, they universalized rhetoric by making it the theory of all kinds of discourse—poetic, scientific, political, philosophical, historical, critical, and the rest. These changes were expressed in textbooks of the next century, and are expressed in texts we use today.

In *The Prospect of Rhetoric*, we find roughly the same universalizing tendency; indeed, we find that by some conceptions of what is rhetorical, hardly anything is nonrhetorical. Two illustrations will suffice. The first is a brief exchange between Larry Rosenfield and Richard McKeon during a session at Wingspread. After a morning session at which the notion of "rhetorical phenomena" had been considerably expanded, Rosenfield—in the afternoon conference—returned to that expansive notion and remarked, with seeming exasperation, "So far as I can tell," the notion of rhetorical phenomena "includes everything but tidal waves." McKeon's immediate quip was "Why not tidal waves?" (Wingspread Conference, audio tape #4).

A second illustration of the universalizing tendency appears in the "Report of the Committee on the Scope of Rhetoric and the Place of Rhetorical Studies in Higher Education." The opening paragraph indicates that the principal object of rhetorical studies should be "the process by which symbols and systems of symbols have influence upon beliefs, values, attitudes, and actions. . . ." And the first recommendation of the same committee is that "rhetorical studies" properly "include any human transaction in which symbols and/or systems of symbols influence values, attitudes, beliefs, and actions . . ." (208, 214). In light of that conception, I find it difficult to find instances of nonrhetorical human transactions.

The history of rhetoric is marked by numerous twists and turns, and so is the history of logic. A couple of centuries ago, it was common to conceive of logic as the art of thinking—or the whole art of correct thought. Philosophers of the last two centuries rejected that conception, and restored logic to its proper and narrower scope and territory. Rhetoric should undergo a similar restoration.

EDWIN BLACK

Emeritus, University of Wisconsin

The Prospect of Rhetoric: Twenty-Five Years Later

The Prospect of Rhetoric was published twenty-five years ago. About a year and half earlier, the event that shaped the book—the Wingspread Conference—occurred. It seemed to me, as an observer at the Wingspread Conference, that Richard McKeon was its dominant presence. It took McKeon about five minutes to get the measure of his colleagues at the conference, and about a day and a half to run out of patience with them. During that day and a half, the conferees were wallowing in a confused, desultory, and increasingly demoralizing conversation. Wayne Booth's essay in *The Prospect of Rhetoric* discreetly alludes to this initial muddle as "games of one-up-man-ship." Supernumeraries, such as I, who were observing these early proceedings from the periphery, saw a disaster in the making. Finally, McKeon, in a monological tour de force, single-handedly pulled the conference together and projected it in a direction that at least flirted with coherence.

I no longer have an exact memory of what McKeon said, but I recall being struck, at the time, by its strong resemblance to another soliloquy that I had heard around fifteen years before. When I was a graduate student undergoing an oral examination, two members of my committee—a philosopher and a social psychologist—fell into an ill-tempered wrangle with one another that to my intensifying horror, became acrimonious and prolonged. Finally my mentor, Herbert Wichelns, after listening to his colleagues in forbearing silence, got his fill of the bickering, and he ended it. He ended it by exuding a platitude so glittering and gaseous that it left the two disputants mute with awe. McKeon engulfed the Wingspread conference with a similarly vaporous benediction. Someday a clever rhetorical theorist will write an essay about this rare and powerful maneuver, perhaps titled "The Uses of Flatulence." The maneuver, whose employment seems confined to elderly savants, resolves irreconcilable differences by pronouncing all the differing parties to be right—ethereally right.

I find it difficult, even now, to disentangle the formidable Richard McKeon whom I observed at the conference from the formidable essay that represents him in *The Prospect of Rhetoric*. The *Quarterly Journal of Speech* carried two reviews of the book. Both were fairly unapproving, but each singled out McKeon's essay for special praise. One reviewer called it the "most thoughtfully produced paper." The other reviewer called it "doubtless the most profound of the papers." Those are persuasive assessments, and it certainly would not be ungenerous to focus briefly on the component of the book that its reviewers regarded as its best. Although some qualities of McKeon's essay are singular, some others are related to the book with a robust typicality.

The intellectual range of McKeon's essay is astonishing; the authority that it radiates is intimidating. It seems to fix, unchallengeably, the history and function of rhetoric as a discipline. But for an essay that is so learned concerning "the separation of wisdom and eloquence," it is, to put the matter delicately, remarkably inelegant. The writing seems uninflected; it seems deficient in the suppleness that denotes precision of expression. And while the unrelenting constancy of McKeon's style may imply to the reader a sense of order and system, and the density of the style may reinforce the reader's sense of profundity, there is also something numbing about it.

Someone may argue—mistakenly, I think—that stylistic considerations are just not as important to a theoretical paper as are argumentative and evidentiary matters. However, at least one property of McKeon's essay is at once stylistic, argumentative, and evidentiary, and it marks as well most of the other essays in *The Prospect of Rhetoric*. That property is abstractness.

Could not one reasonably expect that a theoretical paper contain an allusion or two to the thing the theory is supposed to be about? That is, wouldn't you expect a disquisition on the theory of psychology, for example, to instance one or another mental state? Would you be surprised at a theory of law that referred to no cases? Or a theory of comedy with no citations of comedies, or comedic situations, or even jokes? But perhaps you did not notice that McKeon's essay contains not a single reference to a specific rhetorical phenomenon. Neither do the essays by Wallace or Rosenfield, or two of the three committee reports. And the rare examples of rhetorical phenomena adduced in the other essays are cursory and often vague—with the honorable exceptions of Becker, Johnstone, and Booth.

Richard McKeon was one of the great Aristotelians of the century. He did more than command Aristotle's texts. He actually assimilated the techniques of the Master into his own repertoire. Reading McKeon's essay in *The Prospect of Rhetoric* is almost like reading Aristotle himself: There is the same relentlessly methodical analysis, the same omnivorous inventory and allocation of constituents, the same passion for systematization. But there is one important difference. Despite the fact that our earliest text of Aristotle's *Rhetoric* is the product of fourteen-hundred years of scribal mediation, the treatise is profuse with examples. But McKeon's text is barren of them. Not once does it invoke a specimen of rhetoric. And, as I have mentioned, this vacuity characterizes most of the book.

Yet, even in the face of my reservations about McKeon's essay as a piece of writing, I must grant the majesty of its thesis: Rhetoric is an architectonic art, "an art of structuring all principles and products of knowing, doing, and making"—meaning that it is everywhere, that it saturates human activity. Perelman, of course, advances a thesis of similar latitude: Any expression that can't be mathematicized is rhetoric.

And where do such encyclopedic visions leave us? Well, inspired perhaps, and gratified to be associated with so encompassing a discipline. But let us note that neither our felicity nor the grand definitions that prompted it have yielded a single intelligent observation about a single rhetorical transaction. We may think that we have been brought new information about the term *rhetoric*, but we have been brought no information whatever about the referent of that term. And have we, indeed, made even a definitional advance?

The book displays a troubling flaccidity in its uses of the term *rhetoric*. Corbett observes in his paper that Wallace is the only one of the essayists to offer a definition of *rhetoric*. In one after another of the other essays, *rhetoric* is hypostacized. In much of *The Prospect of Rhetoric*, *rhetoric* is a sovereign entity, moving through history, sometimes flourishing, sometimes languishing: a cultural potency that shapes human experience. The reification of *rhetoric* pervades the book. But we have to remind ourselves that *rhetoric* is only a word.

What is *rhetoric*? It seems to me inescapable that in its disciplinary sense, *rhetoric* is the term used to designate what you and I do professionally. It may also refer to a bit more than that, but within the discursive universe of *The Prospect of Rhetoric*, not much more than that. The meaning of *rhetoric*, as a discipline, is to be found in concrete performances of scholarship, in engagements with specific discourses, in substantive acts of criticism, of analysis, of historical reconstruction. In the absence of such particulars, discussions of *rhetoric* float toward an academic version of the condition that the notable orator, Warren G. Harding, called "bloviation." But have I wandered from the subject of *The Prospect of Rhetoric*? If so, then I must return to it.

Among the more interesting features of the book are its expressions of anxiety. Those expressions have to seem especially poignant to anyone who lived through that painful time. Several of the essays—those by Becker, Johnstone, Booth, Baskerville, and Corbett—explicitly recognize that something was happening in the world that was both material to the subject and alarming. *The Prospect of Rhetoric* is, at places, haunted by the social disquiet that marked the era, by the untidy episodes of "demonstrative rhetoric" that challenged traditional procedures of rational deliberation. The responses within the book to those episodes varied from lamentation to indignation to accommodation to disinterested curiosity, the last expressed by the highly suggestive musings in Henry Johnstone's essay about "the need for an understanding of the rhetoric of the New Left." Behind all of the variable responses was a persistent sense that the upheavals of the time were germane to rhetoric. Our perspective now, twenty-five years after those upheavals, can only confirm their relevance to the subject.

Our campuses were on fire then, and a generation appeared to be in rebellion. Some of the more vocal members of that generation were disposed to resolve crises of personal identity through the medium of political action. That disposition was founded on an ideal. It was an ideal that was bound to produce anxiety in authors of *The Prospect of Rhetoric* because it jeopardized the continued existence of rhetoric as a discipline. That ideal required an abrogation of the conventional distinction between the personal, internal life of the individual and the public and political life of that individual.

It could be argued—and often was twenty-five years ago—that the traditional discrimination between personal and political had been a source of anguish and evil. The anguish was carried in the bosom of every conscientious young person who was in mutiny against institutions that seemed debased by insincerity. The evil had been manifested in a succession of duplicities: from parents who denounced drugs while sipping martinis, to universities that pretended scholarly detachment while prostituting themselves to "the power structure," to an American government that professed democratic and humane values while presiding over a slaughter of innocents in Vietnam. A generation, goaded by the habitual sanctimony of its elders, undertook to remedy this culturally incipient schizophrenia, to amalgamate the personal with the political, and to invest the whole of life with a single set of harmonious motives. Such a harmony was to found in childlike innocence, an innocence that, it was hoped, would finally exorcise that most grievous of vices, hypocrisy. Thus, the "flower children" were born.

One of the more popular slogans of the cultural revolution was "the personal is the political." Those five words encapsulated an apocalyptical agenda: the fusion of the public and private. Another favorite slogan, "Let it all hang out," meant not only that the protuberances of the human body should be liberated from the suffocation of their coverings but also that the secrecies of consciousness should be disclosed. With nothing to conceal, nothing to be embarrassed by, nothing to lie about, falsehood and pretense and hostility would disappear. And there would be born a social order of tolerance, sodality, and peace. Such, at least, were the youthful ideals of those intoxicating times.

And now the sobering question: What would happen to the discipline of rhetoric in a culture of communitarian free-spirits, each of whom has a homogeneous consciousness? The answer is that it would cease to exist. Rhetoric, as a discipline, is deeply implicated in the distinction between public and private. That is because the discipline of rhetoric predicates rhetorical activity as a product of volition rather than instinct. If rhetorical activity were instinctive, spontaneous, uncrafted and uncontrived, then the discipline of rhetoric would lose whatever identity it has sustained for two thousand years and would become a branch of biology. However else the discipline of rhetoric may have been defined historically, its objects of study have always and uniformly been conceived as products of artifice, products of human will, adaptive and purposeful. Such a conception entails a private person regulating a public one. It entails the exercise of scruples and restraint and judgment, all of which are elements of personal conscience. It entails that prior to a social personality is an individual identity that has the capacity of conforming itself to the demands of the civic realm. It entails, in short, the distinction between the public and the private.

It is important to distinguish between the discipline of rhetoric and the object of that discipline's study. Rhetorical activity was certainly compatible with the cultural revolution of the sixties. It is quite possible for rhetorical discourse to advocate, and to advocate successfully, a collection of attitudes that repeal the duality of consciousness. The social order that such attitudes would necessitate, however, would have in it no room for the discipline of rhetoric.

One prominent program of the counterculture, therefore, was paradoxical at its core, and the paradox was that its advocates employed rhetorical procedures—often with great skill—in the hope of achieving a condition in which the artful cultivation of those procedures would be impossible. And those who were attracted by that vision were able to get a foretaste of it by ingesting drugs, which delivered them from the burdensome inhibitions of a divided sensibility.

That the discipline of rhetoric requires, for its existence, a disparity between the public and the private is merely an observation, not an argument for or against anything. The public-private diremption gains no authority from its being a requisite to rhetoric. The discipline of rhetoric is not a moral necessity. I think that it can be justified, but it does not stand as self-justified. And certainly the historic reputation of the discipline has suffered greatly for rhetoric's enmeshment in a cultural regime that elicits deception.

Rhetoric—in any of its regnant definitions, from the most squalid to the most honorific—was antithetical to the cultural revolution. And the anxiety that haunts *The Prospect of Rhetoric* is understandable, originating, as it did, with teachers who were discovering that the conditions necessary for their very field of study were being repudiated by some of their most ardently committed students.

By the most remarkable of coincidences, the twenty-fifth anniversary of *The Prospect of Rhetoric* was the year that disclosed as faithful an embodiment of the cultural revolution as we are ever likely to find. The prototype of what I have been talking about is Theodore Kaczynski, the man suspected of being the Unabomber. He is a paradigm of antirhetoric: a hermit, described even by his nearest neighbors as silent and distant; a man who did not seek—evidently could not even be induced—to engage in an interchange of ideas, to put at risk his diagnosis of society or his prescription for its cure, to open himself to the arguments of others. He inadvertently made himself an exemplary definition of rhetoric: a definition by negation.

The Unabomber, having purged himself of suasory entanglements, left himself with no vehicle for impressing his attitudes upon the world except violence. And his motive was to persuade. The Unabomber said in his April 1995 letter to the *New York Times:* "The people who are pushing all this growth and progress garbage deserve to be severely punished. But our goal is less to punish them than to propagate ideas." The Unabomber said in his manifesto: "In order to get our message before the public with some chance of making a lasting impression, we've had to kill people."

In keeping with his isolation, even his acts of violence were detached, remote, calculated, formulaic. He objectified murder by making its instrument an ingenious device, so that death was simply the predictable consequence of a physical and chemical process that once initiated occurred with autonomous inevitability. Insofar as he could manage it, the substitution of mathematics for rhetorical discourse extended even to his methods of killing.

And whom did he choose to kill? The Unabomber's letter discussed only one of his victims, and the discussion is enlightening:

> We blew up Thomas Mosser last December because he was a Burston-Marsteller executive. Among other misdeeds, Burston-Marsteller helped Exxon clean up its public image after the Exxon Valdez incident. But we attacked Burston-Marsteller less for its specific misdeeds than on general principles. Burston-Marsteller is about the biggest organization in the public relations field. This means that its business is the development of techniques for manipulating people's attitudes. It was for this more than for its actions in specific cases that we sent a bomb to an executive of this company.

The only target that the Unabomber thought worth mentioning was a specialist in rhetorical maneuvering. The life that wanted extinguishing was the one lived by a professional rhetor.

A dream of the cultural revolution is realized in the person of the Unabomber—in that unkempt, uncommunicative, uncompromising votary of what he called "wild nature"—who fused into a monolithic totality the public and private dimensions of himself, and who, in his final, demented fanaticism, transcended the uncertainties of rhetorical engagement to attain the poise of a homicidal self-assurance.

The career of the Unabomber tells us more about rhetoric—its function, its value, the requirements for its existence—than could a woolpack of abstractions. The career was not a theory. It was specific, actual, lethally tangible. Let us occupy ourselves with phenomena.

CAROLE BLAIR

University of California, Davis

"We Are All Just Prisoners Here of Our Own Device": Rhetoric in Speech Communication after Wingspread

This rumination on post-Wingspread rhetoric begins with an understanding of theory as discursive—not as a genre, but as a specific kind of *use* to which languages of various kinds may be put. That is, language practice *becomes* theory when it is used as such, as an interpretive, authorizing, or validating instrument of other discourses or practices. Ordinarily, we limit "theory" to particular kinds of statements that purport to be, or are judged by their capacity as, accurate or empirically verifiable accounts of objects. My invitation to hold such ordinary views in abeyance and to treat theory as use facilitates my goal of using a popular song—the Eagles' 1976 megahit "Hotel California"—as a heuristic, hermeneutic vehicle for understanding post-Wingspread rhetoric in speech communication.

"Hotel California" tells the tale of a traveler in the desert, who grows weary and stops at a place he has glimpsed as a "shimmering light" in the distance—the Hotel California. He is greeted by voices declaring the hotel a lovely place with plenty of room. But not everything is as it appears. The traveler calls for the Captain to bring wine but is informed that "We haven't had that spirit here since nineteen sixty nine." The distant voices now suggest bringing "your alibis." A mysterious woman tells the traveler that "We are all just prisoners here of our own device." The most unsettling scene is in the master's chambers where those gathered for a feast "stab it with their steely knives, but they just can't kill the beast." At that point the traveler seeks a way out: "Last thing I remember, I was running for the door. I had to find a passage back to the place I was before." But the night man tells him, "You can check out any time you like, but you can never leave" (Felder, Henley, and Frey). We are left uncertain about the traveler's fate; although the final lyric suggests that he is trapped in this hauntingly appealing but disturbing retreat, the mysterious woman hints that escape may be volitional.

"Plenty of room at the Hotel California": The "Shimmering Light" in the Desert of Traditional Rhetoric

The story is familiar. The study of rhetoric in mid-century speech departments had become dry and lifeless. Leff and Procario summarize: "The attack centered on scholarship in public address. Existing studies were regarded as 'undistinguished' and 'unimaginative' . . . dismissed as 'stereotyped' and 'banal' . . . and condemned as responsive to only one critical approach, which often was applied in a sterile and mechanical way . . . " (15). Rhetorical study had become a desert—barren, infertile, desiccated. If the rhetorician, like the traveler in Hotel California, found his "head growing heavy and . . . sight growing dim," he could be forgiven. There was, as Donald Bryant suggested, "widespread weariness and disillusionment" (*Prospect* 190).

However, barely visible in the distance was a "new rhetoric." Fogarty glimpsed it, as did Marie Hochmuth ("Kenneth Burke"), as early as the 1950s. By the 1960s the new edifice had become visible to most rhetoricians. Its chief architect was Kenneth Burke, but other theorists were enlisted as well. Their designs were appropriated and amalgamated, force-fitted to a strained synthesis. It would become the role of Wingspread and especially Pheasant Run to validate and promote the new edifice.

The "new rhetoric" surely was a welcome sight for weary rhetoricians' eyes. It was appealing not only because it was new but also because of its capaciousness. Indeed, there was "plenty of room." Rather than accommodating only the persuasive speeches of historically prominent men of British and US politics and pulpit, the "new rhetoric" promised access to other events as well. The Committee on the Advancement and Refinement of Rhetorical Criticism at Pheasant Run mandated that rhetorical criticism "broaden its scope" to examine "media messages, picketing, sloganeering, chanting, singing, marching," etc. (*Prospect* 225), as well as "contemporary rhetorical movements; that is, the rhetoric of the black power movement, the chicano movement, student protest movements, the women's liberation movement . . ." (226). This expansiveness was enabled by a reformulation of rhetoric itself, to include "symbols and systems of symbols" (*Prospect* 208). This focus upon "symbols" provided the ground for expanding the reach of rhetoric to nonplatform-speaking venues. It also represented a radical shift in how rhetoricians would understand and conduct their work.

That the characterization of rhetoric under the sign of "symbols" marked a clear historical turning point is evident in the very different ways rhetoric was described before and after Wingspread. Ehninger suggested in 1972 that rhetoric should be considered "the rationale of symbolic inducement" ("Introduction" 3). Scott and Brock define rhetoric as the "human effort to induce cooperation through the use of symbols" (6).[1] Foss defines rhetoric as "the use of symbols to influence thought and action" (4). While one can still catch a post-Wingspread rhetorician defining rhetoric without the term *symbol* attached somewhere, it is more than a bit unusual (Hart 4). This tendency to equate rhetoric with the occurrence of symbols was *not* typical for pre-Wingspread rhetoricians. Even Marie Hochmuth, writing three years after her introduction of Burke as a representative of the "new rhetoric," takes rhetoric as "verbal activity primarily concerned with affecting persuasion . . . " ("Criticism" 8). Hudson earlier equated rhetoric with persuasion, labeling it a "technique of power" (5, 11).

That rhetoric became more expansive in the *objects* of historical/critical analysis admitted under its rubric in the 1960s and 1970s is the most obvious and laudable entailment of the mid-century redefinition of rhetoric. Worth considering are the conditions that prompted this shift as well as its other consequences.

"We Haven't Had That Spirit Here since 1969": The "Alibis" of Theory and Symbolicity

Two conditions stand out as the most obvious and consequential in the overdetermined definitional transformation of rhetoric from persuasive discourse to symbolic conduct.[2] The first seems clear in the Pheasant Run plea to expand the range of practices available for rhetorical criticism. If we attend to the examples targeted for rhetorical study, it seems obvious that these rhetoricians sought to understand, perhaps even influence, their political context. There are more than hints in *The Prospect of Rhetoric* that rhetoricians could and should be involved in these conflicts and that rhetoric had something to offer in arenas of political engagement. To expand the range of rhetorical practices to include any symbolic gesture would allow rhetoricians the capacity to deal directly with contemporary events. Perhaps "we haven't had that spirit here since 1969," but the character of our disciplinary work was profoundly reshaped by that spirit of struggle over political and ethical action in the 1960s.

Another condition that certainly influenced rhetoricians to mark rhetoric as a study of symbolic activity was the mid-century rapprochement between rhetoric and communication in speech. The professional ideology of those interested in communication demanded that knowledge be unified—under the sign of a disciplinary group (Nothstine, Blair, and Copeland 46-47). Thus, whatever reconciliation could be achieved between rhetoric and communication scholars would have to be accomplished not by granting difference but by declaring mutual interest and direction. It certainly is uncontentious to claim that communication scholars of the 1960s and since have claimed symbolic behavior as their principal territory. Indeed, *meaning*—the referential resources of symbols—would become rhetoric's principal domain.

One final set of terms for the truce between rhetoric and communication scholars contributed to the same effect. Rhetoricians in the 1960s and 1970s began to cast their goals differently; since then the focal goal of rhetorical study in speech communication has been to "contribute to theory." Nothstine, Blair, and Copeland trace this impulse to a wholesale acceptance on the part of rhetoricians of a scientized understanding of intellectual work, borrowed from their communication compatriots (24-25, 40-41). The tendency is obvious in *The Prospect of Rhetoric*. The Committee on the Advancement and Refinement of Rhetorical Criticism put the case this way: "Whether rhetorical criticism ought to contribute to theory seems to us to be beyond question" (*Prospect* 222). A similar statement, if not a stronger one, is found in almost every rhetorical criticism text written in the past twenty-five years. Represented in such statements is a reconfiguration of a theory-practice affinity assumed in earlier formulations of rhetoric and articulated by Thonssen and Baird: "Rhetorical criticism . . . serves as an effective link between the theory of public address and the outside world" (21). Although criticism *might* lead to theory construction, in their view, it neither always nor necessarily did or should (21).

The reunderstanding of rhetoric as symbolic, coupled with the revaluing of theory, would have the positive consequence of putting a seeming end to the rhetoric-communication battles and expanding the study of rhetoric into areas that had been closed to it. However, unproblematically equating rhetoric with symbolicity and marking theory contribution as the unquestioned goal of rhetorical studies also assigned rhetorical practice and its effectivity—its political capacity to do things in the world—to disciplinary oblivion.

Symbolicity diverts us from rhetoric's fundamental capacity to do things, rather than simply *mean* something. As Hochmuth claimed, the new rhetoric "is concerned not with persuasion as a specific end, but with the meanings of statements in any type of discourse" ("I. A. Richards" 9). Theory construction also diverts the rhetorician from the capacity of rhetoric to *do* things, by detaching rhetorical study from the civil and pedagogical tasks that rhetoric had formerly taken to be its own—those of having voice in civil affairs and assisting others to be so enabled (Cohen xi). The rhetorical practices we study become merely "data" (Becker, *Prospect* 41; Brockriede, *Prospect* 128) upon which to build generalizations, rather than materially consequential events to which we might respond in kind (Nothstine, Blair, and Copeland).

When rhetoricians decided to stop for the night at their own "Hotel California," they inadvertently brought their alibis—symbolicity and theory construction. It is clear in the documents from Pheasant Run and Wingspread that the participants were overwhelmingly concerned with the political dimensions of rhetoric. But that interest would be virtually impossible to pursue because of the singular goal of theory contribution posited for rhetorical study and the definitive symbolic character assigned to rhetorical practice.

"They Stab It with Their Steely Knives, But They Just Can't Kill the Beast": Rhetoric Still *Does* Have Consequences

To whatever degree rhetoricians may have internalized and naturalized the depoliticizing implications of defining rhetoric as symbolic and of taking their task to be theory building, rhetorical practice still has material consequences. No matter how many times the beast of "effect" is stabbed, it will not die; rhetoric still does things. Some of us might even suggest that that is rhetoric's definitive characteristic. Bryant's distinction between "the treatment of artifacts as significant primarily for what they *are* and the treatment of them as primarily significant for what they do" remains the clearest articulation (*Rhetorical* 27). We may identify the wealth of meanings harbored by a symbolic construction, but we have not *thereby* identified what happens when that symbolic construction is mobilized in a social context.

The beast of effect is still very much alive. The beast certainly showed up for Pheasant Run. The Committee on the Scope of Rhetoric suggested that "the study of what is happening when [one] talks or listens is rarely available, or when it occurs, is unsystematic and superficial" (*Prospect* 212). Karl Wallace seems to have seen it the same year. In *Understanding Discourse* he implored the rhetorician to "think again about the value and meaning of 'effect'. . . . Does 'effect' carry the same meanings as the concept does when one thinks of a cause and effect relationship? Does one distinguish between the effect and the consequences of an act of communication?" (20).

Since the 1970s, scholars as diverse as Black, McGee, and Farrell recognize that effect is a problem still inadequately addressed. While none of these authors suggests explicitly that symbolicity is at the root of the difficulty, enough of them propose other "units of analysis"—speech act, utterance, ideograph, etc.—to make the case more compelling. Their proffered alternatives for understanding instances of rhetorical practice imply that the symbol is not coterminous with rhetoric. They also suggest by implication that if effectivity is a definitive, essential dimension of rhetoric, it seems more productive to acknowledge and understand it than to ignore or attempt to subdue it.

"You Can Check Out Any Time You Like, But You Can Never Leave": Can We Find a Passage [Back]?

It may be worthwhile to seek a passage out of the "new rhetoric" if not back to where we were before. A mere return to the pre-Wingspread space seems neither desirable nor even conceivable. It is not desirable because the "new rhetoric" represented by Wingspread and Pheasant Run has given us something we should take with us when we leave—an expanded view of the range of rhetorical practices. It probably is impossible to go back anyway. While we have been inside rhetoric's Hotel California, the terrain outside of it has changed sufficiently to suggest that there is no "there" to go back to. The desert has been irrigated and planted by an upstart, interdisciplinary group, loosely going under the name of "cultural studies." The territory rhetoric began exploring in the early part of the twentieth century and then abdicated—a territory marked by the political vectors of rhetoric—has been occupied by this group, in many cases, with great productivity and to great advantage.[3] We too need to embrace and explore rhetoric's character as consequential, rather than deny it or suppress it by calling it symbolic.

The night man is wrong—we really *can* leave when we check out. In fact, we had already left at the beginning of this essay. My invitation to suspend disbelief about what could count as theory, to the degree it received even grudging or contingent consent, suggested that we had found our way. The invitation represented a precise reversal of what the "new rhetoric" would have us do. One would never have used a song to study theoretical or historical formulations; one might study songs and build theoretical formulations on the basis of them. The "new rhetoric" left unsettled how it is that critics/historians actually do their work, but the unsettledness did not (arguably could not, given the scientistic timbre of the position) entice rhetoricians to explore the character or practices of their own intellectual labor. That investigation has begun, and among the things we have to learn from it is a very different view of theory. If we can believe the reports of rhetoricians, theory is a tertiary support for our work, rather than the prize we seek at the end of it (Frentz and Rushing 157-58). We do not choose our theories by any apparently rational or even very systematic process (Taylor 418-19; Brummett). We end up choosing them for what they allow us to do or say, or because we have had occasion to attend to them recently (Mechling and Mechling 120; Nothstine 234; Leff 324). All of this suggests that "theory" is a function of discourse or a use to which we put it, not an allegedly accurate, testable hypothesis about a range of objects.

It is difficult to say what a post-"new rhetoric" might become, but if this tour through post-Wingspread has served to mark out issues that matter now, certainly the most urgent ones seem to be how it is we will deal with rhetoric as a consequential instrument of power and how it is we will understand theory. Such work already has begun in particular quarters, another indication that we have slipped past the night man after all.[4]

Notes

[1] This definition has remained through subsequent editions.

[2] Thanks to Jerry Murphy, who saved materials from his role as a Steering Committee member for the National Developmental Project. The two conditions I have specified—political activities of the 1960s and the rhetoric-communication tiff—are topics in almost all of the position papers submitted by would-be participants in Pheasant Run.

[3] The questions posed by the position papers written by those who applied to participate in the Pheasant Run conference are striking in their resemblance to contemporary cultural studies. Ehninger suggested that rhetoricians must not only deal with the techniques of "cajoling or persuading those who are like us in background and values" but also learn to "speak across class, race, age, and culture lines to those who are in some way 'different'" (4). Smith posed as the most important task for Pheasant Run to address the question of whether rhetoric is a uniquely Western phenomenon (24). Although issues of "otherness" are not the only ones that cultural studies poses and explores to advantage, they are among the most prominent. And they have to do always with issues of power and of what rhetoric *does*.

[4] There is little agreement about what a post-"new rhetoric" should be, and perhaps there need be no agreement. Generally speaking, however, there are two "camps"—one that values the return and reformation of public address studies, in the narrow sense of formalist or structuralist readings of public, persuasive speeches, and one that values cultural readings of rhetorical practices and that has as its chief patrons French poststructuralism, critical race theory, feminism, and British and American cultural studies. The two camps do not agree on very many significant issues, for example, on the import of audience response, symbolicity/materiality, or political effectivity of discourse. However, both tend to place traditional notions of theory in a subordinate position to rhetorical practices.

Works Cited

Bitzer, Lloyd F., and Edwin Black, eds. *The Prospect of Rhetoric: Report of the National Developmental Project*. Englewood Cliffs, NJ: Prentice, 1971.

Black, Edwin. "The Mutability of Rhetoric." *Rhetoric in Transition: Studies in the Nature and Uses of Rhetoric*. Ed. Eugene E. White. University Park: Pennsylvania State UP, 1980. 71-85.

Brummett, Barry. "Rhetorical Theory as Heuristic and Moral: A Pedagogical Justification." *Communication Education* 33 (1984): 97-107.

Bryant, Donald C. *Rhetorical Dimensions in Criticism*. Baton Rouge: Louisiana State UP, 1973.

Cohen, Herman. *The History of Speech Communication: The Emergence of a Discipline, 1914-1945*. Annandale, VA: SCA, 1994.

Ehninger, Douglas. "Introduction." *Contemporary Rhetoric: A Reader's Coursebook*. Ed. Douglas Ehninger. Glenview, IL: Scott, 1972. 1-14.

——. Position paper, compiled with "Statements by Conference Participants." Pheasant Run Conference, May 10-15, 1970. 3-4.

Farrell, Thomas B. "On the Disappearance of the Rhetorical Aura." *Western Journal of Communication* 57 (1993): 147-58.

Felder, Don, Don Henley, and Glenn Frey. "Hotel California." Cass County Music/Red Cloud Music ASCAP, 1976. The Eagles. *Hotel California*. Elektra/Asylum/Nonsuch Records, 1976.

Fogarty, Daniel, S. J. *Roots for a New Rhetoric*. New York: Teachers College, Columbia University, 1959.

Foss, Sonja K. *Rhetorical Criticism: Exploration and Practice*. Prospect Heights, IL: Waveland, 1989.

Frentz, Thomas S., and Janice Hocker Rushing. "Commentary." *Critical Questions*. Ed. William L. Nothstine, Carole Blair, and Gary Copeland. 155-60.

Hart, Roderick P. *Modern Rhetorical Criticism*. Glenview, IL: Scott, 1990.

Hochmuth, Marie. "The Criticism of Rhetoric." *A History and Criticism of American Public Address*. Vol. 3. Ed. Marie Hochmuth. New York: Russell, 1955. 1-23.

——. "I. A. Richards and the 'New Rhetoric.'" *Quarterly Journal of Speech* 44 (1958): 1-16.

——. "Kenneth Burke and the 'New Rhetoric.'" *Quarterly Journal of Speech* 38 (1952): 133-44.

Hudson, Hoyt. "The Field of Rhetoric." *Quarterly Journal of Speech* 9 (1923): 167-80. Rpt. in *Historical Studies of Rhetoric and Rhetoricians*. Ed. Raymond F. Howes. Ithaca: Cornell UP, 1961. 3-15.

Leff, Michael C. "Commentary." *Critical Questions*. Ed. William L. Nothstine, Carole Blair, and Gary Copeland. 323-26.

Leff, Michael C., and Margaret Organ Procario. "Rhetorical Theory in Speech Communication." *Speech Communication in the 20th Century*. Ed. Thomas W. Benson. Carbondale: Southern Illinois UP, 1985. 3-27.

McGee, Michael Calvin. "The 'Ideograph': A Link Between Rhetoric and Ideology." *Quarterly Journal of Speech* 66 (1980): 1-16.

Mechling, Elizabeth Walker, and Jay Mechling. "Commentary." *Critical Questions*. Ed. William L. Nothstine, Carole Blair, and Gary Copeland. 118-24.

Nothstine, William L. "Commentary." *Critical Questions*. Ed. William L. Nothstine, Carole Blair, and Gary Copeland. 233-37.

Nothstine, William L., Carole Blair, and Gary Copeland, eds. *Critical Questions: Invention, Creativity, and the Criticism of Discourse and Media*. New York: St. Martin's, 1994.

Nothstine, William L., Carole Blair, and Gary A. Copeland. "Professionalization and the Eclipse of Critical Invention." *Critical Questions*. Ed. William L. Nothstine, Carole Blair, and Gary Copeland. 15-70.

Scott, Robert L., and Bernard L. Brock. "An Introduction to Rhetorical Criticism." *Methods of Rhetorical Criticism: A Twentieth-Century Perspective*. Ed. Robert L. Scott and Bernard L. Brock. New York: Harper, 1972.

Smith, Arthur L. Position paper, compiled with "Statements by Conference Participants." Pheasant Run Conference, May 10-15, 1970. 24-25.

Taylor, Bryan C. "Commentary." *Critical Questions*. Ed. William L. Nothstine, Carole Blair, and Gary Copeland. 417-22.

Thonssen, Lester, and A. Craig Baird. *Speech Criticism: The Development of Standards for Rhetorical Appraisal*. New York: Ronald, 1948.

Wallace, Karl R. *Understanding Discourse: The Speech Act and Rhetorical Action*. Baton Rouge: Louisiana State UP, 1970.

PATRICIA BIZZELL

College of the Holy Cross

The Prospect of Rhetorical Agency

The Prospect of Rhetoric seems most prophetic of our interests today in the collection's extended definition of rhetoric. Although Karl Wallace speaks for tradition in limiting the domain of rhetoric to "public discourse" only (9), most contributors follow the lead of Richard McKeon in defining rhetoric as an "architectonic art" (52ff), organizing virtually all forms of language use under its aegis. Johnstone explicitly includes the discourse of philosophy, and Perelman that of science, in rhetoric's domain, and the three reports that conclude the volume all advance very broad definitions. Ehninger's committee argues that rhetoric embraces no less than "all forms of human communication" (208). I think most scholars in rhetoric and composition studies today would agree with this broad definition, and its effects can be seen not only in our field but also in the so-called rhetorical turn of many contemporary academic disciplines, where the constitutive power of disiciplinary language has become a major focus of study.

At the same time, *The Prospect of Rhetoric* seems most distant from our concerns in its treatment of rhetorical agency. The contributors envision communication as taking place among internally unified, rational individuals who can more or less freely choose among available means of persuasion. Here Wallace sets the tone when he defines the "fundamental concepts belonging to the dynamics of the [rhetorical] act" as "the notions of end and its cousins, purpose, intent, motive, and goal; the material and substantial basis of action; form, structure, order, place, and position; the concepts of maker or artist, and of thing made or artifact" (5). By and large, the contributors disturb this purposeful picture of crafted structure only to suggest that strictly objective logic may not suit rhetorical persuasion. They invoke new respect for Aristotelian *phronesis* or probablistic reasoning, which, they say, should be served by a newly revived, nonscientific kind of invention. Here is how the final report to the NEH characterizes what is required:

> Most of our problems, including the great social and political issues, are moral, or humane; the analysis and resolution of humane problems requires the application of methods to uncover facts, to be sure, but also to determine relevant criteria, to form new

definitions, to critique values and hierarchies of value, to bring sentiments and feelings into relation with thoughts. (239-40)

The authors of the report set these methodical processes of deliberation in explicit contrast to the "non-rational immediacy" of the verbally and physically violent campus protests that were swirling around them in 1970, the year I graduated from college (239).

What's wrong with this picture? From a postmodern perspective, it gives far too much control to the participants in communicative acts. It assumes that they have independent agency. Lester Faigley provides a good summary of the contrasting postmodern view, in which the communicating entity is no longer a person, or "man" as we find most commonly in *Prospect* but rather a genderless "subject":

> Postmodern theory . . . would situate the subject among many competing discourses that precede the subject. The notion of 'participation' itself becomes problematic in its implication that the subject can control its location and moves within a discourse. By divorcing the subject from prevailing notions of the individual, either the freely choosing individual of capitalism or the interpellated individual of Althusserian Marxism, postmodern theory understands subjectivity as heterogeneous and constantly in flux. . . . The subject, like judgments of value and validations, has no grounding outside contingent discourses. (226-27)

The subject would appear to be an entity with little or no agency; rather, the subject finds itself mouthing the words of preexisting discourses without even understanding why this particular discourse is the one using it as a means of expression. There is no way to determine the "authenticity" or "sincerity" of a subject's discourses, since there is "no grounding," no essential identity outside of discourse, against which a subject's discourses could be measured. And if the subject cannot even establish its own authenticity, how much less able is it to make any claims on others to acknowledge the validity of its value judgments and evidence? Faigley argues that this effect is accelerated by what he calls the "dispersal of the subject in electronic communications technologies," in which crafted purposes and consensual methodologies give way to the anonymous free play of discourses (227).

If I were entirely happy with this postmodern view of the subject, then I could simply thank *The Prospect of Rhetoric* for its one valuable contribution of enlarging the definition of rhetoric, and dismiss it (except possibly for the essay by Samuel Becker).[1] I'm not entirely happy, however, and neither are many other scholars in composition studies and rhetoric, as the large number of articles and books on the "problem" of the postmodern subject, Faigley's among them, suggests. But let me say first, I'm not entirely unhappy with this view, either.

For me, its main virtue is that it makes possible the acknowledgement of a far greater heterogeneity within audiences and within persons than the more unitary views in *Prospect* do. This may be the place to mention the almost total absence of people of color and white women not only from the list of contributors but from references or virtually any mention in the volume at all. It could be argued that the *Prospect* contributors' limited view of who comprises their own immediate community influences them to devise such a univocal, quasi-rational model of communication. Indeed, it has been argued by many major thinkers of postmodernism that a broader awareness of disenfranchised perspectives on the margins of culture destabilizes the unified world view on which such a traditional view of agency depends. I admit that many of *Prospect's* contributors note a new heterogeneity in the rhetor's audience. Indeed, it is a major point of Wayne Booth's. But the point tends to be made in the context of an argument to find ways to reassert the traditional model in spite of this heterogeneity, or more, as a sort of "cure" for it.

Faigley likes the postmodern subject for reasons similar to mine. He uses it to attack the notion of community, or discourse community, which has been an important concept in composition studies, because he fears that thinking of language use in terms of community "tends to suppress differences among its members and exclude those who are labeled as different" (231). A discourse community would be a group of people who are held together by shared values and discursive practices. But evidently the postmodern subject makes such community impossible. The postmodern subject is so decentered that it cannot be said securely to possess *any* values or discursive practices, and therefore it cannot "share" any because in order to "share," you have to have some control over what you are sharing. Against the notion of community, Faigley prefers a vision of the urban world he derives from the work of Iris Young, in which each subject is "a play of differences that cannot be reduced to a whole," a subject "open to the possibilities of interacting with strangers" and passing through different neighborhoods—both spatial and discursive—with equanimity (232).

Faigley and I are caught in a similar logical contradiction, however. We both like the postmodern subject because we see the concept working against unjust discrimination on the basis of difference. But if we are postmodern subjects ourselves, then we have no way of establishing our implicit claim that working against unjust discrimination is valuable. Faigley attempts to get himself out of this difficulty with the assistance of Jean-François Lyotard. If the postmodern condition of competing discourses constitutes what Lyotard calls the "differend," in which all value discourses are incommensurate and adjudication happens on the basis of brute political power, then, Faigley suggests, following Lyotard, all we can do is to accept responsibility for continually examining and questioning the ethical positions that are created when we use language—an inherently value-laden medium—even though, as Faigley notes, there is "no external discourse to validate" the taking on of this responsibility (237). This responsibility presumably includes examining positions that exclude on the basis of difference or that "celebrate" it.

Faigley does not so much resolve the contradiction, then, as move beyond it by an existential act of will. In effect, he says, we will agree to assume responsibility for our language use even though we know there is no compelling reason for us to do so. And once we have reached this agreement, then we can talk about communicative acts in terms of purposes, strategies, and choices. That is, we can talk about them in terms not so uncongenial to the *Prospect* contributors after all. This will not be difficult because in spite of our understanding of ourselves as agency-less postmodern subjects, we *feel* when we are using language as if we have at least some control. We feel like agents, and moreover, I submit that we feel as if our students are agents. I seriously doubt that there are any teachers of language use—be they teachers of writing or speech—who simply go into class, announce that we are all constituted by discourse, and fold their hands. In other words, the world pushes us into action.

Faigley's modus operandi gives us a way of dealing with our feelings of purposefulness. But is that all there is? Only a sort of pacifying self-deception? If so, therein lies the crux of my dissatisfaction with the postmodern subject. It seems inaccurate to me to deny that sense can be made of individual human lives. I accept that sense is not created by individual choices autonomously, but it seems to me that sense for the individual emerges in large part from the personal and communal histories that converge in her. As Faigley says, "historical positioning shapes the production and participation in discourses" (239). Thus positioned, the postmodern subject is more than a randomly jostled mote, adrift in discourses. Direction and meaning emerge from the convergence of histories. At the very least, the subject becomes the agent of these histories. But more, the subject can become critically aware of, though not distanced from, these histories—and the more historical consciousness, the more potential to bring the individual's unique creative energy or serendipity to bear on the mix. In other words, historical consciousness plus serendipity equals rhetorical agency for the postmodern subject.

It follows that we can enhance rhetorical agency by enhancing historical consciousness. Interestingly, a version of this view is also important in the conclusions drawn in *The Prospect of Rhetoric*. Several *Prospect* contributors call for increased study of history, both rhetorical history specifically (see Bitzer 180-81) and more general cultural history (e.g., what Wallace calls "the materials of public discourse" [9]). Lawrence Rosenfield links the broad redefinition of rhetoric to what he calls "a more general effort to regenerate historico-critical thought" (64). Not surprisingly, this attention to history is connected in *Prospect* to schemes for liberal education, where rhetoric is seen as central.

Today we cannot simply call for direct teaching of historical information, as the *Prospect* contributors seem to do. We know how such schemes lead to tendentious exclusions. Indeed, I detect in their curricular recommendations the germs of an argument for cultural literacy, which I don't want to rehearse again (see Bizzell "Arguing"). Perhaps what we need instead is a new kind of historical imagination, such as Bruce Herzberg and I have begun to try to demonstrate in our American rhetoric text, *Negotiating Difference*. Here Herzberg and I define the pedagogical problem for rhetoric not simply in terms of students' lacking particular cultural and historical information but of their lacking a kind of vision of how such information might be constructed, interpreted, and used. Herzberg and I think that they, and we all, need to imagine that it would be possible to understand something about one's own histories and the histories of one's interlocutors, and to use that understanding to build rhetorical bridges, to help join together in mutual examination of incommensurate discourses.

The goal here is much more modest that those articulated in my earlier quotation from *Prospect* in which methods to "critique values and hierarchies of value" were confidently anticipated (240). To actually reach agreement about such things is a utopian horizon receding beyond our reach. Moreover, there's no promise to get at the "truth" about anyone's cultural histories. Rather, we would simply become more reflective language users together.

Aware that I have no foundation on which to base such a recommendation, particularly in attempting to persuade students, I would invoke a highly contingent set of values, contingent, that is, on the social fabric in which we find ourselves, namely the values of a multicultural democracy. I can't count on all students sharing my commitment against unjust discrimination. But I can hale them as my fellow citizens. I can claim that they need to know more about their own and others' cultural histories in order to be effective participants in our multicultural democracy. To the objection that the notion of the postmodern subject mocks the idea of effective participation, I can respond with my attempt to suggest a new view of this subject in which rhetorical agency is achieved through historical consciousness and the serendipity of the individual imagination. And as I said earlier, the world pushes us into action. The exigencies of the times will influence what we wish to believe possible of rhetoric, just as they did in *The Prospect of Rhetoric*. I prefer to teach in that hope.

Note

[1] Becker focuses on electronic media of communication, emphasizing "the complexities of this communication environment" that bombard the individual with "an immense number of fragments or bits of information on an immense number of topics" (26, 33). This perspective gives him a decentered, almost postmodern view of communicative interaction between people. Using media coverage of the Vietnam war as a prime example, he says:

> The message to which a receiver is exposed is scattered through time and space, disorganized, has large gaps; he is exposed to parts of it again and again; and there is great variance with the message to which other receivers are exposed. Many of the new arts provide a paradigm of the contemporary message. . . . The traditional director in the theatre has been much like the traditional critic or theorist of rhetoric. In studying a script for ideas on its direction, he looks for "through lines of action"—for an organizing principle—so that his conception and direction are relatively linear, a "meaningful" succession of images. In the new theatre, directors arrange random multiple images and whatever meaningful organization is given to these images is given by the individual member of the audience. Thus it is with the Vietnam message and the rest of our communication environment. (31-32)

This begins to sound like a postmodern world view. We even get an almost Jameson-like analysis of the emergence of postmodern fragmentation in contemporary art. However, even in Becker, we still have the unitary individual who can give "meaningful organization" to the barrage. In fact, Becker can still characterize this individual from a limited perspective, as a "man in a modern . . . society," one of whose annoyingly ubiquitous information sources is his wife (26).

Works Cited

Bizzell, Patricia. "Arguing about Literacy." 1988. Rpt. in *Academic Discourse and Critical Consciousness*. Pittsburgh: U of Pittsburgh P, 1992. 238-55.

Bizzell, Patricia, and Bruce Herzberg. *Negotiating Difference: Cultural Cases for Composition*. Boston: Bedford, 1996.

Black, Edwin, and Lloyd F. Bitzer, eds. *The Prospect of Rhetoric*. Englewood Cliffs, NJ: Prentice, 1971.

Faigley, Lester. *Fragments of Rationality: Postmodernity and the Subject of Composition*. Pittsburgh: U of Pittsburgh P, 1992.

MARY GARRETT

Ohio State University

How Far We've Come;
How Far We Have To Go

Most of my research has been on the Chinese rhetorical tradition, and I assume I was asked to be on part of the RSA conference plenary for that reason. When I received the invitation, I was reminded of a cartoon I saw long ago, in which a dragon is standing at a podium, facing an audience of knights in shining armor. The dragon says, "First, let me say that the very fact that I'm speaking to you here today shows how far we've come." This dragon's observation will be my theme for these remarks: how far we've come, and how far we have to go.

As I reread *The Prospect of Rhetoric* in preparation for the plenary, and then considered the kind of work rhetoricians—and RSA rhetoricians in particular—have been accomplishing, it struck me that the original conferees would be surprised, and then proud, to see how far we've come. If you read through the final committee reports and lists of recommendations from the Wingspread conference and the National Conference on Rhetoric and then skim through the programs for recent Rhetoric Society of America conferences, or browse through the titles at the publishers' table here, you'll notice that many of the recommendations are being realized, and probably far beyond anyone's expectations twenty-five years ago.

Let me just remind you of a few of the committees' conclusions and recommendations as they appeared in *The Prospect of Rhetoric*. The conferees agreed to define rhetorical studies as "any human transaction in which symbols and/or systems of symbols influence values, attitudes, beliefs, and actions" (214). They expanded rhetorical criticism to include

> subjects which have not traditionally fallen within the critic's purview: the non-discursive as well as the discursive, the non-verbal as well as the verbal, the event or transaction which is unintentionally as well as intentionally suasive. The rhetorical critic has the freedom to pursue his study of subjects with suasory potential or persuasive effects in whatever setting he may find them, ranging from rock music and put-ons, to architecture and public forums, to ballet and international politics. (221)

In a similarly expansionist mood, they remarked, "As rhetorical critics we should undertake the examination of the rhetoric of such areas of study as sociology, political science, psychology, anthropology, English, history, education, speech, and so forth" (226). The other committees also advocated broadening rhetoric's scope. For instance, the committee on rhetorical studies in higher education encouraged, among other things, "curricular investigations of cross-cultural, inter-cultural, and intra-cultural communication" (215).

Of course, we've also had expansions in ways not envisioned by the conferees. We've gone far beyond the advice to examine "contemporary rhetorical movements; that is, the rhetoric of the black power movement, the chicano movement, student protest movements, the women's liberation movement, and so forth" to the point of switching the assumed perspective (226). Now rhetoricians engage in deep questioning and rethinking of rhetorical theory starting from feminist standpoints, from the perspective of critical race theory, or queer theory. We've gone beyond the suggestion to examine the rhetoric of disciplines directly associated with communication, moving on to the "rhetoric of inquiry" project and related studies of the sciences. Rhetoric has reached out to semiotics, to critical theory, to cultural studies, and to postmodernism, with hopeful and exciting results.

Before turning to the question of how far we still have to go, I'd like to note that it is precisely those people who are self-reflexive, open to suggestion, responsive to criticism, and willing to change in the face of good argument who are the most promising audience for exhortation, admonishment, and advice. It is in the faith that you are such an audience that I venture to sketch out two areas where we can make even more progress. My jumping-off point for these reflections is Lloyd F. Bitzer's 1970 essay, "More Reflections on the Wingspread Conference." In that essay he observes that

> The crucial problems of the next decades will be solved, if at all, either by the assistance of campaigns of discourse or by coercion. The great contemporary problems facing rhetorical practice are plain to people of intelligence and humane sense: eliminating war and instruments of war, and developing world community; solving the problems of hunger and poverty; adjusting world populations to the capabilities of our planet and technology; making urban areas not just habitable but desirable; ending the senseless corruption of the environment; assuring human rights to all. (201)

Bitzer goes on to propose that "we view rhetoric as a discipline and art whose practical mission is realization of the great aspirations of the human community," so that "The question before you becomes, therefore—what steps must we take to effectively engage rhetoric with this subject-matter?" (202).

I suggest two steps for those of us who wish to join Bitzer in this enterprise. First, if we truly wish to understand "*human* transaction[s] in which symbols and/or systems of symbols influence values, attitudes, beliefs, and actions," we must include the symbolic transactions of all humans. As part of her commencement address to Oberlin College on May 29, 1989, Audre Lord read this untitled poem:

> The US and the USSR are the most
> powerful countries
> in the world
> but only 1/8 of the world's population.
> African people are also 1/8 of the world's
> population.
> of that, 1/4 is Nigerian.
> 1/2 of the world's population is Asian.
> 1/2 of that is Chinese.
>
> There are 22 nations in the middle east.
>
> Most people in the world
> are Yellow, Black, Brown, Poor, Female
> Non-Christian
> and do not speak English.
>
> By the year 2000
> the 20 largest cities in the world
> will have one thing in common
> none of them will be in Europe
> none in the United States. (qtd. in Mohanty 1)

A move of inclusion, a move toward studying the rhetorical practices of "most people in the world," should not mean abandoning traditional objects of rhetorical study. Rather, these need to be put into perspective and contextualized, as Lord does. They are the practices of a group that is, globally, a minority, but a minority that remains extremely powerful and influential—a group that may not be disregarded if we wish to respond to Bitzer's summons. But for rhetoricians to attend to global problems and issues of world community, it is not enough to appreciate and speak only to and about those in this minority tradition.

Broadening our horizons to encompass the global range of rhetorical practices also requires that we reach out to understand the rhetorical theories and traditions that developed along with these practices, the various theories and traditions that in turn shape the patterns of creation and reception of discourse. Right now China, India, African cultures, the Arab world, all remain more or less blank spaces on the map to us as far as rhetorical theory, pedagogy, or textbooks are concerned. It is true that working outside one's own cultural context and native tongue is daunting, and even dangerous. But without such efforts, rhetoricians cannot respond effectually to Bitzer's challenges.

When I look at the many recent scholarly works on the Greek sophists, I'm fascinated by the analyses and impressed by how much energy and intellectual brilliance has been devoted to them, especially considering how meager the sources are. But I am also saddened that while these fragments of alternative perspectives have been mined so thoroughly, vast troves of sophisticated theories and practices from other cultures lie neglected.

My second recommendation to you is that we continue to reflect on, incorporate, and apply the concepts of cultural studies and critical theory to rhetorical theory and criticism. If we wish to address the challenges Bitzer lists for rhetorical studies, such incorporation is essential; for we must understand the relations among power, cultural, discourse, and material relations at the micro- and at the macrolevels—and these are the defining concerns of cultural studies and critical theory. To further illuminate this network of relations, we can bring to bear the concepts, tools, and analytic frames of rhetorical theory and criticism, and this combined approach is potentially comprehensive and powerful.

Let me give an example of the kinds of questions cultural studies and critical theory would bring to rhetorical studies. Right now there is growing interest among rhetoricians, as there should be, in cutting-edge communication technologies, such as online discussion groups, Web pages and hypertext, video-conferencing, interactive games, and virtual reality. Naturally, attention is drawn to how these new communication experiences seem to differ from previous kinds of communication. In some ways they level power differentials (as in anonymous discussion groups), allow greater freedom of expression (set up your own Web page!), and empower citizens and researchers by making immense amounts of information readily available.

These new technologies also raise fascinating questions about such foundational rhetorical issues as the definition of the speaker or author, the nature and the boundaries of the text, the author/audience relation, characterization of public space, and so on. Hypertext, scrolling screens, and transitory texts encourage a process of interaction that is reader-constructed but nonlinear, fragmented yet seemingly self-contained, and always shifting.

At the same time, it is important to contextualize these new communication phenomena, both geographically and socioeconomically, and to consider the power relations they create and reinforce. It has been estimated that about half of the world's population has never used a telephone. And telephone competence is easier to acquire than basic literacy. (The graduate secretary at my department recently enlisted a Bengali speaker to contact a potential graduate student in India. He was able to communicate the information to the maid, but she was not able to take it down because she could not write.) Even those who are connected to the World Wide Web can't necessarily access the images or, now, the videos because doing so requires more technology than they have.

We need to keep these same concerns in mind when we restrict ourselves to talking about the United States. According to the best estimate, the study by O'Reilly and Associates, in 1995 3.68 percent of the US population (about 9.7 million people) was online, with a prediction that 5.95 percent (15.7 million) would be online in 1996 (Rickard). True, in many places libraries offer online services, but it takes a certain amount of time and cultural capital to use these. It also requires some adaptability; my mother no longer uses her public library because the card catalog is now entirely online, and she fears it. (This age bias is confirmed by the O'Reilly study, according to only 6.5 percent of people online were over 55.) In addition, being online requires functional literacy, which roughly 15-20 percent of the American population lacks. Again, such computer-based communication practices are the practices of a minority, though, again, a powerful and influential minority. Not surprisingly, about half of online users have annual household incomes between $35,000 and $75,000.

A friend of mine recently moved to Alabama, and when she went to the licensing office, there was a sign at one window that said, "If you can't read, stand here." The people standing in that line—leaving aside the question of how they figured out they should stand there—as well as many others, are outside the enchanted circle of Internet and Web connections. To the extent that information is power, and I believe that in many ways it is, and to the degree that accessing information requires more and more technology and expertise, these people are increasingly cut off. If we are concerned about contributing to the global community, we must keep everyone in mind.

Questions about connections among text, power, culture, and material relations can be raised for those inside the enchanted circle as well. Online shopping and services offer not self-contained texts but texts that refer to, and indeed depend upon extratextual events and objects. Online pornography offers a perfect example. Such texts and transactions reflect and are enmeshed in the economic relations of late capitalism. Once security for online use of credit cards is established, we can expect ever greater use of point-of-transaction information gathering, marketing, and surveillance.

I conclude with a few remarks on the extremely seductive and profitable video games. As a rhetorician analyzing these games, I ask questions about what beliefs and values are being reinforced, what patterns of emotional response are encouraged, how are these things done, and what kind of person is being created through these hours of voluntary training. Now I also add questions about power, culture, and the material world. In whose interest is it that children, as well as adults, wish to play these games? In whose interest is it that the games require little learning, indeed, are extraordinarily "user-friendly," but also require lots of expensive equipment? Why are new versions of the games needed? And in whose interests is it that children are conditioned to be violent, sexist, and acquisitive?

The people constructing these games are clever—but not as clever as we are! Based on what we have done in the twenty-five years since *The Prospect of Rhetoric* appeared, I have faith that we can make these expansions of our field and that we can contribute, as rhetoricians, to ameliorating some of the grave problems we face. Much of the legacy of the sixties is good, and *The Prospect of Rhetoric* is among those lasting achievements.

Works Cited

Bitzer, Lloyd. "More Reflections on the Wingspread Conference." *The Prospect of Rhetoric: Report of the National Developmental Project*. Ed. Lloyd F. Bitzer and Edwin Black. Englewood Cliffs, NJ: Prentice, 1971. 200-07.

Mohanty, Chandra Talpade. "Introduction: Cartographies of Struggle." *Third World Women and the Politics of Feminism*. Ed. Chandra Talpade Mohanty, Ann Russo, and Lourdes Torres. Bloomington: Indiana UP, 1991. 1-47.

Rickard, Jack. "The Internet by the Numbers—9.1 Million Users Can't Be Wrong." *Boardwatch Magazine* 9.12 (Dec. 1995), at www.boardwatch.com/mag/95/dec.

STEVEN MAILLOUX

University of California, Irvine

Rhetoric 2000: The New Prospects

I want to begin this otherwise theoretical paper with an example, a concrete rhetorical performance to which I can refer. Indeed, most of my paper is simply a gloss on this example:

RHETORICIANS OF THE WORLD UNITE!
THE MOMENT OF OUR TRIUMPH IS AT HAND!

This is an example of what the 1971 "Report of the Committee on the Scope of Rhetoric" called "revolutionary rhetoric." The Report had this to say as an engaged description, not a negative evaluation, of such language use: "The rhetoric of revolution is based on an intuition, apprehension, or assumption of a true belief, a cause, a faith. Revolutionary rhetoric is meant to induce religious conversion; its expression may be fanatical—certainly in many instances, it is frenetic" (Ehninger 210).

I believe that it was not a mistake that *The Prospect of Rhetoric*, which included this Report, focused so intensely on its contemporary scene of late sixties protest. It was acting responsibly to examine the political effectivity of trope and argument in the establishment- and counterculture of its day. In the words again of the Report: "Rhetorical studies are not in themselves the solution to social, political, or personal problems. They are, however, by their nature and functions relevant to the tasks of social betterment. Rhetorical studies are humanistic studies" (Ehninger 210).

I will return at the end of my paper to the present scene of a larger rhetorical politics extending beyond the academy, but now I want to concentrate on the present disciplinary meaning and possible institutional effects of a call, frenetic or otherwise, that rhetoricians of the world unite. Rhetorical study today offers us a unique opportunity; it has the potential to lead scholars and teachers into a new interdisciplinary, transdisciplinary, or even postdisciplinary future. What exactly are these new prospects of rhetoric? I'll begin an answer with some general claims about universities and the role of the humanities.

As producer and conduit of knowledge, the university has often had an ambivalent relationship to the society that supports it. While supplying the basic intellectual tools for carrying out established cultural functions, the university has also been among those institutions providing a space for criticism of societal principles and practices. Central to these conventional missions of transmitter and producer, supporter and critic are the disciplines organized under the name of "humanities."

The humanities provide the basic core and the cutting edge of the university today. These fields study and develop the linguistic practices (foreign languages, rhetoric and composition, oral performance) and cultural knowledges (literature, philosophy, history) forming the core of the traditional university. That is, humanities disciplines analyze the fundamental techniques of communication used by other components of the whole educational system and the larger society, as well as criticize those techniques and the cultural web of beliefs in which they are practiced. It is this critical function, so necessary for the production of new knowledges, that establishes the humanities as perhaps the most important site of cultural critique and intellectual transformation.

In their current shape within American higher education, schools of humanities bring together these analytical and critical functions, these core and transformative activities, to focus on new areas of interest throughout the academy and broader culture: interests that might be called "critical literacy" or, better, "cultural rhetoric." These studies investigate traditional and emerging rhetorical techniques and contexts, including the new *technologies* of communication (the electronic media revolution) and the multicultural and global *conditions* of communication (cultural diversity within a democratic society and cultural difference in a transnational setting). The examination of lariguage and its effects is central to cultural rhetoric study. Language can be understood broadly as any means of signification and narrowly as specific vernaculars relevant to national and transnational interactions. If language is understood broadly, then one crucial research focus of cultural rhetoric is electronic media, which is being conceptualized and applied in a range of humanistic disciplines, from the postmodern theorizing of cyber-culture to the pedagogies of e-mail and websites in writing courses. In addition, the study of cultural rhetoric interprets the use of specific languages within ethnically diverse democracies and across different national cultures. It plays a central role in analyzing and criticizing the multicultural conversation in which the members of this diverse democracy will participate throughout the next century.

Now if there is something in all this that smacks a bit of facile boosterism, I attribute that effect to the institutional origin and rhetorical intention of the preceding claims. I first wrote something very like these words in my role as Associate Dean last summer when the Dean of Humanities asked me to help draft a brief profile for the School that could be used to explain to the higher administration, mostly scientists, the current nature of the humanities and the role its departments will play in the future of research universities. Frankly, this was an internal press release that aimed to persuade nonhumanists to give the School of Humanities more money in the years ahead.

Whatever its rhetorical success or failure in that context at UCI, I offer it to you here as part of my rough, imperfect attempt to sketch the new prospects of rhetoric. In the future rhetorical study will help organize and reconceptualize the humanities and the interpretive social sciences, meeting the intellectual and political challenges of its historical moment, as it did twenty-five years ago in the book we are honoring in this session, *The Prospect of Rhetoric*.

But this is a repetition with a difference. As we approach the end of this millenium, rhetorical study is in a rather different historical position than previously. I have already alluded to the rapid changes in technology and cultural demographics we have experienced. But another transformation in our rhetorical context can also be named: the intellectual effects of the postmodern. In reference to these effects, I make this rather crude prognostication: The next decade or so will be a period of consolidation and possible reconfiguration within the humanities and between the humanities and the interpretive social sciences. I say "consolidation" not "downsizing" because I am not here referring to the economic situation before us though that must certainly be taken into consideration in making predictions. No, I use the term *consolidation* to refer to the intellectual dynamic of academic disciplines in the years immediately ahead. I predict we will see more and more methodological and substantive reintegration, in which no new initiatives of thought comparable to poststructuralist theory will gain wide currency. This means that we will participate in a period of consolidation in which the so-called humanistic tradition will come to intellectual terms with postmodernism in both a more open and a more covert way than it has heretofore.

And it is precisely in this period of consolidation that I see rhetorical studies playing an increasingly active role. It is the field of rhetoric that offers both an analytic of cultural change and a hermeneutic of intellectual transformation. By an "analytic of cultural change," I mean, among other things, a useful, nuanced rhetorical account of how new ideas are resisted, accepted, and translated within the cultural conversations inside and outside the university. By a "hermeneutic of intellectual transformation," I mean an interpretive strategy for tracking rhetorical traditions in the movement *of* and as a topic *for* the history leading to our postmodern present. That is, though some of its enemies and advocates argue that poststructuralist thought is a dramatic break with the so-called humanistic tradition, much of that thought was developed during this century from within are interpretation of the very humanistic tradition it supposedly rejects. This, of course, is news only to those who have not read Nietzsche, Heidegger, and Dewey, seminal thinkers for contemporary critical theory, or much of that contemporary theory itself. I'm thinking especially of the critical engagement with or even reversal of

Platonism in Derrida, Irigaray, Deleuze, Foucault, Lyotard, Rorty, Fish, Butler, and many, many others. Rhetoric, especially sophistic rhetoric, plays a prominent role in the development of these thinkers' theories, which have in turn significantly affected the new forms of cultural studies. Assumptions about this historical agon between Platonic philosophy and sophistic rhetoric form a significant part of what I am calling contemporary rhetoric's hermeneutic of intellectual transformation.

Thus, it is my claim that rhetorical study today offers the academic human sciences both a way of critically analyzing their current evolution (an analytic) and a way of historically interpreting the pomo humanism or, if you like, posthumanism that is emerging in this coming period of consolidation (a hermeneutic). Rhetorical studies also provide tools for rethinking the relation between what has been seen as radically different methodologies, humanistic and scientific. That is, rather than seeing, for example, the humanities and the behaviorial sciences as offering competing modes of inquiry into rhetoric, rhetoric can be seen as offering a framework for analyzing these fields generally and for remapping their similarities and differences more specifically. The new prospects of rhetoric, then, include the opportunity for using a comprehensive analytic of cultural change, a powerful hermeneutic of intellectual transformation, and a practical framework for transdisciplinary studies.

In this moment of opportunity for rhetorical studies, I am rather amazed that speech communication departments have not more aggressively stepped forward and taken advantage of their disciplinary strengths to become leaders in the human sciences within the university. I am also a little disconcerted that some rhetoric and composition specialists in English departments hesitate to unite with rhetoric-oriented critical theorists or practitioners of rhetorically focused cultural studies to reconceptualize *together* literature-centered English Studies. (Of course, I am not surprised that many literary historians and critics resist such collaboration and continue in blissful ignorance of the developing field of rhet/comp.) And I am particularly disappointed that the different professional language organizations—MLA, SCA, NCTE, RSA—have not formed a coalition to produce the kind of manifestoes written by just one of these organizations in *The Prospect of Rhetoric* twenty-five years ago.

Yet I do remain hopeful. I am hopeful because there are writing programs such as the one at Syracuse proposing a new Phd in Composition and Cultural Rhetoric. Hopeful because there are English departments integrating rhet/comp and history of rhetoric into their graduate training in literature studies. Hopeful because some historians of rhetoric are now using archival work to reexamine issues in poststructuralist critical theory. Indeed, there are now enough theorists around working in the intersection of the ancients and the postmoderns that we might borrow a term from Susan Jarratt and Victor Vitanza and call the present age a Third Sophistic.[1] In this "Third Sophistic," much critical work agrees with Edward Schiappa and Thomas Cole that rhetoric and philosophy, the use of language and the search for truth, are not separate enterprises, that we are with the Older Greek Sophists who taught the two together under the study of logos prior to Plato's invention of the term *rhêtorikê*. But whether you buy this claim or not, I am also hopeful because much of the most interesting scholarship in cultural studies is rhetorical through and through even when the term *rhetoric* is never used. Here I am thinking of not only new historicisms, feminisms, and neo- and postmarxisms but also various versions of what calls identity studies, even and especially when the very concept of identity is called into question: critical race theory, gender and sexuality studies, multicultural and postcolonial inquiries. In their critical work, these sociopolitical analyses could very easily adopt such definitions of *rhetoric* as "the political effectivity of trope and argument in culture" and become part of a new rhetorical studies attempting to reconceptualize and reorganize the human sciences within the future university.[2]

It is to its great credit that *The Prospect of Rhetoric* advocated several points—the promotion of theory, the rhetorical analysis of social movements, an interpretive focus on the contemporary scene—all directly related to these new propects for Rhetoric 2000. At the present moment, we should respond vigorously to calls for critical rhetorics and "radical rhetorical studies" (Reed 174, n.5). But the examination of the political effectivity of trope and argument in culture must also look closer to home (and at the trope of "home"). The academic humanities today struggle with their critical relation to the society in which they reside. The culture wars are with us still, and rhetorical studies have a crucial function to play in those wars. While continuing debate over the future role of public intellectuals in North America, cultural rhetoricians should analyze, discuss, and respond forcefully to the political challenges now facing the professionalized humanities: diminished job prospects for graduate students, radical restructuring of higher education, attacks on the NEA and NEH, and threats to affirmative action programs.

These, then, are today's challenges; these are the new prospects of rhetoric.

Notes

[1] See Vitanza 45; and Mailloux, "Introduction" 1-22.

[2] Mailloux, *Rhetorical Power* xii; for more on cultural rhetoric studies, see Mailloux, "Rhetorically Covering Conflict."

Works Cited

Cole, Thomas. *The Origins of Rhetoric in Ancient Greece*. Baltimore: Johns Hopkins UP, 1991.

Ehninger, Douglas, et al. "Report of the Committee on the Scope of Rhetoric and the Place of Rhetorical Studies in Higher Education." *The Prospect of Rhetoric: Report of the National Development Project*. Ed. Lloyd F. Bitzer and Edwin Black. Englewood Cliffs, NJ: Prentice, 1971. 208-19.

Mailloux, Steven. "Introduction: Sophistry and Rhetorical Pragmatism." *Rhetoric, Sophistry, Pragmatism*. Ed. Steven Mailloux. Cambridge: Cambridge UP, 1995. 1-31.
——. *Rhetorical Power*. Ithaca: Cornell UP, 1989.
——. "Rhetorically Covering Conflict: Gerald Graff as Curricular Rhetorician." *Teaching the Conflicts*. Ed. William E. Cain. New York: Garland, 1994. 79-94.
Reed, T. V. *Fifteen Jugglers, Five Believers: Literary Politics and the Poetics of American Social Movements*. Berkeley: U of California P, 1992.
Schiappa, Edward. *Protagoras and Logos: A Study in Greek Philosophy and Rhetoric*. Columbia: U of South Carolina P, 1991.
Vitanza, Victor J. "Critical Sub/Versions of the History of Philosophical Rhetoric." *Rhetoric Review* 6 (1987): 41-66.

Part II

Positions and Perspectives: Rhetoric, Community, and Social Action

HENRY W. JOHNSTONE, JR.

Pennsylania State University

Some Further Trends in Rhetorical Theory

In 1970, having edited *Philosophy and Rhetoric* for just two years, I thought I had spotted a number of trends in rhetorical theory, and I listed them in the paper I gave in 1970 at Wingspread under the title "Some Trends in Rhetorical Theory." This paper became a chapter of *The Prospect of Rhetoric*. The supposed trends that I listed were the following: (1) theories that attempt to give an account of the rhetoric of the New Left; (2) attempts to elicit the ethics of rhetoric; (3) examinations of Wittgenstein's attitude toward rhetoric; (4) discussions of the relation between rhetoric and communication and of the rhetoric of information and of the mass media; (5) inquiries into the ontological and phenomenological basis of rhetoric; (6) approaches to rhetoric from the point of view of ordinary language philosophy, including that of John Austin; (7) rhetoric as viewed from the perspective of General Semantics; (8) the study of Topics as generalized from the status accorded them by Aristotle to cover arguments in science and philosophy; (9) the attempt to vindicate the claim that legal rhetoric is *sui generis*; (10) work on the relation between rhetoric and formal logic; (11) expositions of the nature of dialectic and of how it is distinguished from rhetoric; and (12) inquiries into the nature of philosophical argumentation.

This list sounds a little like the list of categories in the Chinese encyclopedia as cited by Jorge Luis Borges. Perhaps it is worse. For it is doubtful that the topics I have just listed were all in fact *trends*, or for that matter that I even actually *regarded them as* trends. Perhaps I was just kidding myself (I was, after all, only fifty years old!). As I survey the situation twenty-six years later, it seems to me that in most cases the topics suggested themselves to me as *problems*. It is a problem, for example, to state the relation between rhetoric and formal logic, or to expose the ontological foundations of rhetoric; but the attempt to deal with these problems can become a trend only if it has exercised many thinkers over a long period of time, and it is necessary for the culture to have encouraged and sustained concerted attention for many years.

One reason for doubting that all the problems I elicited in 1970 were in fact trends is insufficiency of evidence; no one can be certain that a series of events is a trend until after the series has terminated, and one can see whether the series was a flash in the pan or a genuine trend. The two-year accumulation of contributions at my disposal in 1970 was scarcely a reliable basis for a sound generalization. But there is also a second reason for skepticism, namely that I wonder whether editors in their role as editors are in principle qualified to speak about trends even if their editorial experience is extensive. They are, after all, not professional trend-watchers; they do not take polls or write social history. Their primary business is not to make generalizations about contemporary culture. They receive information about this culture much as a person on a desert island might acquire data about the outside world by finding bottles containing messages. An envelope that arrives containing a manuscript is such a bottle.

Trends are evinced by all arriving manuscripts, not by those only that are eventually published. If a trend has indeed been established, it will serve as a context in which scholarly work is being done, a motive from which unacceptable manuscripts as well as important ones are written.

Yet the situation is in fact a little more problematic than I have yet admitted it to be. There are nowadays far more many rhetorical-theory journals receiving messages in bottles than there were 26 years ago. There is accordingly a strong likelihood that not all the journals are receiving messages of the same sort. To the extent that this is the case, no one editor can make trustworthy generalizations about trends.

Indeed, it may well be the case that particular trends are associated with particular journals. Outside of rhetorical theory, this is often clearly the case. In a great many areas there are certainly trendy journals. Yet I would hesitate to label *Rhetorica*, *Rhetoric Review*, or *Rhetoric Society Quarterly* as trendy. Perhaps in some cases the epithet "specialized" would apply. But specialties and trends seem to me to be quite distinct.

With all these warnings and provisos, I shall plunge ahead. There are several directions in which I might move. I could comment more extensively than before on my 1970 list from a contemporary perspective. That would be without much redeeming value; the list is water under the bridge. I could try to list the trends that have emerged during the entire history of *Philosophy and Rhetoric*. But any interest constant over the total period of twenty-eight years would, I think, have to be considered an interest central to rhetorical theory, not a mere trend. In addition, the twenty-eight-year sweep includes an eleven-year period during which I was not giving full attention to the concerns of the journal; I refer to the period during which *Philosophy and Rhetoric* was being edited by Donald Verene. A more felicitous venture, I think, would be to consider what trends, if any, seem to have manifested themselves over the period of my second regime as editor, beginning with the third issue of 1987.

I turn to what seem to me to be the present trends in rhetorical theory, at last as I judge them on the basis of what I find in bottles washed ashore on my island. It is in the first place to be expected that the Deconstructionist movement would have a profound impact on rhetorical theory. Perhaps the most vivid evidence of this effect is at the moment still in press, scheduled to appear in our August issue. This is the recent radical enlargement of the scope of studies associating Plato and rhetoric. A vast amount had hitherto been written and still is being written on Plato's rhetorical theory, especially as expressed in the *Phaedrus* and the *Gorgias*. This is no trend; it is of the essence. What I have been noticing in the past five years or so, however, is an interest in a different linkage between Plato and rhetoric. Studies of this linkage examine the rhetorical force of the Platonic texts themselves. They concern not Plato's rhetorical theory, but Plato's rhetoric.

Perhaps this trend has manifested itself in other places, and you are already aware of it. If not, I must simply ask you to take my word until August. (If you then find that I have overstated my case, you can accost me with that charge at the "After Tucson" panel in San Diego.) But there is in fact a precursor to this movement. In 1989 we published an article by Livio Rossetti on "The Rhetoric of Socrates." Since there is no Socratic text, this is not quite comparable to the Plato studies it preceded; but as an examination of the rhetorical strategies of Plato's teacher, it has a bearing on the rhetorical strategies of Plato himself. (Rossetti elaborated his description of Socrates' deployment of rhetoric in a 1993 discussion of a 1992 article by Joseph Vincenzo: "Socrates and Rhetoric: The Problem of Nietzsche's Socrates." Vincenzo was also criticized by Domino in the same year.) With this exchange Farness (1987) ought to be compared.

The deconstruction of Plato is but one manifestation of the influence that Derrrida and his successors have had on rhetorical theory. On the pages of *Philosophy and Rhetoric*, such influence has over the past decade been expressed or criticized by such writers as Biesecker (1989), Nuyen (1992), Khushf (1995), and Rowland (1995).

While the report I have just given on studies of Plato's rhetoric points to a copious amount of material on what is perhaps to some an unexpected topic, my report on our publication of articles on feminist rhetoric concerns a topic certainly to be expected but surprisingly uncopious in comparison with the total page-count of our journal. I do not know how to explain this discrepancy. I don't think we have a reputation for treating feminists badly. If we had, we might have expected a torrent of contributions in protest. I do not think, on the other hand, that we are guilty of having treated feminism too well. The fact remains that since 1987 our only writers on feminist rhetoric have been Barbara Biesecker (1992, 1993), Karlyn Kohrs Campbell (1993), and A. T. Nuyen (1995), all appearing fairly recently.

But it is, as I have already said, not so much the manuscripts we have published as those we have received that evince trends. So I shouldn't restrict my attention to contributions we have actually published. Indeed, if I narrow the focus to what we have actually printed, I could be accused of creating the very trends I say I simply find. We have, to be sure, received manuscripts on feminist rhetoric that we have not published, just as we have on all other relevant topics. If you want me to spot trends in all the contributions the journal has received over the past decade, you are asking more of me than I can easily glean from our records, especially in view of the fact that we do not retain rejected manuscripts for more than a limited time.

I fluctuate between calling informal logic a trend and thinking that attention to it is one of the standard preoccupations of rhetorical theory. In any event, if we believe that there is a logic governing the rhetorical force of arguments—even of those standardly dismissed as fallacies—we can understand why informal logic has been regarded as an important adjunct to rhetorical theory. It has been an object of concern since early in the history of *Philosophy and Rhetoric*, even though in 1970, my earlier *terminus ante quem*, it was not yet in evidence. The series of studies of informal logic we have been publishing began in earnest in 1974, with the publication of Woods and Walton's *Argumentum ad Verecundiam* article in Volume 7. These two authors followed up in Volume 9 (1976) with a more generally oriented discussion, "Fallaciousness Without Invalidity?" About this time we also printed articles on the appeal to force—an article by Van de Vate (1975a) and a criticism by Yoos (1975), followed by a rebuttal by Van de Vate (1975b)—and the fallacies of composition and division by Broyles (1975). This trend has continued into my second stab at being editor with articles by Levi (1987), Jacquette (1989a, 1989b), Sorensen (1989), Johnson (1990a, 1990b, 1991), Suber (1990), and Walton (1994).

Closely allied with this project is that of defining "argument," thus distinguishing argumentative from nonargumentative contexts. Among the toilers in this vineyard have been Rowland (1987), Reboul (1988), Adler 1992), Verene (1989 and 1993), Walton (1993), and Rowland (1995).

Another topic that is either a trend or interwoven with the fabric of rhetorical theory is metaphor. Clearly a metaphor is a sort of argument, perhaps an enthymematic one, falling within the province of rhetoric rather than that of standard logical theory. The first article on metaphor to appear on our pages was by Stewart in Volume 4 (1971); it was followed by Paul's contribution in the next volume (1972). Since 1987 we have had articles by Nuyen (1989), Hidalgo-Serna (1990), Hausman (1991), and Heckmann (1991). Others are still in press. I expect contributions on this topic to continue unabated.

Surely epistemic rhetoric, based on the contention that rhetoric issues in knowledge, is a genuine trend, even though it may by now have peaked—a trend the origins of which are to be seen in Robert L. Scott's 1973 article "On *Not* Defining Rhetoric." The names most closely associated with this movement, at least so far as *Philosophy and Rhetoric* is concerned, are those of Hikins and Cherwitz (1990); Cherwitz and Darwin (1994, 1995), Bineham

(1990), and Zhao (1991) have also contributed to the literature on this topic issued by our journal.

"The rhetoric of science" is surely a trend, one that can plausibly be said to have been initiated by Thomas Kuhn in 1962. On our pages it has been carried forward by such investigators as Zagacki and Keith (1992). Lewin made an important contribution to this topic in 1994. But I must confess that I think that many manuscripts illustrating this trend must have been borne by an adverse current away from my island. We have simply not received all that I might have hoped to.

The rhetoric of science, like the rhetoric of feminism, cannot be shown to be a trend merely on the evidence of what has actually appeared on our pages. No doubt my judgment on this matter is somewhat subjective. Later, I will name a trend of which I can identify only one member, at least in print in our journal.

The relation between rhetoric and hermeneutics is a further topic that seems to me to have the makings of a trend. Dascal (1989), Kent (1992), Malpas (1992), Scult (1994), Bineham (1994, 1995), and Zuñiga (1995) have all contributed to what we have printed on this topic.

Lastly, there are the trends in rhetorical theory consisting of studies of thinkers trendy in their own right. These include Kenneth Burke, Martin Heidegger, and Friedrich Nietzsche. The case for including this last writer in the list was established, if it needed establishment, by our publication in 1994 of an issue devoted to his rhetoric and views on rhetoric. Prior to these articles by Conway, Crawford, Gilmour, and Porter, we had printed a relevant study by Heckman in 1991.

Studies of Heidegger have been contributed at an accelerating pace lately by Grassi (1987), Crosswhite (1989), Hyde (1994), Scult (1994), and Ramsey (1993). Burke studies are represented both in their presence in our table of contents and in their absence therefrom. Crusius in 1988 published a relevant article; several others have also been submitted. But something tells me that Burke studies are a trend in rhetorical theory, even if I can mention only one member.

That you are all already familiar with the canons of rhetorical theory strongly suggests an equal familiarity with its trends. So probably not much of what I have just said is news. But it would be a mistake to hope for news from an inhabitant of a desert island. If he is solitary, the only news he can tell is about himself. Even Robinson Crusoe can do better; he has news to report not only about himself but also about the man Friday, who was no mere message in a bottle.

Works Cited

GENERAL

Johnstone, Henry W., Jr. "Some Trends in Rhetorical Theory." *The Prospect of Rhetoric.* Ed. Lloyd F. Bitzer and Edwin Black. Englewood Cliffs, NJ: Prentice, 1971.

Kuhn, Thomas. *The Structure of Scientific Revolutions.* Chicago: U of Chicago P, 1962.

WORKS ILLUSTRATING TRENDS

I. Rhetoric and Deconstruction

Biesecker, Barbara. "Rethinking the Rhetorical Situation from Within the Thematic of *Différance.*" *Philosophy and Rhetoric* (Henceforth "*P&R*") 22 (1989): 110-30.

Farness, Jay. "Missing Socrates: Socratic Rhetoric in a Platonic Text." *P&R* 20 (1987): 41-59.

Khushf, George. "Grammatacentrism and the Transformation of Rhetoric." *P&R* 28 (1995): 30-44.

Nuyen, A. T. "The Role of Rhetorical Devices in Postmodernist Discourse." *P&R* 25 (1992): 183-94.

Rossetti, Livio. "The Rhetoric of Socrates." *P&R* 22 (1989): 225-28.

Rossetti, Livio. "'If we Link the Essence of Rhetoric with Deception': Vincenzo on Socrates and Rhetoric." *P&R* 26 (1993): 311-21.

Rowland, Robert C. "In Defense of Rational Argument: A Pragmatic Justification of Argumentation Theory and Response to the Postmodern Critique." *P&R* 28 (1995): 350-64.

Vincenzo, Joseph. "Socrates and Rhetoric: The Problem of Nietzsche's Socrates." *P&R* 25 (1992): 162-82.

II. Rhetoric and Feminism

Biesecker, Barbara. "Coming to Terms with Recent Attempts to Write Women into the History of Rhetoric." *P&R* 25 (1992): 140-61.

Biesecker, Barbara. "Negotiating with Our Tradition": Reflecting Again (Without Apologies) on the Feminization of Rhetoric." *P&R* 26 (1993): 236-41.

Campbell, Karlyn Kohrs. "Biesecker Cannot Speak for Her Either." *P&R* 26 (1993): 153-59.

Nuyen, A. T. "The Rhetoric of Feminist Writings." *P&R* 28 (1995): 69-82.

III. Informal Logic

Broyles, James E. "The Fallacies of Composition and Division." *P&R* 8 (1975)" 108-13.

Jacquette, Dale. "The Hidden Logic of Slippery Slope Arguments." *P&R* 22 (1989): 59-70.

——."Epistemic Blood from Logical Turnips." *P&R* 22 (1989): 203-11.

Johnson, Ralph H. "Hamblin on the Standard Treatment." *P&R* 23 (1990): 153-67.

——. "Acceptance is not Enough: A Critique of Hamblin." *P&R* 23 (1990): 271-87.

——. "In Response to Walton." *P&R* 24 (1991): 362-66.

Levi, Don S. "In Defense of Informal Logic." *P&R* 20 (1987): 227-47.

Sorensen, Ray. A. "A Slipping Off the Slippery Slope: A Reply to Professor Jacquette." *P&R* 22 (1989): 195-202.

Suber, Peter. "A Case Study in *Ad Hominem* Argument: Fichte's *Science of Knowledge.*" *P&R* 23 (1990): 12-42.

Van de Vate, Dwight, Jr. "The Appeal to Force." *P&R* 8 (1975): 43-60.

——. "Reasoning and Threatening: A Reply to Yoos." *P&R* 8 (1975): 177-79.

Walton, Douglas. "Hamblin on the Standard Treatment of Fallacies." *P&R* 29 (1994): 353-61.

Woods, John, and Douglas Walton. "*Argumentum ad Verecundiam.*" *P&R* 7 (1994): 135-53.

——. "Fallaciousness Without Invalidity?" *P&R* 9 (1976): 52-54.

Wreen, Michael. "A Bolt of Fear." *P&R* 22 (1989): 131-40.

Yoos, George E. "A Critique of Van de Vate's 'The Appeal to Force.'" *P&R* 8 (1975): 172-76.

IV. The Nature of Argument

Adler, Jonathan E. "Even-Arguments, Explanatory Gaps, and Pragmatic Scales." *P&R* 25 (1992): 22-44.

Reboul, Olivier. "Can there be Non-Rhetorical Argumentation?" *P&R* 21 (1988): 220-33.

Rowland, Robert C. "On Defining Argument." *P&R* 20 (1987): 140-59.
Verene, Donald Phillip. "Philosophy, Argument, and Narration." *P&R* 22 (1989): 141-44.
——. "The Limits of Argument: Argument and Autobiography." *P&R* 26 (1989): 1-8.
Walton, Douglas. "Alethic, Epistemic, and Dialectical Modes of Argument." *P&R* 26 (1993): 302-10.

V. Metaphor
Hausman, Carl R. "Language and Metaphysics: The Ontology of Metaphor." *P&R* 24 (1991): 25-42.
Heckman, Peter. "Nietzsche's Clever Animal: Metaphor in "True and False." *P&R* 24 (1991): 301-21.
Hidalgo-Serna, Emilio. "Metaphorical Language, Rhetoric, and Comprehensio: J. L. Vives and M. Nizolio." *P&R* 23 (1990): 1-11.
Nuyen, A. T. "The Kantian Theory of Metaphor." *P&R* 22 (1989): 95-109.
Paul, Anthony M. "Metaphor and the Bounds of Expression." *P&R* 5 (1972): 143-58.
——. "Metaphor and the Bounds of Expression." *P&R* 5 (1972): 143-58.
Stewart, Donald. "Metaphor and Paraphrase." *P&R* 4 (1971): 111-23.

VI. Epistemic Rhetoric
Bineham, Jeffery L. "The Cartesian Anxiety in Epistemic Rhetoric: An Assessment of the Literature." *P&R* 23 (1990): 43-62.
——. "Beyond Reductionism in Rhetorical Theories of Meaning." *P&R* 27 (1994): 313-29.
Cherwitz, Richard A., and Thomas J. Darwin. "Toward a Relational Theory of Meaning." *P&R* 28 (1995): 17-29.
Hikins, James W., and Richard A. Cherwitz. "Irreducible Dualisms and the Residue of Common Sense: On the Inevitability of Cartesian Anxiety." *P&R* 23 (1990): 229-41.
Scott, Robert L. "On Not Defining Rhetoric." *P&R* 6 (1973): 81-96.
Zhao, Shanyang. "Rhetoric to Praxis: An Alternative to the Epistemic Approach." *P&R* 24 (1991): 255-66.

VII. The Rhetoric of Science
Lewin, Philip. "Categorization and the Narrative Structure of Science." *P&R* 27 (1994): 35-62.
Zagacki, Kenneth S., and William Keith. "Rhetoric, *Topoi*, and Scientific Revolutions." *P&R* 25 (1992): 59-78.

VIII. Rhetoric and Hermeneutics
Bineham, Jeffery L. "Displacing Descartes: Philosophical Hermeneutics and Rhetorical Studies." *P&R* 27 (1994): 300-12.
——. "The Hermeneutic Medium." *P&R* 28 (1995): 1-16.
Dascal, Marcelo. "Hermeneutical Interpretation and Pragmatic Interpretation." *P&R* 22 (1989): 239-59.
Kent, Thomas. "Hermeneutical Terror and the Myth of Interpretive Consensus." *P&R* 25 (1992): 124-39.
Malpas, J. E. "Analysis and Hermeneutics." *P&R* 25 (1992): 93-123.
Scult, Allen. "Heidegger's Hermeneutics and the Rhetoric of Biblical Theology." *P&R* 27 (1994): 397-409.
Zuñiga, Joaquin. "Hermeneutics in Ordinary Language Expressions." *P&R* 28 (1995): 365-76.

IX. Studies of Trendy Thinkers
Burke
Crusius, Timothy W. "Orality in Kenneth Burke's Dialectic." *P&R* 21 (1988): 116-30.

Heidegger
Crosswhite, James. "Mood in Argumentation: Heidegger and the Exordium." *P&R* 22 (1989): 28-42.
Grassi, Ernesto. "The Originary Quality of the Poetic and Rhetorical Word: Heidegger, Ungaretti, and Neruda." *P&R* 20 (1987): 248-60.
Hyde, Michael J. "The Call of Conscience: Heidegger and the Question of Rhetoric." *P&R* 27 (1994): 374-96.

Ramsey, Ramsey Eric. "Listening to Heidegger on Rhetoric." *P&R* 26 (1993): 266-76.
Scult, Allen. "Heidegger's Hermeneutics and the Rhetoric of Biblical Theology." *P&R* 27 (1994): 397-409.

Nietzsche
Conway, Daniel W. "Parastrategesis, Or Rhetoric for Decadents." *P&R* 27 (1994): 179-201.
Crawford, Claudia. "A Genealogy of Worlds according to Nietzsche." *P&R* 27 (1994): 202-17.
Gilmour, Douglas A. "On Language, Writing, and the Restoration of Sight: Nietzsche's Philosophical Palinode." *P&R* 27 (1994): 245-69.
Heckman, Peter. "Nietzsche's Clever Animal: Metaphor in 'True and False.'" *P&R* 24 (1991): 301-21.
Porter, James I. "Nietzsche's Rhetoric: Theory and Strategy." *P&R* 27 (1994): 218-44.

LEAH CECCARELLI

Pennsylvania State University

The Ends of Rhetoric:
Aesthetic, Political, Epistemic

In 1970 Wingspread Conference participants were asked to develop "the essential outline of a conception of rhetoric useful in the second half of the twentieth century." Twenty-five years later, we have the opportunity to reexamine their answers, and project the future for "a conception of rhetoric" in the next century. My paper will argue that there is no *one* conception of rhetoric that could be said to dominate the thinking of scholars, either today, twenty-five years ago, or even twenty-four hundred years ago; consequently, there is no reason to believe that there will be a single definition sufficient for rhetoricians of the future. Instead, rhetoric will continue to grow along at least three parallel lines that correspond to the three different *ends* of rhetorical thought. These ends are the aesthetic, the political, and the epistemic. It is the assumption of this paper that an "essential outline" of these three ultimate goals will help us to better appreciate, use, and understand the various *multiple* conceptions of rhetoric that appeared in our past, inhabit our present, and will emerge in our future.

In the first half of my paper, I will trace the ends of rhetoric for the ancient Greek thinkers Gorgias, Isocrates, and Plato. Through a close reading of primary texts, I will argue that Gorgias sought a rhetoric that extolled the power of eloquent speech to affect an audience, Isocrates sought a rhetoric that produced practical discourse to work for the good of the community, and Plato sought a rhetoric that assisted the soul in its efforts to disclose the truth. These three conceptions of rhetoric competed with each other because they corresponded to three very different views of the proper purpose of rhetorical thought and action.

In the second half of my paper, I will propose that contemporary rhetoricians are guided by variations of these three competing ends. Some are most interested in the persuasive artistry of a discourse, some are most interested in the way that discourse inspires humans to recognize and act on civic values, and some are most interested in how rhetoric aids humans in their attempts to gain knowledge. It is my argument that many of the conflicts between and within various schools of rhetoric can be attributed to the different *ends* that guide our scholarship.

The Ancients

One of the few fragments of Gorgias that survives is his treatise "On the Nonexistent," where he argued that either nothing exists, or if it exists, it is inapprehensible to humans; and even if it is apprehensible to humans, it is without a doubt incapable of being expressed or explained to the next person (*The Older Sophists* 82 B 3). Gorgias also questioned human access to truth in his *Encomium of Helen*, where he argued that because it is not easy for humans "to recall the past nor to consider the present nor to predict the future," they must "take opinion as counselor to their soul" (82 B 11.11). Astronomers, debaters of logic, and philosophers all show through their attempts to reveal truth that logic merely substitutes opinion for opinion (82 B 11.13). Although Gorgias developed rational arguments in his speeches, he didn't seem to think that those arguments would serve to reveal a higher truth.

Neither did Gorgias seem to think that his speeches would serve the greater social good of the community. Instead of consistently arguing for the good of a particular political philosophy, Gorgias seemed more interested in the immediate reaction of his audience to an image of improvement. He found power in the eloquence of speech, but it was a temporary power, not a lasting political good; it was the power to "stop fear and banish grief and create joy and nurture pity" (82 B 11.8).

The philosophy of rhetoric that Gorgias developed in his *Encomium of Helen* emphasizes the aesthetic power of speech. Says Gorgias:

> Speech is a powerful lord, which by means of the finest and most invisible body effects the divinest works. . . . Fearful shutterings and tearful pity and grievous longing come upon its hearers . . . through the agency of words, the soul is wont to experience a suffering of its own. (82 B 11.8-9)

Notice that it's the aesthetic effect of speech, its ability to create an emotional experience in the souls of its hearer, that makes it divine, not the social good or other worldly truth that it discloses. The same aspect of speech is stressed when Gorgias compares rhetoric to a drug that dispels secretions from the body that can "distress" or "delight," cause "fear," or make one "bold" (82 B 11.14). Gorgias later lays out a conception of visual art that is "analogous to [the] spoken," where perfectly formed pictures are engraved on the mind, and this delights the sight or causes one to grieve (82 B 11.17-18). In both his descriptions of spoken and visual rhetoric, Gorgias focuses his attention on the psychological power of the aesthetic composition.

In contrast, Isocrates' speech on Helen argues that the woman is worthy of praise not simply because men found pleasure in her beauty but because her beauty was able to inspire Theseus, who was the embodiment of practical discourse working for the good of the community. Similarly, Isocrates was not impressed by the beauty of rhetoric but by the political virtue it could inspire in the Athenian citizen. The goal of rhetorical education, said Isocrates, is to pursue the political good, which means "to instruct pupils in the practical affairs of our government and train to expertness therein" (§4-5).

According to Isocrates, both truth and beauty are important only as they relate to the ultimate end of the well-lived social life. Isocrates makes a double attack against the aesthetic and epistemic ends of rhetoric in a section near the beginning of his treatise on Helen. In this section Isocrates attacks those like Plato who seek exact knowledge of the "divine ideas" divorced from practical affairs and those like Gorgias who play with language, praising bumble-bees and salt instead of speaking "on subjects recognized as good or noble, or of superior moral worth" (§12).

Also, it is interesting to note that while Gorgias developed an incipient theory of aesthetic effect in his speech on Helen, Isocrates developed an incipient theory of public action. According to Isocrates, Alexander chose Helen not for the pleasure of her beauty but for very practical, political reasons: He wanted to pass the birthright of Zeus to his children because "he foresaw that this choice would be to the advantage to all his race" (§42-44). Even the Trojan and the Greek armies, who were ostensibly fighting as eager champions of their affronted leaders, were actually fighting with the larger political good on their minds: They fought "in the belief that the land in which Helen resided would be the more favored of Fortune" (§50-51). In Gorgias's speech people respond to impulses stamped upon the mind by the power of language; in Isocrates's speech people take deliberate action on political motives. Under these different philosophies of human behavior, it is not surprising that Gorgias saw the guiding purpose of rhetoric in eloquence, and Isocrates saw it in "virtue and justice" (*Antidosis* §67).

In contrast to both Gorgias and Isocrates, Plato believed the purpose of rhetoric was to assist the soul in beholding the "real eternal absolute" that resides in heaven (*Phaedrus* §247). In the *Phaedrus*, Plato says the rhetor must "know the truth," rather than be the sort of person who "has only gone about chasing after opinions" (§262). This begins his direct attack on Gorgias and other sophists who "make it seem that probabilities are more highly esteemed than truths," who "make trifles seem important and important things seem trifling," and who "rouse a crowd to anger and sooth anger by their spells" (§267). Plato claims that the sophist does not practice the art of rhetoric any more than someone who knows how to apply drugs to induce fever and make people vomit is a doctor (§268). For Plato the visceral effect of a speech is not the goal of rhetoric, as it is for Gorgias.

But neither is the ultimate goal of Plato's rhetoric the achievement of practical good for the community, as it is for Isocrates. Although the "world of affairs" must be known by the student of rhetoric, the most important knowledge to be gained is the ideal connection between different kinds of speech and different classes of soul (§271, §277). This requires "leisurely discussion, or stargazing, if you will, about the nature of things" (§270). The finished orator needs "that loftiness of mind that by all means and at all times strives to attain perfection" (§270). Plato's rhetoric is therefore part of a larger search for knowledge, a search for the truth of the gods rather than the opinions of mortals, a search for the sort of "exact knowledge" of the nonpractical that Isocrates belittled. For Plato rhetoric is guided by this epistemic goal.

I hope that at this point I have convinced you that the aesthetic, the political, and the epistemic are the three ultimate ends pursued by Gorgias, Isocrates, and Plato. I do not think these categories should be viewed rigidly; but as long as we understand the terms comparatively, and as long as we see them as the ultimate *ends* of rhetoric for these three thinkers, I believe that "eloquence," "political good," and "truth" do much to describe the guiding *topoi* and the evaluative criteria they apply to their discourse.

Contemporary Rhetoricians

Let us move now to the "ends" of contemporary rhetoricians. Before I start, I want to make it clear that my intent is not to suggest that the ancients informed our more recent views of rhetoric; the projects of the Greeks were neither transferred directly to the projects of twentieth-century rhetoricians, nor were they less-evolved versions of the later accounts.

Also, I want to make it clear that I will not try to force broad schools of contemporary rhetoric into my rough outline of the "ends of rhetoric." A close look at the particular theoretical and critical writings of several contemporary rhetoricians will show that there are scholars of all stripes who seem to privilege one ultimate end over the others.

A contemporary version of the aesthetic end is described by Steve Whitson and John Poulakos in their 1993 article, "Nietzsche and the Aesthetics of Rhetoric." They argue that "rhetoric has survived both metaphysical (mis)treatments and moralistic (ab)uses" and should now return to an aesthetic impulse (131). Like Gorgias they reject the notion that truth exists and can be described and argue instead that the goal of rhetoric is to move an audience through eloquence. They say: "Aesthetic rhetoric focuses on the human body as an excitable entity, an entity aroused by language. . . . the task of rhetoric is to speak words appealing to the bodily senses . . . aesthetic rhetoric draws its strength from seeing an audience affected by its message" (141). According to Whitson and Poulakos, this affect is one that benefits the rhetor's audience, but only temporarily. They say that

> Understood aesthetically, rhetoric allows people to suspend willingly their disbelief and be exposed to a world other or seemingly better than the one with which they are familiar, all too familiar. That is why the rhetorical art asks not for dialectically secured truths but for linguistic images that satisfy the perceptual appetites or aesthetic cravings of audiences. These appetites can only be satisfied temporarily through artistic creations. (138)

Although Whitson and Poulakos describe their aesthetic rhetoric so as to most directly oppose it to an epistemically driven rhetoric, a close reading of their article shows that it is also opposed to a politically driven rhetoric. The aesthetic perspective does not displace power to build a better social order. Instead, it associates power with "charming words, words that can veil the terrors of existence" (142). Adversity in the community is *masked*; it is not eliminated and replaced by an existence that reaches toward the political good. An aesthetic rhetoric can claim no such higher ground. Instead, it remains at the primordial level of affect, steeped in the sensual process of seduction, while taking its audience to an artistic world more enchanting and more sufferable than the one they currently inhabit (142).

Whitson and Poulakos's article calls for the type of scholarship that would seek an aesthetic end. But are there any contemporary rhetorical critics who have been guided by this end? Barbara Warnick seems to think so; she describes an aesthetically driven rhetorician when she defines "artistic criticism," a type of rhetorical criticism that "has as its primary goal appreciation rather than understanding" (233). According to Warnick, Edwin Black uses words artistically to evoke emotion and sensation. And even though he does this by writing perceptive criticism rather than speeches designed for public presentation, I would say that his purpose is the same as Gorgias's. For critics like Black, the end of rhetoric is to be moved by the tragedy and amused by the farce, and to share that affective response with an audience. His purpose is to "recreate the work, to enhance the appreciation of its artistry" (233).

Of course, in today's academy there are certain economic and political realities that make it difficult for one to admit that an aesthetic appreciation is the goal of one's scholarship. Nevertheless, this impulse does seem to drive some "close readers." For example, an aesthetic end is sought when Michael Leff traces the "intentional dynamics" and reveals the "artistic integrity" of an historical text (223). Likewise, when Tom Benson inquires "into the states of thought or feeling an audience is invited to experience," he evokes those states for his audience (235). This type of rhetorical scholarship doesn't claim to uncover the "true" effect of a text on an audience, nor does it offer an addition to political theory that promises to alter our social lives. Instead, it helps us celebrate the "brilliant achievement" and be alert to the "potential deceptiveness" of a rhetorical masterpiece (Benson 261). In plumbing the depths of an artistic work, these essays expose us to a world other than the one we recognize on a mundane, surface inspection, and in so doing, they help satisfy our perceptual appetites and aesthetic cravings. Although this is not always considered a "legitimate" end for scholars in the late twentieth century, I find this type of rhetorical scholarship most appealing. And perhaps because they neither claim a higher truth nor a better political-ethical rule, I find it easy to agree with their arguments.

Of course, many contemporary rhetoricians do not share my taste for rhetorical scholarship with an aesthetic end. In a 1993 article, Tom Farrell complains that the aestheticized cult of textuality "has had the effect of blinding many of us to . . . the places where real material grievances are stored and sometimes lost" (149). Instead, says Farrell, we should study public argument, and do so from an engaged position (156). In a 1989 article, James Aune also argues that we should stop studying the formal artistry of public address. Aune argues that textual critics should view public address documents not as "masterpieces" but as "concrete instances of political judgments, embodiments of political philosophy" (49). He says this would require us to inquire into the "nature of the 'good speech' and the nature of the regime which would best nurture such speech" (44). Many other rhetoricians agree with the sentiments of Farrell and Aune. They argue that the rhetorical critic should be "morally engaged" and "move beyond description of the rhetorical strategy to comment on the social form promoted" (Klumpp and Hollihan 87, 90). They argue that critics should take an "ideological turn" that "carries us to the point of recognizing good reasons and engaging in right action" (Wander 31). They believe that theorists should no longer focus on the aesthetic form of discourse but on the "political and ethical values that apply to public discussion" (Wallace 249). Likewise, they contest the epistemic view of rhetorical theory, arguing that "the task of rhetoric is to generate normative knowledge which guides human action rather than to search for factual knowledge which conforms to reality" (Zhao 256). In short, they promote a politically engaged criticism that seeks as its end what is good for the social body. This gives the field of rhetorical studies a cultural importance that it does not have with either the morally and politically agnostic aesthetic end or with the presumably dispassionate and impartial epistemic end.

Even so, it is probably the epistemic end that is most "legitimate" by the standards of the twentieth-century knowledge industry. Lawrence Rosenfield has argued that an overly interested political end is unreliable by academic standards of good scholarship because it "distorts the critical object or event that it confronts in order to meet the commentator's ideological preconceptions" (120). Likewise, James Hikins argues that an aesthetic purpose makes us vulnerable to elimination by forces of power in the academy (374). In contrast, a relatively disinterested study that adds new knowledge to the scholarly record is highly valued by academic standards.

Our view of "truth" may be very different from the one promoted by Plato, but it is still the search for knowledge that guides much of our contemporary rhetorical scholarship. Perhaps the strongest evidence for the influence of the "epistemic end" is the explosion of "rhetoric of inquiry" literature in the latter part of this century. Some scholars believed that rhetoric could overcome its "second rate status" in the academy by coming to understand the actual way that knowledge is shaped (Weimer 20). Whether it was to claim that science was rhetorical without remainder or to merely to claim that rhetoric had a place in the production and dissemination of academic knowledge, the epistemic end of rhetoric was secured in the study of inquiry itself (Gross; Bokeno; Lyne).

Of course, the rhetoric-of-inquiry movement is not the only place where the epistemic end has been promoted recently. In 1985 Dick Gregg argued that our best criticism ought to "suggest hypotheses regarding human rhetorical behavior that . . . provide generalizable understandings of the human rhetorical condition" (60). In 1979 Michael Hyde and Craig R. Smith claimed that "rhetoric's primordial function is the making-known of meaning in and through interpretive understanding" (355). And at the Wingspread conference twenty-five years ago, Samuel Becker called for systems and theories of rhetoric "which explain the complex web of interactions among ideas, messages, and men, and which are *testable* in some fashion" (22). Whether rhetoric is tied to the study of symbolic inducement, hermeneutics, or social science, it seeks to understand, explain, and analyze for a scholarly audience. In other words, it seeks to add to our accumulated knowledge.

The epistemic end is sought in public address scholarship, too. In a 1986 article, Rod Hart argues that we should stop trying to write history and instead "be concerned insistently and exclusively with the *conceptual record* because . . . it is that record and that record alone that will insure the continued intellectual vitality of this field of inquiry" (284). In a 1989 article, Martin Medhurst says that to produce scholarship that "is both intellectually respectable and potentially productive of various sorts of critical knowledge," our public-address studies must be "aimed at articulating general truths to a broad-based, scholarly audience" of both rhetoricians and historians (36, 39). So although Hart and Medhurst disagree about which part of the scholarly record we should be concerned with, both take it as self-evident that the aim of rhetorical study is to build knowledge by adding to the scholarly record.

Now that I have traced the aesthetic, political, and epistemic ends of rhetoric in ancient and contemporary scholarship, I would like to argue briefly that there is value in doing so. By using this schema, we do more than develop another convenient way to categorize work in our field. Recognizing the purposes that drive scholars helps us to better appreciate their scholarship. It also allows us more adequately to engage in the controversies that arise from that scholarship and more fully understand the assumptions that keep us from resolving those conflicts.

One interesting aspect of this conceptual schema is that its lines of demarcation do not parallel the most contentious division that has polarized our field of late. There are both modernist and postmodernist thinkers who believe scholarship should pursue one of these ends to the exclusion of all others. Rhetorical critics driven by the aesthetic end may be close readers who help us appreciate the formal intricacy of an historical masterpiece, or they may be deconstructive wizards who help us unravel a contemporary music video. Rhetorical critics who believe their work supports the political health of our social body might rail against the postmodern loss of a shared public life, or they might find hope in the postmodern attack on the hegemonic practices of patriarchy. Rhetorical critics who believe their work adds to the conceptual record may think of what they do as a part of the larger scientific enterprise, or they may believe that they are offering a postmodern alternative to realist conceptions of truth and knowledge. By viewing our scholarship through the "ends" that typically lie beneath the surface of awareness (and yet do so much to drive our work), we will be able to recognize affinities and understand conflicts that may not have make sense before. For example, a modernist and a postmodernist who share an aesthetic end may find that they are more able to communicate with one another than two postmodernists who hold different conceptions of the proper purpose of rhetoric. In short, I think that this lens may help us to better appreciate, use, and understand each other's scholarship. And no matter what you think the end of rhetoric is, this would be a positive change.

Works Cited

Aune, James Arnt. "Public Address and Rhetorical Theory." *Texts in Context: Critical Dialogues on Significant Episodes in American Political Rhetoric.* Ed. Michael C. Leff and Fred J. Kauffeld. Davis, CA: Hermagoras, 1989. 43-51.

Becker, Samuel L. "Rhetorical Studies for the Contemporary World." *The Prospect of Rhetoric: Report of the National Developmental Project.* Ed. Lloyd F. Bitzer and Edwin Black. Englewood Cliffs, NJ: Prentice, 1971. 21-43.

Benson, Thomas. "The Rhetorical Structure of Frederick Wiseman's High School." *Communication Monographs* 47 (1980): 233-61.

Bokeno, Michael. "The Rhetorical Understanding of Science: An Explication and Critical Commentary." *Southern Journal of Speech Communication* 52 (1987): 285-311.

Farrell, Thomas B. "On the Disappearance of the Rhetorical Aura." *Western Journal of Communication* 57 (1993): 147-58.

Gregg, Richard B. "The Criticism of Symbolic Inducement: A Critical-Theoretical Connection." *Speech Communication in the 20th Century.* Ed. Thomas W. Benson. Carbondale: Southern Illinois UP, 1985. 41-62.

Gross, Alan. "Rhetoric of Science Without Constraints." *Rhetorica* 9 (1991): 283-99.

Hart, Roderick P. "Contemporary Scholarship in Public Address: A Research Editorial." *Western Journal of Speech Communication* 50 (1986): 283-95.

Hikins, James W. "Nietzsche, Eristic, and the Rhetoric of the Possible: A Commentary on the Whitson and Poulakos 'Aesthetic View' of Rhetoric." *Quarterly Journal of Speech* 81 (1995): 353-77.

Hyde, Michael J., and Craig R. Smith. "Hermeneutics and Rhetoric: A Seen but Unobserved Relationship." *Quarterly Journal of Speech* 65 (1979): 347-63.

Isocrates. *Antidosis.* Trans. George Norlin. New York: Putnam's, 1929.

——. *Helen.* Trans. LaRue Van Hook. Cambridge: Harvard UP, 1961.

Klumpp, James F., and Thomas A. Hollihan. "Rhetorical Criticism as Moral Action." *Quarterly Journal of Speech* 75 (1989): 84-97.

Leff, Michael C. "Things Made by Words: Reflections on Textual Criticism." *Quarterly Journal of Speech* 78 (1992): 223-31.

Lyne, John. "Rhetorics of Inquiry." *Quarterly Journal of Speech* 71 (1985): 65-73.

Medhurst, Martin J. "Public Address and Significant Scholarship: Four Challenges to the Rhetorical Renaissance." *Texts in Context: Critical Dialogues on Significant Episodes in American Political Rhetoric.* Ed. Michael C. Leff and Fred J. Kauffeld. Davis, CA: Hermagoras, 1989. 29-42.

The Older Sophists: A Complete Translation By Several Hands of the Fragments in Die Fragmente Der Vorsokratiker *Edited by Diels-Kranz.* Ed. Rosamond Kent Sprague. U of Southern Carolina P, 1972.

Plato. *Phaedrus.* Trans. W. C. Helmbold and W. G. Ravinowitz. New York: Macmillan, 1956.

Rosenfield, Lawrence W. "Ideological Miasma." *Central States Speech Journal* 34 (1983): 119-21.

Wallace, Karl R. "The Substance of Rhetoric: Good Reasons." *Quarterly Journal of Speech* 49 (1963): 239-49.

Wander, Philip. "The Ideological Turn in Modern Criticism." *Central States Speech Journal* 34 (1983): 1-18.

Warnick, Barbara. "Leff in Context: What is the Critic's Role?" *Quarterly Journal of Speech* 78 (1992): 232-37.

Weimer, Walter B. "Science as a Rhetorical Transaction: Toward a Nonjustificational Conception of Rhetoric." *Philosophy and Rhetoric* 10 (1977): 1-29.

Whitson, Steve, and John Poulakos. "Nietzsche and the Aesthetics of Rhetoric." *Quarterly Journal of Speech* 79 (1993): 131-45.

Zhao, Shanyang. "Rhetoric as Praxis: An Alternative to the Epistemic Approach." *Philosophy and Rhetoric* 24 (1991): 255-66.

JAMES F. KLUMPP

University of Maryland, College Park

The Rhetoric of Community at Century's End

To a young graduate student, "Wingspread" sounded like an exotic place. It was, of course, uniquely American that leaders of the discipline of 1970 would go off on a bucolic pilgrimage to invent the future. When I saw the first product of that conference—a copy of the report of the Committee on Rhetorical Invention slipped to me in a seminar—excitement was hard to contain. When *The Prospect of Rhetoric* reached my bookshelves, I was ready to endorse the practice of American business to have all great meetings in these bucolic Meccas.

That book was absolutely crucial in the quarter century since. It preached a bit—I remember particularly the absolutely compelling essay by Hugh Duncan—but served us well by setting forth an agenda of questions that we should be asking, material we should be examining, and approaches we should be taking. But mostly, I think, the book served as a legitimizer for the generation of scholars who have worked since that time. When we wanted to do something different, to challenge those tacit barriers that a profession establishes to proscribe ideas that stray too far from the common, there was *Prospect* from which to select a juicy quotation to challenge the tradition we were confronting. The conference and its volume shaped the work of our generation.

It is entirely appropriate that we should reprise Wingspread this quarter of a century later. It is not so much the magic of the silver anniversary that is important, but the fact that we have somehow survived the turbulent sixties, moved through the deadening seventies, the narcissistic eighties, half-way through the angry nineties, and lie on the verge of the twenty-first century with new challenges for rhetoric. For the spirit of Wingspread was to examine the state of rhetorical study with an eye to the times and the social context and to reenvision the discipline's tasks as meet that assessment.

In this essay I focus on the crisis of public life and community at the end of the century. I consider the rhetorical dimensions of that problem and the resources of rhetorical scholarship that can be brought to addressing the problem in the coming years. My argument is that the task of our time is to develop rhetorical theory and criticism that strengthens communities and their ability to adapt to change.

The Crisis in Public Life

The National Developmental Conference on Rhetoric fell at the end of the calendar decade of the 1960s, and in the midst of the social decade of great change that we know today simply as "The Sixties." The sixties were marked by confrontations of power, initiated and opposed by human will. The changes were loudly urged and heralded, and the opposition harsh and polemic. Today, we once again live in the midst of change. A globalization ushered in by the computer age brings fundamental economic and social changes that we must confront daily. Yet, the crisis of our time is not to contain the raging cacophony of human will; rather we strain to discern the voices of others who pass through this time with us. Ours is a crisis of isolation seeking the strength of human will. Battered by forces often greater than we can comprehend, we search in vain for an attitude that would allow us to negotiate their impact upon us. We can see old securities fading and feel the jarring inappropriateness of old patterns of living, but how to orient ourselves to our new experiences is painfully unclear.

At times like these, we turn to others. When rhetoric serves us properly, we recognize that times of change are shared by others. Through our discursive powers, we join to texture the change in ways that we recognize and to weave approaches that frame human choices that negotiate the change. Our rhetorical action transforms our private disorientation into a search for public direction. Today, traditional rhetorical institutions fail to provide meaningful access to public life, and we have so far failed to invent new ways of achieving the dialogue that would provide orientation. The crisis of our time is that public life remains elusive.

The most obvious symptom of this problem is the failure of our political system. The American electorate swings wildly in search of leaders who can articulate the character of the change and marshall commitment to negotiate the new age. None are found. The result is a cynicism toward political institutions. When the political system approaches this problem in the way it knows—the opinion poll—it easily finds the evidence of its crisis. "Trust" in governmental institutions is at an all-time low. The *Washington Post* reports that "In 1964, three in four Americans trusted the federal government all or most of the time, a view shared by one in four persons today" (Morin and Balz). The *Post* found that the result was not a shift of trust to other institutions but a general deterioration in trust in any institutions and even in other people, in human nature. "Americans with low trust in human nature are more likely to see themselves as politically powerless and to see politicians as unsympathetic to their needs" (Morin and Balz).

Furthermore, this lack of faith is largely justified. Our political system still operates in a traditional theory of rhetoric grounded in persuasion. We have, in a real sense, perfected that theory into a mechanical system that cannot respond to the needs of our time. Our politics today are marked by reduction: Public opinion is reduced to opinion polls; responsibility to participate is reduced to voting; messages are reduced to sound bites; and politicians are reduced to strategists of, and deliverers of, messages. The logic driving our political decisions has become a weighing of competing interest groups. The emotion has been diverted into a two-valued, polemic portrayal of opposition. In the face of our problems, government is paralyzed to take effective action. After voting for change in 1992 and finding none, and voting for change again in 1994 and finding none, the voters' cynicism has deepened. The political system's own measure of its faith—the percent of the electorate who vote—struggles to break 50 percent. A President of the United States is inaugurated upon receiving the endorsement of about one-fourth of the eligible voters. The 1994 election witnessed only 38.7 percent of the electorate going to the polls (Claiborne). Legitimacy is supported only by the machinations of the political culture.

The techniques of modern politics are designed and are most appropriate for late-capitalistic bureaucratic administration. The system has developed a rationale for its state that sheds the responsibility onto the victims. Typical is columnist Chris Black's charge that the cynicism of youth results from their ignorance about basic responsibilities of citizenship. A more systemic view of the process is far too rare. Polls reduce public opinion to defined demographics and narrowly defined responses. Managers formulate messages to echo the reductions of the polls. Candidates reduce leadership to service in office and view their incumbency as depending on their obedience to the managers. The media's fascination with providing play-by-play of this closed process constitutes our politics in a rhetoric of the game. Those governed are constituted as markets, segmented and activated by diverse targeted messages.

Structurally, the cycle of interest-group influence, campaign contributions, and the necessity of funding for campaigns is nearly impossible for successful political candidates to break. The commodification of our political system and the tremendously expensive "campaign industry" of managers, pollsters, reporters, and candidates demands more and more wealth to contend for governmental office at the national level. The decline of the mass media and the growth of narrow casting magnifies the problem. The fragmented audience presents new demands for more specific polling, ever more targeted messages, and the much more expensive technology of mass mailing.

Yet, if my students are any measure, the cynicism toward the political process—government is the way they think about it—is not matched by a desire to abandon public life. They recognize that not all of their problems are private and that not all the responsibilities for their community should be born in isolation. They sense the dramatic economic changes brought by globalism and the dawn of postindustrialism. They recognize that the increasing diversity of their classes and their world beyond the classroom poses the problem of constructing a multicultural community that thrives off difference rather than suppressing it. They wish to reach out to others, to define a purpose for action by their community, and to join with others in accomplishing what they consider good.

But in the face of the alienation from politics, we are left without alternative institutions for generating and directing public cohesiveness. How does the public develop commitment to work together in addressing the vicissitudes of their lives? Who can command their attention and use the voice to develop community will? These are questions raised in what colleagues and I have called the "postpolitical" age (see Hollihan et al.; Klumpp et al.; Riley et al.). The need that we face today is to pursue the rhetorical resources available to us for building public life. How do we construct viable communities that provide human choice and human will as we negotiate the problems that we face?

Developing Rhetorical Notions of Community

Twentieth-century rhetorical theory and criticism has had a heavy stake in the political system that has failed us. Teaching of rhetorical technique throughout the century has been dominated by a rhetoric of personal persuasion. The entire, commodified, expensive political communication machine is based in a neo-Aristotelian theory of personal appeal. The rhetoric of our century has highlighted institutional sites for rhetoric and portrayed democracy as a deliberative arena. Our portrayal of audience as respondent to rhetorical appeals creates the image that has fed the reduction of public opinion. Perhaps most importantly, we have invested in political communication in a way that has left a reduced notion of the importance of discourse to a democracy.

Yet, a different orientation—a rhetoric that emphasizes the building of communities as a central rhetorical task—has been a prominent feature of rhetorical theory and criticism late in the current century. The extensive frameworks of Kenneth Burke and Richard Weaver have provided direction to such study. Burke's most prolific decade—the 1930s—focused his thought on the place of language in defining community as a context for social change. Burke describes the use of rhetorical resources to negotiate the dialectic of permanence and change—the first of many dialectical tensions in Burke's work. These are dialectically related stresses copresent in successful rhetorical action, *permanence* assuring the sense of continuity that creates human subjectivity through the resources of narrative and *change* providing the sense of adjustment that connects daily life to the evolution of our material and social environment. The Burkean notion of dialectic also stresses symbolic motivation: that the strategic resources of language empower human communities to define human choice by melding these copresent forces into motives learned, applied, and evolved in daily activity. In *Attitudes Toward History*, Burke explores the place of ritual in the development of motives that place humans into history with a sense of power in their daily lives. This basic framework for working with the rhetorical construction of community gives life to many of the familiar resources for strategically defining life situations.

Burke's dialectic tension between identity and identification places the focus precisely on the problem we are delineating. *Persuasion*, Burke asserts, is the term for traditional rhetoric, *identification* for the new rhetoric (*Rhetoric* xiv). The rhetorical discourse of a community transforms the tension between the assertion of individual identity and the embracing of community identification into the energy that creates discourse about values and the identity of the community. Thus the identity/identification pair is not in the same relationship as the individual/community pair. Rather these pairs work on each other to transform themselves into their paradoxical opposites. Rhetoric invents self by appropriating patterns (Burke calls them "form," of course) that attain power from their appeal in community. The assertion of self-identity is articulated in the recognizable language of the community, and assertion of identity is an act of identification that not only asserts the character of the individual but also negotiates the character of the community.

In its political roots, Richard Weaver's participation in the conservative movement spawned by the Southern agrarians contrasts with Kenneth Burke's flirtation with communism. Yet Weaver's notion about what he calls "the cultural role of rhetoric" shares many of Burke's assumptions. Weaver's conservatism stressed the traditional, to be sure, but there was in Weaver the notion of change embodied in dialectic. In "Dialectic and Rhetoric at Dayton, Tennessee," Weaver argues that rhetoric was a necessary counterpart to dialectic because only with rhetoric was community formed.

Encouraged by the reports of the Committees on Rhetorical Criticism and Rhetorical Invention in the *Prospect of Rhetoric*, assumptions such as these spawned study of social movements and processes of community construction in rhetoric. Other major projects entered the dialogue. Walter Fisher's work with narrative focused attention on this rhetorical power. Jürgen Habermas's project proposed to develop a normative-based ethic of discourse in public life. Thomas Farrell's recent *Norms of Rhetorical Culture* is an attempt to provide a more Aristotelian-based theory of public life. The direction of this work was away from existing institutions and from a focus on deliberation as the archetypal democratic discourse. Attention turned to seeing discourse's role in developing, critiquing, and nurturing values that guide public life far beyond the political process. Celeste Condit's work on "Crafting Values" comes to mind as this sort of work.

Other work has combined criticism with theory to point toward processes of community construction. Maurice Charland's work with "the constituted audience" stressed the work that rhetoric does in creating civic identity. Michael McGee's work on the ideograph of <people> and Celeste Condit and John Louis Lucaites' work with <equality> stressed the power of discourse to work through civic identity. Theorizing the powers of such a rhetoric and opening the vision of such a rhetoric in criticism points the way toward a reinvigoration of participation in the lifeworld and a viable postpolitical public life.

There is reason to believe that a focus on a rhetoric that builds public community will have a warm reception. PBS recently sponsored a National Issues Forum at the University of Texas. Focus groups were constituted using standard statistical polling techniques, and those selected were flown to Austin to meet and discuss public issues. Issues to be discussed were strictly controlled, and wandering from the subject was discouraged. Despite all these heavy-handed controls on the breadth of public discussion, the limits of such control were soon exceeded. Groups were nearly irrepressible in diverting discussion into subjects that they viewed as more relevant than those urged on them by the masters of the process. In addition, interviews with participants following the Forum revealed that they were most energized by the differences that they encountered in the discussion. Far from seeking like-minded interactants with whom they could form identity enclaves, these participants expressed eagerness to hear from people who had different life experiences. A rhetorician listening to these interviews easily observed the difference between the rich rhetoric of "experience" and the embracing of difference among those who participated in the focus groups and the reductive rhetoric of demographics, attitudes, and "changes in polling results" among those who set up the experiment and tried to contain it.

An Agenda for Working toward Rhetorical Community

The notion of rhetoric places language at the necessary merger of identity and identification. Words are a constant in our lives because we use them to negotiate our relationship to others in response to the events of our lives. Emphasizing the power rhetorical skill gives *individuals* in that negotiation is an arbitrary punctuation of the rhetorical act. It is the punctuation that has dominated the twentieth century. The equally viable but so far less-explored punctuation that emphasizes the vitality of rhetoric as the key to *communities* successfully negotiating times of change is now a critical priority. Central problems remain in this latter strain of rhetorical scholarship. The postmodern condition compels close scrutiny of the nature of agency in the dialectic between identity and identification. Similarly, notions of self and the power to construct subjectivity are not fully resolved. Authority becomes a particularly difficult rhetorical problem in a postpolitical community. The dialectical tension between coherence and hegemony remains to be fully explored.

Such work is crucial to our future, however. The postindustrial world that we have entered promises disorientation as profound as that experienced in the shift from an agrarian to an industrial world a century ago. The postmodern condition defines a need for orientational powers more difficult than experienced in the familiar confines of modernity. The globalization of daily life requires new concepts of community that transcend the nation-state. The globalization of corporate culture voids past arrangements to humanize the excesses of that culture and challenges us to develop new institutions to control new material structures. This is a broad agenda made urgent by the rapid approach of the crisis of public life. The challenge in the new century is to use the prospect of rhetoric to address the possibilities.

Works Cited

Bitzer, Lloyd F., and Edwin Black, eds. *The Prospect of Rhetoric*. Englewood Cliffs, NJ: Prentice, 1971.

Black, Chris. "America's Young Have Tuned Out on Politics." *Boston Globe* 13 May 1990: A17.

Burke, Kenneth. *Attitudes Toward History*. 3rd ed. Rpt. Berkeley: U of California P, 1984.

———. *Permanence and Change*. 3rd ed. Rpt. Berkeley: U of California P, 1984.

———. *Rhetoric of Motives*. Rpt. Berkeley: U of California P, 1969.

Charland, Maurice. "Constitutive Rhetoric: The Case of the *Peuple Québécois*." *Quarterly Journal of Speech* 73 (1987): 133-50.

Claiborne, William. "38.7% of Eligible Americans Vote, A 12-Year, Non-Presidential High." *Washington Post* 12 November 1994:A3.

Condit, Celeste Michele. "Crafting Virtue: The Rhetorical Construction of Public Morality." *Quarterly Journal of Speech* 73 (1987): 79-97.

Condit, Celeste Michele, and John Louis Lucaites. *Crafting Equality*. Chicago: U of Chicago P, 1993.

Farrell, Thomas. *Norms of Rhetorical Culture*. New Haven: Yale UP, 1993.

Hollihan, Thomas A., Patricia Riley, and James F. Klumpp. "Greed versus Hope, Self-Interest versus Community: Reinventing Argumentative Praxis in Post-Free Marketplace America." *Argument and the Postmodern Challenge: Proceedings of the Eighth SCA/AFA Conference on Argumentation*. Ed. Raymie E. McKerrow. Annandale, VA: SCA, 1993. 332-39.

Klumpp, James F., Patricia Riley, and Thomas A. Hollihan. "Argument in the Post-Political Age: Emerging Sites for a Democratic Lifeworld." *Special Fields and Cases*. Vol. 4. *Proceedings of the Third ISSA Conference on Argumentation*. Ed. Frans H. van Eemeren, Rob Grootendorst, J. Anthony Blair, and Charles A. Willard. Amsterdam: SicSat, 1995. 318-28.

McGee, Michael Calvin. "In Search of 'The People': A Rhetorical Alternative." *Quarterly Journal of Speech* 61 (1975): 235-49.

Morin, Richard, and Dan Balz. "Americans Losing Trust in Each Other and Institutions." *Washington Post* 28 January 1996: A6.

Riley, Patricia, James F. Klumpp, and Thomas A. Hollihan. "Democratizing the 21st Century: Evaluating Arguments for New Democratic Sites." *Argumentation and Values: Proceedings of the Ninth SCA/AFA Summer Conference on Argumentation*. Ed. Sally Jackson. Annandale, VA: SCA, 1996. 254-60.

Weaver, Richard. *The Ethics of Rhetoric*. Rpt. Chicago: Regnery, 1965.

———. *Language Is Sermonic*. Ed. Richard L. Johannesen, Rennard Strickland, and Ralph T. Eubanks. Baton Rouge: Louisiana State UP, 1970.

CHARLES BAZERMAN

University of California, Santa Barbara

Genre and Social Science:
Renewing Hopes of Wingspread

The Wingspread Conference, as represented in *The Prospect of Rhetoric*, struck many prophetic themes. Several are close to my heart: concern for communicative transactions other than the persuasive, an interest in the changing technology of communication, and calls for the rhetoric of science and technology, the rhetoric of the everyday, and the rhetoric of the many institutional and bureaucratic settings of modern society. Speakers at that conference recognized that the complexity of modern differentiated society has created many locales of communication with new dynamics and tasks. Further, several of the speakers, most explicitly Wayne Booth, Wayne Brockriede, and Hugh Duncan, suggested that to understand rhetoric in its new circumstances we take up the tools and knowledge of the social sciences.

There were, to be sure, voices on the other side, arguing for the autonomy and special knowledge of rhetoric, pointing out that rhetoric, long subordinated to the empirical social sciences, has its own special message that needs to be delivered forcefully. I am too much an outsider to communications departments to attempt a survey of the historical and continuing tensions between classicists and moderns. Nor will I attempt to sort how the rediscovery of rhetoric in writing programs—housed within English Literature departments—has reinforced those divisions. Nor will I consider how literary theory's versions of rhetoric have turned the dialogue in different directions; nor will I survey how the social sciences themselves have engaged lines of rhetorical and discursive inquiry.

Rather I will simply present one domain where rhetoric and the social sciences have converged—namely, the study of genre within social action. This convergence has been only partly recognized on both sides, but it is proceeding. From rhetoric's side the initial and key gesture in this convergence was Carolyn Miller's use of Alfred Schutz's concept of social typification in the production and phenomenology of everyday life. Miller built on an already vital concern for genre within speech rhetoric, documented in her article and soon to produce several major volumes such as Campbell and Jamieson's *Deeds Done in Words*. Nonetheless, seeing genre as typified social action had particular hold for writing researchers trying to understand the social location of writing, a problem not nearly as puzzling for students of speech.

For this audience I don't need to rehearse Miller's arguments, the consequent elaborations by others of relations between genre and typified social action, typified knowledge production, typified social relations, and social structure. I might mention, however, that the door for me (as I was already engaged with sociology) was a two-way door, one that helped me see the conceptual resources rhetoric had to offer in unpacking issues in science studies and scientific communication. I also don't need to rehearse how interest in genre spread within writing programs and writing research, perhaps first starting in areas of professional and technical writing (see, for example, the work of Berkenkotter and Huckin; Russell; Journet; Schryer) but now applied to all domains including classroom genres, freshman writing genres, expressive, and humanistic genres (see, for example, the forthcoming volume edited by Bishop and Ostrom).

Early in this exploration of genre as typified social action, there was a mutually discovered intersection with applied linguistics. About fifteen years ago, I heard of the work of John Swales, who used the functional linguistic concept of moves to explore the structure of introductions to scientific articles. I meant to write him, but before I could get around to it, he wrote me. In the applied linguistic specialty of English for Specific Purposes, many have followed Swales's and his students' lead in mapping out the formal structures of genres of professional writing. Other applied linguists, such as Tony Dudley-Evans, Vijay Bhatia, Aviva Freedman, Amy Devitt, Dwight Atkinson, Patrick Dias, Anthony Pare, and Pete Medway, have been developing mixed composition and linguistic elaborations of genre. A further force in this intersection was the more technical elaboration of genre within the Australian Structural Functional Linguistic school, led by Halliday; Hasan, Martin, and Christie particularly concerned themselves with the role of genre in the SFL system and its application to the public schools, arousing more than a little controversy in Australia. Gunther Kress then took the issues back to Britain, but with an interpretation of genre that foregrounds more its relation to both critical linguistics (see also Fairclough) and to American composition expressivist interests. Cope and Kalantzis elaborate this linguistic perspective.

Genre soon formed another bridge with social studies of science, across the notion of social typification as a means of regularizing scientific communication and practice. This occurred within a turn of science studies to discourse analysis as a means of illuminating social constructionism (Latour and Woolgar; Latour; Knorr-Cetina). Among the more radical social-constructivist epistemologists, the recognition and reaction against existing disciplinary genres led to the movement known as new literary forms—essentially sociologists discovering new ways to write that would expose their reflexive understanding of their own work (Woolgar; Gilbert and Mulkay). Historians of science, such as Shapin and Schaffer, and Dear, influenced by the social studies of science, began looking into the discursive formation of science, and paying attention to the forms of scientific communication. A number of us from rhetoric entered into the dialogue with science studies to examine the activities, social roles, and social mechanisms of controlled conflict embedded within the genres of scientific communication.

Simultaneously with the rhetorical turn of the social studies of science, a number of disciplines in the social sciences took their own reflexive rhetorical turns to evaluate the limitations of their traditional forms of professional discourse. Anthropology (led by such figures as Geertz; Clifford and Marcus; Rosaldo) began a deeply disturbing and broadly influential examination of the genre of ethnography and economics (led by McCloskey; Klamer; Henderson) developed a critique of the narrowly mathematical forms of economic argument as not reflecting the full range of issues at stake.

Anthropologists, building on the longstanding interest in cultural norms and in linguistics, once attuned to the powerful force of genre, began to use genre as a substantial tool in cultural analysis. Bauman, in studying the cultural production of folk tales, explored the implications of genre and made salient the role of genre in prior anthropological work (see Briggs and Baumann). Goffman's ideas of framing and footing and Gumperz's concept of contextualization clue made the link between microinteractional linguistic data and the larger forms of social recognizability realized in genre, a lead that was followed by Hanks and Duranti.

In sociology several lines of work building on Schutz's comments on typification discovered genre and genre-like issues. Schutz's student, Thomas Luckmann (well known for his book with Berger on *The Social Construction of Reality*), came to see genre as one of the primary mechanisms by which we constructed social realities (see Bergmann and Luckmann). In turn his students began to explore the sociological implications of genre (Guenther and Knoblauch). The most elaborate piece of work from this tradition to this date has been Bergmann's *Discreet Indiscretions* that explores the moral and phenomenological dimensions of the genre of gossip.

Ethnomethodology and conversational analysis, again starting with Schutz and the idea of social typification, began examining how we construct and hold ourselves accountable to social forms (see Garfinkel; Sacks). This work has most explicitly touched back on genre in a recent essay by Schegloff that includes comments on how extended turns are produced and recognized through the invocation of perceivable discursive forms, such as jokes that hold the floor until punchlines are reached.

In trying to find a phenomenologically plausible agent-oriented sociology that reconciles microscopic accounts of behavior with macroscopic issues of social structure, an entirely different strain of sociology has developed accounts of typified action that are compatible with an interest of genre—namely

Bourdieu's account of habitus and Giddens' of structuration. While these sociologies themselves have not yet recognized genre as a useful resource, genre studies have found them useful for understanding how individual utterances shaped within generic regularities reproduce and carry forward larger patterns of social organization.

Two more interdisciplinary conjunctions need to be mentioned to fill out the complex of genre studies as they currently stand. The first ties genre studies back to one of their longstanding homes: literary studies. Bakhtin's career-long concern for the ways in which genres represent utterances and recognizable voices within novels led ultimately to his late essay on "The Problem of Speech Genres." That essay in breaking away from the world of literary representation has led to a revivification of genre studies in literature, with the message most explicitly carried by Todorov but also lending weight to the longstanding interest of Ralph Cohen, and recently extended by Beebee. This new literary work is more savvy about the relationship between textual forms, social transmission, individual consciousness, and ideology than prior literary work on genre. The work of Bakhtin also has made the circuit of linguistics, sociology, and anthropology, giving energy and literary panache to genre work in the social sciences.

Finally, Cultural Historical Activity Theory (CHAT)—building on Vygotsky and other Soviet psychologists but now being extended in relation to organizational theory (Engestrom) and Cognitive Science (Hutchins, Nardi)—has been a useful umbrella for a number of the genre theorists to bring together their observations about genre as a form of social activity that itself helps structure those activities, mediates relationships, and provides tools for the growth of individual cognition. Russell, Freedman, Medway, Dias, Berkenkotter, Prior, Winsor, Blakeslee, and I, among others, have been incorporating activity theory in our work, and genre has become an increasingly visible concept in the activity theory world (most visibly present in the journal *Mind, Culture, and Activity*).

What do we get from this convergence of disciplinary interests over the concept of genre? First, we have more people of different orientations studying different kinds of genres from different cultural locales. We have moved far from the agora and the three genres of epideictic, forensic, and deliberative and far from the standard arrangement of exordium, narrative, proof, and peroration. The scientific article, the ethnography, and the kaffee-klatsch stand beside the Polynesian Laugo, chronicles of colonial Mexico, and the jive-talking put-on. Each has its most salient features, but each also has been examined from the particular perspective of the examiners, exposing cultural, ideological, linguistic, interactional, formal, epistemic, phenomenological, and social structural vitality in the generic utterance. We are seeing more of what is at stake in genre.

The example of genre also suggests how rhetoric stands in the middle of an interdisciplinary study of human life, intertwined, as human life is, with our intentional and reflective use of language. But rhetoric gets transformed as it enters in dialogue with the human sciences, which over the last century have documented and contemplated much about our lives. The last time there was a thoroughgoing attempt to rethink rhetoric in light of our understanding of the human was in the eighteenth century—addressing the kinds of psychological and interpersonal problems posed by Hume, but that initiative ossified as it found temporary answers in sympathy, then sentiment, and then belles-lettristic aesthetics. In this century we have had some sporadic attempts to rethink rhetoric in light of new observations about humans and human society by a few individuals, most notably Burke, but these have been partial and had little systematic impact. They were expressed more in the hopes than in the practice.

Genre's interdisciplinary history suggests how such a rethinking of rhetoric might proceed. The rhetorical tradition contains a series of concepts that point to features of language use that have appeared salient to language users within a group of related cultural traditions. These reflective categories are clues as to what people have made of language and thus provide some strong clues about what language has become. However, these uses of language need to be compared to the explicit reflections on language used in other cultures (as is now beginning in the comparative rhetoric movement) and to the actual practices, whether or not an explicit reflective vocabulary has developed for them and whether or not the practices themselves follow that reflective vocabulary. Then we need to place our understanding of these language practices and reflective vocabularies within a much broader inquiry into the role of language in human life, in its many dimensions. At that point we will be in a better position to examine the relationship between the explicit vocabularies and pedagogies of language use and the actual social practices. And we will be in a better position to develop new reflective vocabularies and pedagogies to fit the changing communicative needs of historically evolving societies.

Works Cited

Atkinson, Dwight. *Scientific Discourse in Sociohistorical Context: The Philosophical Transactions of the Royal Society of London, 1675-1975.* Mahwah, NJ: Erlbaum, 1997.

Bakhtin, Mikhail. *The Dialogic Imagination.* Austin: U of Texas P, 1986.

——. *Speech Genres & Other Late Essays.* Austin: U of Texas P, 1986.

Bauman, Richard. *Story, Performance, and Event.* Cambridge: Cambridge UP, 1986.

——. "Contextualization, Tradition, and the Dialogue of Genres." *Rethinking Context.* Ed. Allesandro Duranti and Charles Goodwin. Cambridge: Cambridge UP, 1992. 77-99.

Bazerman, Charles. *Shaping Written Knowledge: The Genre and Activity of the Experimental Articles in Science.* Madison: U of Wisconsin P, 1988.

——. "Social Forms as Habitats for Action." *Festschrift for Ralph Cohen.* Lexington: U of Kentucky P, 1997.

——. "Systems of Genre and the Enactment of Social Intentions." *Rethinking Genre*. Ed. A. Freedman and P. Medway. London: Taylor & Francis, 1994. 79-101.

——. "Whose Moment?: The Kairotics of Intersubjectivity." *Constructing Experience*. Carbondale: Southern Illinois UP, 1994. 171-93.

Bazerman, Charles, and James Paradis, eds. *Textual Dynamics of the Professions*. Madison: U of Wisconsin P, 1991.

Beebee, Thomas O. *The Ideology of Genre: A Comparative Study of Generic Instability*. University Park: Pennsylvania State UP, 1994.

Berger, Peter, and T. Luckmann. *The Social Construction of Reality*. New York: Doubleday, 1966.

Bergmann, Joerg R. *Discreet Indiscretions: The Social Organization of Gossip*. New York: DeGruyter, 1993.

Bergmann, Joerg R., and Thomas Luckmann. "Reconstructive Genres of Everyday Communication." *Aspects of Oral Communication*. Ed. Uta Quasthoff. Breling: DeGruyter, 1994.

Berkenkotter, Carol, and Tom Huckin. *Genre Knowledge in Discipliinary Communication*. Hillsdale, NJ: Erlbaum, 1995.

Bhatia, Vijay. *Analysing Genre: Language Use in Professional Settings*. London: Longman, 1993.

Bishop, Wendy, and Hans Ostrom, eds. *Genre and the Teaching of Writing*. Upper Montclair, NJ: Boynton/Cook, 1997.

Bitzer, Lloyd, and Edwin Black. *The Prospect of Rhetoric*. Englewood Cliffs, NJ: Prentice, 1971.

Blakeslee, Ann. *Rhetoric in Science: Social and Rhetorical Practice in Ordinary Science*. Mahwah, NJ: Erlbaum, forthcoming 1998.

Bourdieu, Pierre. *The Field of Cultural Production*. New York: Columbia UP, 1993.

——. *Language & Symbolic Power*. Cambridge: Harvard UP, 1991.

——. *Outline of a Theory of Practice*. Cambridge: Harvard UP, 1991.

Briggs, Charles L. "Generic versus Metapragmatic Dimensions of Warao Narratives: Who Regiments Performances." *Reflexive Language*. Ed. John Lucy. Cambridge: Cambridge UP. 179-212.

Briggs, Charles L., and R. Bauman. "Genre, Intertextuality and Social Power." *Journal of Linguistic Anthropology* 2 (1992):131-72.

Campbell, Karlyn Kohrs, and Kathleen Hall Jamieson. *Deeds Done in Words*. Chicago: U of Chicago P, 1990.

Christie, Francis. "The Morning News Genre." *Language and Education* 4 (1990): 161-79.

Clifford, James, and George Marcus. *Writing Culture*. Berkeley: U of California P, 1986.

Cohen, Ralph. "Do Postmodern Genres Exist?" *Genre* 20 (1987): 241-57.

Cohen, Ralph. "History and Genre." *New Literary History* 17 (1986): 203-18.

Cope, Bill, and Mary Kalantzis. *The Powers of Literacy: A Genre Approach to Teaching Writing*. Pittsburgh: U of Pittsburgh P, 1993.

Dear, Peter. *Discipline and Experience*. Chicago: U of Chicago P, 1995.

Dear, Peter, ed. *The Literary Structure Of Scientific Argument*. Philadelphia: U of Pennsylvania P, 1991.

Dear, Peter. "Totius in Verba." *Isis* 76 (1985): 145-61.

Devitt, Amy. "Intertextuality in Tax Accounting: Generic, Referential, and Functional." Charles Bazerman and James Paradis. *Textual Dynamics of the Professions*. Madison: U of Wisconsin P, 1991. 336-80.

——. *Standardizing Written English*. Cambridge: Cambridge UP, 1989.

Dias, Patrick, Anthony Pare, Aviva Freedman, and Peter Medway. *Writing in Academic and Workplace Settings: Affordances and Constraints*. Mahwah, NJ: Erlbaum, 1997.

Dudley-Evans, Tony. "Genre Analysis: An Investigation of the Introduction and Discussion Sections of M.Sc. Dissertrations." *Talking About Text*. Ed. M. Coulthard. Birmingham: English Language Research, 1986. 128-45.

Duranti, Alessandro. *From Grammar to Politics*. Berkeley: U of California P, 1994.

——. "Laugo and Talanoago: Two Speech Genres in a Samoan Political Event." *Dangerous Words: Language and Politics in the Pacific*. Ed. Donald Brenneis and Fred Myers. New York: NYU P, 1984: 217-42.

Duranti, A., and C. Goodwin. *Rethinking Context: Language as an Interactive Phenomenon.* Cambridge: Cambridge UP, 1992.

Engestrom, Yrjo. "Developmental Studies of Work as a Testbench of Activity Theory: The Case of Primary Care Medical Practice." Ed. S. Chaiklin and J. Lave. *Understanding Practice.* Cambridge: Cambridge UP, 1993. 64-103.

Fairclough, Norman. *Discourse and Social Change.* London: Polity, 1991.

Freedman, A. "Reconceiving genre." *Texte* 8/9 (1990): 279-92.

Freedman, Aviva. "Show and Tell? The Role of Explicit Teaching in the Learning of New Genres." *Research in the Teaching of English* 27 (1993): 5-35.

Freedman, A., C. Adam, and G. Smart. "Wearing Suits to Class: Simulating Genres and Simulations as Genre." *Written Communication* 11 (1994): 193-226.

Freedman, Aviva, and Peter Medway. *Genre in the New Rhetoric.* London: Taylor, 1995.

——. *Learning and Teaching Genre.* Portsmouth, NH: Heinemann, 1994.

Garfinkel, Harold. *Studies in Ethnomethodology.* Englewood Cliffs, NJ: Prentice, 1967.

Geertz, Clifford. "Blurred Genres: The Refiguration of Social Thought." *Local Knowledge.* New York: Basic, 1983. 19-35.

Giddens, Anthony. *The Constitution of Society.* Berkeley: U of California P, 1984.

Gilbert, Nigel, and Michael Mulkay. *Opening Pandora's Box.* Cambridge: Cambridge UP, 1984.

Goffman, Erving. *Forms of Talk.* Philadelphia: U of Pennsylvania P, 1981.

——. *Frame Analysis.* New York: Harper, 1974.

Guenther, Susanne, and Huber Knoblauch. "The Analysis of Communicative Genres—Linking Detailed Sequential Analyses of Verbal Activities with Cultural Speaking Practices and Communicative Norms." Manuscript, 1994.

Gumperz, John. "Contextualization and Understanding." *Rethinking Context.* Ed. A. Duranti and C. Goodwin. Cambridge: Cambridge UP, 1992. 229-52.

——. "The Linguistic and Cultural Relativity of Conversational Inference." *Rethinking Relativism.* Ed. J. Gumperz and S. Levinson. Cambridge: Cambridge UP, 1995.

Halliday, Michael. *Spoken and Written English.* Oxford: Oxford UP, 1989.

Halliday, Michael, and James Martin. *Writing Science.* Pittsburgh: U of Pittsburgh P, 1993.

Hanks, William F. "Discourse Genres in a Theory of Praxis." *American Ethnologist* 14 (1987): 668-92.

——. *Referential Practice.* Chicago: U of Chicago P, 1990.

Hasan, Ruqaiya. "The Structure of Text." *Language, Context, and Text.* Ed. M. Halliday and R. Hasan. Geelong: Deakin UP, 1985. 52-69.

Henderson, W., et al., eds. *Economics and Language.* London: Routledge, 1993.

Hutchins, Edwin. *Cognition in the Wild.* Cambridge: MIT P, 1995.

Journet, Debra. "Interdisciplinary Discourse and 'Boundary Rhetoric': The Case of S. E. Jelliffe." *Written Communication* 10 (1993): 510-41.

Klamer, A, D. McCloskey, and R. Solow, eds. *The Consequences of Economic Rhetoric.* Cambridge: Cambridge UP, 1988.

Kress, Guther. "Genre as Social Process." *The Process of Literacy: A Genre Approach to Teaching Writing.* Ed. Bill Cope and Mary Kalantzis. Pittsburgh: U of Pittsburgh P, 1993.

Knorr-Cetina, Karin. *The Manufacture of Knowledge.* Oxford: Pergamon, 1981.

Latour, Bruno. *Science in Action.* Cambridge: Harvard UP, 1987.

Latour, Bruno, and Steve Woolgar. *Laboratory Life.* London: Sage, 1979.

Luckmann, Thomas. "On the Communicative Adjustment of Perspectives, Dialogue and Communicative Genres." *The Dialogical Alternative.* Ed. Astri Heen Wold. Oslo: Scandinavian UP, 1992. 220-34.

Martin, James R. *English Text: System and Structure.* Philadelphia: Benjamins, 1992.

McCloskey, Donald. *The Rhetoric of Economics.* Madison: U of Wisconsin P, 1986.

Medway, Peter. *Discourse in Architecture.* Mahwah, NJ: Erlbaum, forthcoming, 1998.

Miller, Carolyn. "Genre as Social Action." *Quarterly Journal of Speech* 70 (1984): 151-67.

Nardi, Bonnie, ed. *Context and Consciousness.* Cambridge: MIT P, 1996.

Pare, Anthony, and Graham Smart. "Observing Genres in Action: Towards a Research Methodology." *Genre and the New Rhetoric.* Ed. A. Freedman and P. Medway. London: Taylor, 1994. 146-54.

Prior, Paul. *Writing/Disciplinarity: A Sociohistoric Account of Literate Activity in the Academy.* Mahwah, NJ: Erlbaum, forthcoming, 1998.

Rosaldo, Renato. "Where Objectivity Lies: The Rhetoric of Anthropology." *The Rhetoric of the Human Sciences.* Ed. John Nelson, Allan Megill, and Donald McCloskey. Madison: U of Wisconsin P, 1987. 87-110.

Russell, David. "Activity Theory and Its Implications for Wrtiting Instruction." *Reconceiving Writing, Rethinking Writing Instruction.* Ed. Joseph Petraglia. Mahwah, NJ: Erlbaum, 1995. 51-78.

Sacks, Harvey. *Lectures on Conversation.* Oxford: Blackwell, 1995.

Sacks, H., E. A. Schegloff, and G. Jefferson. "A Simplest Systematics for the Organization of Turn-Taking for Conversation." *Language* 50 (1974): 696-735.

Schegloff, Emanuel. "Turn Organization: One Intersection of Grammar and Interaction." Manuscript, 1994.

Schryer, Catherine. "Records as Genre." *Written Communication* 10 (1993): 200-34.

Schutz, Alfred, and Thomas Luckmann. *The Structures of the Life-World.* Evanston: Northwestern UP, 1973.

Shapin, Steven, and Simon Schaffer. *Leviathan and the Air Pump.* Princeton: Princeton UP, 1985.

Shapin, Steven. *The Social History of Truth.* Chicago: U of Chicago P, 1994.

Swales, John. *Genre Analysis.* Cambridge: Cambridge UP, 1990.

Todorov, Tzvetan. *Genres in Discourse.* Cambridge: Cambridge UP, 1990.

Vygotsky, Lev. *Mind In Society.* Cambridge: Harvard UP, 1978.

——. *Thought and Language.* Trans. Alex Kozulin. Cambridge: MIT P, 1986.

Winsor, Dorothy. *Writing Like an Engineer: A Rhetorical Education.* Mahwah, NJ: Erlbaum, 1996.

Woolgar, Steve, ed. *Knowledge and Reflexivity.* London: Sage, 1988.

DAVID SEBBERSON

St. Cloud State University

Is the Prospect of Rhetoric Antirhetorical?
Or Rhetoric's Critical Impulse

I begin with two quotations. The first is from Stephen Spender, written in 1951 and recalling an observation from the 30s:

> To divide humanity into irreconcilable groups with irreconcilable attitudes, having no common language of truth and morality, is, ultimately, to rob both groups of their humanity. They will be inhuman first to one another, and lastly to their own followers. (136)

The second quotation from Todd Gitlin's *The Twilight of Common Dreams* was written last year. After considering the difference between what he calls "the late New Left politics of separatist rage . . . [and] the early New Left politics of universalist hope" (146), Gitlin argues that

> Identity politics confronts a world in flux and commands it to stop. . . . Today, some cultural fundamentalists defend the formulas of "multiculturalism.". . . Other fundamentalists . . . claim that multiculturalism, racial preferences, and the like are instruments of an elite. . . . What frightens both is the flimsiness of a culture where everything is in motion. . . . In the minds of all fundamentalists, porousness makes for corrosiveness. A porous society is an impure society. The impulse is to purge impurities, to wall off the stranger. (223)

Spender's reflection and Gitlin's urgency reflect a concern that has been around for sixty years and more—a concern for communicating across huge gaps of identity, huge chasms of difference.

While neither Spender nor Gitlin was concerned directly or explicitly as a rhetorician surveying the prospect of rhetoric, a similar concern by rhetoricians was present twenty-five years ago in *The Prospect of Rhetoric*, situated chronologically half way between Spender's then and Gitlin's now. Baskerville, for example, raised the specter of communication failed in a violent New-Left noise (152), and Wayne Booth, to cite another example, reflected on a crisis in rhetoric and failed understanding (113). What, then, is the prospect of rhetoric when those prospects have remained so bleak for so long? Gitlin's lament and urgency leave him wondering how a left politics can possibly survive when, to use Spender's words criticizing Stalin-era communist ideologues, "humanity is reduced into irreconcilable groups with irreconcilable attitudes."

In a nonpartisan way, Carolyn R. Miller raises a similar issue for rhetoricians, articulating it in the configuration of the one and the many. Noting problems in both the communal and the liberal-individual, for example, Miller identifies a problematic aspect of community when she writes that "The domination of the communal over outsiders is both a political and a rhetorical problem" (86). Similarly, Miller identifies a problem of individualism as articulated in classical liberalism, which "promotes anomie and disaffection and ultimately the conviction that reasoned argument is not possible because each individual is entitled to his or her conception of the good incommensurable by definition with everybody else's" (87). Consequently, Miller calls for "a rhetoric of pluralism [that] must speak not only to the diversity within any community but also to the diversity of communities that co-exist and overlap each other" (91). Such a rhetoric may be characterized, according to Miller, as "a rhetoric of play, of experiment, of advocacy that is both tentative and committed of dialogic agonism that is exploratory and possessive" (91). Inviting rhetoricians to consider such a prospect for rhetoric, Miller offers some caveats. The first has to do with "essentializing the plural" and fragmentation, articulating concerns similar to Spender's and Gitlin's (91). Another of Miller's caveats is "to resist the aestheticizing of play, the apolitical impulses within postmodernism lest we be left again with a rhetoric of only declamation and trope catalogs" (91).

I would like to take up Miller's invitation by paying special attention to her last caveat and by casting the question this way: How do we think responsibly about rhetoric in relation to power? How do we avoid fetishizing it in a postleft Babel or ignoring it, disingenuously, in a posthumanist, free market of storytellers? I would like to suggest that reconsidering a pair of theorists at different ends of historical and even political spectra—namely Plato and Habermas—as a way to take up Miller's challenge as well as to address the frustrations expressed between Spender and Gitlin. Now it is not self-evident, nor even easily argued, that Plato and Habermas can be ushered in to reconstruct a postmodern rhetoric that is democratic. Currently, it is sophistic rhetoric rather than Platonic rhetoric that is enlisted to serve democratic ends. Indeed, from sophistic perspectives, Plato is an enemy of democracy. Similarly, Habermas is seen less as a postmodernist committed to democratic pluralism and partiality than as the last proponent of Western enlightenment. So why in the name of a left politics and a rhetoric of democracy would one turn to two theorists that seem most problematic from those perspectives?

Plato and Habermas are both controversial figures in the history and theory of rhetoric not only because of their own statements against rhetoric but also because of currently prevalent theoretical positions that situate their work as antirhetorical, antidemocratic, or both. Last summer, for example, at the ISHR conference, Brian Vickers argued that in *Phaedrus* Plato set out not to reform but rather to destroy rhetoric. Moreover, Plato is typically considered seminal to the Western tradition culminating in a modernism wedded to invidiously constructed hierarchies. Kaufman, for example, argues that in Plato rhetoric is reduced to justice, which in turn is reduced to hierarchies (113). More damning, however, is Kaufman's assertion that for Plato "All expression in the state . . . is censored to serve the ends of the state. This kind of rhetoric, I assert, is unworthy of praise." Habermas, on the other hand, has been characterized, for example by Aronowitz, as the last modernist, the inheritor of the Enlightenment that Plato prefigured (238ff). Both conceptualize in universals; both posit the ideal. What could either have to offer to the situated, pragmatic discourses of democracy? Moreover, while the early Habermas saw that "the orator was engaged in the philosophical transaction of practical prudence with the specific sphere of Politics" (*Theory and Practice* 80), more recently he has allowed himself from time to time to collapse the rhetorical into the literary, reducing, for example, the rhetorical simply to the "poetic" and "figures that shape style" (*Philosophical Discourses* 209, 188) in particular: precisely the reduction of rhetoric that Miller wants us to avoid.

New sophistic histories of rhetoric organized to oppose theoretical axes of Western enlightenment such as the Plato-Habermas one just sketched out have their own internal logic difficult to dispute, and they have been effective in opening up fields of rhetoric and discourse of which only the intellectually agoraphobic could despair. I am not looking, however, to a simple or nostalgic adoption of either Plato or Habermas but rather to reconstruct a particular theoretical impulse that I find common in their radically different endeavors, providing a prospect of rhetoric that brings into view a critical impulse that can be considered antirhetorical only insofar as rhetoric would eschew the critical all together. I wish to suggest a reconstruction of Plato and Habermas to conceptualize rhetoric as a critical practice that problematizes, on the one hand, identity and power while theorizing, on the other, the possibility of negotiating multiple perspectives.[1]

Reconstructing Plato

While Havelock's important work clearly does much to legitimate the work of the sophists (see, for example, Vickers' *In Defence of Rhetoric* 121ff), I would use Havelock in the reconstruction of Plato. First, Havelock demonstrates how Plato creates the critical. In exploring the transition from an oral tradition, represented by Homer, to that of a written one represented by Plato, Havelock argues that this transition involved moving from an uncritical, imagistic, and mimetic way of thinking to a critical, conceptual, and autonomous way of thinking. Thus Havelock writes that the oral, poetic tradition relies on a sort of "self-surrender" and "automatism" (198). It is Socrates, Havelock argues, who redefines the soul as having a critical capacity (197). Later Havelock points out that the Greek term, *philosophia*, would identify

> that capacity which turns a man into a student by defying the pressure of his. . . . passionate emotional identification with persons and stories of heroes. . . . Instead, the "philosoph" is the one who wants to learn how to restate these in a different language of isolated abstractions . . . imposing the rule of principle in place of happy intuition . . . and substituting reasoned analysis in its place as the basic mode of living. (282-83)

It is this theoretical move of critique and disruption, of spell-breaking, that is the key salvageable element of Platonic rhetoric. Without this theoretical framework, it is impossible to stand aside and gain perspective. Without this capacity for critically distancing oneself from "passionate emotional identification," it is impossible to make a space for commonality where different perspectives can be not only presented but also negotiated.

The critical impulse of Platonic rhetoric, then, provides a necessary corrective, for example, to Protagorean rhetoric, complementing it when it finds itself, in Thomas Conley's words, "deprive[d] . . . of . . . criteria to distinguish what is true or false or between what is right or wrong. . . . [and] degenerating into dialogue between two equally misguided parties" (7). The Protagorean impulse to "consensus (*homonoia*) arrived at by debate and eloquence" may be necessary but not sufficient (Conley 23). Without setting aside the *dissoi logoi* and democratic impulses of Protagorean rhetoric, we have to acknowledge the need for establishing a critical stance—a way other than simply appealing to majority rule, market forces, and perfect access to their institutional bases, assuming as these all do, equilibrium of power—to address krisis and judgment. In its basic formulation, Protagorean rhetoric assumes that power is not an issue and that consensus is nonproblematic. Plato, I would argue, conceptualizes the critical space necessary, if by itself not sufficient, for negotiating both power and difference. Habermas will convert that space into a public sphere by positing an ideal speech situation where power is confronted and pluralism is grounded in critique rather than identity.

Reconstructing Habermas[2]

In reconstructing Habermas for the purpose of rhetoric, we must heed Richard J. Bernstein: "Habermas is frequently misread as if he were proposing an ideal form of life in which all conflicts would be settled by rational discussion, an ideal form of life where all violence would disappear. But this is a caricature" (205). Bernstein goes on to note that "Habermas rejects any philosophy of history . . . committed to a grand teleological narrative. . . . [while] affirm[ing] . . . communicative dialogical reason['s] stubbornly transcending power" (205). The transcendental moment that Bernstein refers to is an instance of that critical impulse necessary for rhetoric to sustain a space where different perspectives can be articulated, negotiated, and judged in light not only of the stronger argument but also of power relations.

Power figures explicitly in Habermas first when he distinguishes communicative action from strategic action, and again when he distinguishes openly strategic action from covertly strategic action—deception—and yet again when he distinguishes conscious deception or manipulation from unconscious deception or "systematically distorted communication . . . [where] at least one of the participants is deceiving *himself or herself* regarding the fact that he or she is actually behaving strategically, while he or she has only apparently adopted an attitude orientated to reaching understanding" ("A Reply to my Critics" 264). Habermas's distinction between communicative action oriented toward understanding and strategic action oriented toward success is an important one for the issue of power, keeping it always present, always unbracketable.

At the same time, the ideal speech situation makes space for the principle that *every* speech act raises a set of validity claims that articulate relations to the world—truth, rightness or appropriateness, or truthfulness—and that in principle are always criticizable. "In the attitude oriented toward reaching understanding," says Habermas,

> the speaker raises with *every* intelligible utterance the claim that the utterance in question is true (or that the existential presuppositions of the propositional content hold true), that the speech act is right in terms of a given normative context (or that the normative context that it satisfies is itself legitimate) and that the speaker's manifest intentions are meant in the way that they are expressed. (*Moral Consciousness* 136-37)

Because every intelligible utterance not only raises these three validity claims but also places different emphases on them given the task at hand, Habermas argues that there is a "decentered understanding of the world," which allows for reflection from different perspectives—decentered understanding—and for critique—the criticizability of validity claims (*Moral Consciousness* 137-38).

In effect, Habermas theorizes a space for both a critical rhetoric and what Georgia Warnke has called "critical pluralism" by triangulating the ideal speech situation, communicative action, and strategic action.[3] It is through the play of these parameters that rhetoric eschews the reiterative monotony of alienated individualism, essentialized pluralism, and dominating communitarianism for the critical multivocality of political and cultural autonomy. Habermas's theoretical space is at once a sort of conceptual public sphere and *konoi topoi* that first recognizes the legitimacy of different voices, but then insists on openly validating them in relation to the criticizeability of their claims, in the context of power, and against the possibilities of systematically distorted communication. It is this critical impulse in Habermas that is necessary to sustain a healthy multivocality, where the insistence on tolerance is reduced to neither the cacophony of intolerance nor the silence of disingenuous consensus.

Space has been the governing metaphor of my argument, for without space there cannot be perspective, and without perspective the prospect of rhetoric is dim. Without space and perspective, there can be only the worst kind of identification—claustrophobic—a sort of infernal metonymy that is always reducing the one into the many, the many into the one. To disrupt this sort of identification, to displace it with difference that can both tolerate difference and provide for negotiated, unified practices, requires critical impulses like those in Plato and Habermas. Without such a critical impulse, is there a prospect of rhetoric at all?

Notes

[1] Habermas makes these useful distinctions in defining the practice of reconstruction: "The word *restoration* signifies the return to an initial situation that had meanwhile been corrupted. . . . *Renaissance* signifies the renewal of a tradition that has been buried for some time. . . . *[R]econstruction* signifies taking a theory apart and putting it back together again in a new form in order to attain more fully the goal it has set for itself. This is the normal way . . . of dealing with a theory that needs revision in many respects but whose potential for stimulation has still not been exhausted" (*Communication and Evolution* 95).

[2] Thomas B. Farrell does considerable work integrating Habermas into the "norms of rhetorical culture." Here however, I do not build so much on Farrell's work as complement it, maintaining a greater tension between the aesthetic and the rhetorical than Farrell does. Thus Farrell remains outside the immediate scope of my argument.

[3] I am grateful to Warnke for this term and more: A careful critic of Habermas, Warnke argues for the value of Habermasian theory as it allows multiple perspectives—cultural ones, for example, and feminist ones—while at the same time, in the case of feminism, "insisting on the legitimacy of a unified feminist practice" ("Discourse Ethics and Feminist Dilemmas" 260).

Works Cited

Aronowitz, Stanley. *Dead Artists Live Theories and Other Cultural Problems*. New York: Routledge, 1994.

Baskerville, Barnet. "Responses, Queries, and a Few Caveats." *The Prospect of Rhetoric: Report of the National Developmental Project*. Ed. Lloyd F. Bitzer and Edwin Black. Englewood Cliffs, NJ: Prentice, 1971. 151-65.

Bernstein, Richard J. *The New Constellation: The Ethical-Political Horizons of Modernity/ Postmodernity*. Cambridge, MA: MIT P, 1992.

Booth, Wayne C. "The Scope of Rhetoric Today: A Polemical Excursion." *The Prospect of Rhetoric: Report of the National Developmental Project*. Ed. Lloyd F. Bitzer and Edwin Black. Englewood Cliffs, NJ: Prentice, 1971. 93-114.

Conley, Thomas M. *Rhetoric in the European Tradition*. New York: Longman 1990.

Farrell, Thomas B. *Norms of Rhetorical Culture*. New Haven: Yale UP, 1993.

Gitlin, Todd. *The Twilight of Common Dreams: Why America Is Wracked by the Culture Wars*. New York: Holt, 1995.

Habermas, Jürgen. "A Reply to my Critics." *Habermas: Critical Debates*. Ed. John B. Thompson and David Held. Cambridge, MA: MIT P, 1982. 219-83.

——. *Communication and the Evolution of Society*. Trans. Thomas McCarthy. Boston: Beacon, 1979.

——. *Moral Consciousness and Communicative Action*. Trans. Christian Lenhardt and Shierry Weber Nicholsen. Cambridge, MA: MIT P, 1990.

——. *The Philosophical Discourse of Modernity; Twelve Lectures*. Trans. Frederick G. Lawrence. Cambridge, MA: MIT P, 1987.

——. *Postmetaphysical Thinking: Philosophical Essays*. Trans. William Mark Hohengarten. Cambridge, MA: MIT P, 1992.

——. *Theory and Practice*. Trans. John Viertel. Boston: Beacon, 1973.

Havelock, Eric A. *Preface to Plato*. Cambridge: Harvard UP, 1963.

Kaufman, Charles. "The Axiological Foundations of Plato's Theory of Rhetoric." *Landmark Essays on Classical Greek Rhetoric*. Ed. Edward Schiappa. Davis, CA: Hermagoras, 1994. 101-16.

Miller, Carolyn R. "Rhetoric and Community: The Problem of the One and the Many." *Defining the New Rhetorics*. Ed. Theresa Enos and Stuart C. Brown. Newbury Park, CA: Sage, 1993. 79-94.

Spender, Stephen. *World Within World: The Autobiography of Stephen Spender*. New York: St Martin's, 1994.

Vickers, Brian. *In Defence of Rhetoric*. New York: Oxford UP, 1988.

——. "Plato's Phaedrus and the 'Reform' of Rhetoric." International Society for the History of Rhetoric, 10th Biennial Conference. Edinburgh, UK, July 18-22, 1995.

Warnke, Georgia. "Communicative Rationality and Cultural Values." *The Cambridge Companion to Habermas*. Ed. Stephen K. White. Cambridge, UK: Cambridge UP, 1995. 120-42.

——. "Discourse Ethics and Feminist Dilemmas of Difference." *Feminists Read Habermas: Gendering the Subject of Discourse*. Ed. Johanna Meehan. New York: Routledge, 1995. 247-61.

MARTHA COOPER

Northern Illinois University

A Feminist Glance at Critical Rhetoric

The pervasive sense of frustration, despair, powerlessness, and alienation present in some groups, and in other groups a disregard for, misunderstanding of, or unwillingness to accept different images that people have of themselves have produced polarized types of language in our society: an establishment rhetoric and a rhetoric of revolution. . . . The most immediate social responsibility of rhetorical scholarship in the United States is to ameliorate, insofar as scholarship can, the diremption that has occurred in our public language, to investigate further the reasons for that fissure and, more challenging still, the prospects for transcending it.
—*Douglas Ehninger et al., 1971*

There is a rising sentiment that we are coming to the close not only of a century and a millennium but of an era, too. . . . The idiom we have favored since the beginning of the modern era fails to inspire conviction or yield insight; the language of those who are proclaiming a new epoch seems merely deconstructive or endlessly prefatory. . . . The language of postmodernism has crucial critical force. But much of it seems idle; very little of it gives us a helpful view of the postmodern divide or of what lies beyond it. How can we hope, then to find a discourse in which to explore this watershed and find our way across it?
—*Albert Borgmann, 1992*

Twenty-five years ago, participants in the Project on Rhetoric recommended broadening our concept of rhetoric beyond persuasion and public address to include "any transaction involving the use of symbols between human beings" and advocated "increasing a student's awareness of what is happening when he [sic] uses symbols and responds to them" as a way to deal with problems in society (Ehninger et al. 212). They concluded with a call "to replace the 'scientific stance' and the 'analytic stance' with a 'rhetorical stance' in humanistic and social affairs" (Bitzer and Black 244). Their call for a rhetorical stance reflected a general recognition that the master narratives of modernity held little promise for coping with contemporary social problems and thus laid the ground for rhetorical scholarship that would incorporate postmodern thinking.

Among the more influential assimilations of postmodern thought into rhetorical studies is "critical rhetoric," an orientation first outlined by McKerrow that promotes critique as the primary feature of a rhetorical stance. While critical rhetoric clearly holds promise for increasing our awareness of how symbolic action creates effects of power and knowledge and thus advances the struggle against dogmatic and oppressive power/knowledge systems, it does not provide much guidance for how to cope with the fragmentation, isolation, and anomie that follow from losing our certainty in universals. To move beyond the postmodern divide requires a rhetorical stance that includes more than critique, a rhetorical stance that includes creation alongside critique. In this essay I turn to feminist theory and practice to describe such a rhetorical stance.[1] Feminist scholarship suggests a rhetorical stance that creates social transformation through a vigorous rhetoric of resistance. Before exploring feminist contributions, however, a closer review of critical rhetoric and its problems is in order.

McKerrow describes critical rhetoric as an orientation toward rhetoric that, following Foucault, foregrounds the relation between discourse and knowledge/power and proposes critique as the primary mode of rhetoric appropriate to a postmodern world ("Theory"; "Postmodern"; *Argument*). As Charland summarizes the project: "Critical Rhetoricians would no longer be in the business of teaching princes and citizens how to formulate arguments, but would be engaged in an ongoing struggle against the oppressive formations of power specific to their own context" (71). In order "to constantly challenge the status quo to be other than it is," to enhance "the possibility of change through critique," McKerrow advocates both a critique of domination—ideology critique—and a critique of freedom—self-reflexiveness about power in everyday relations ("Postmodern" 75; "Theory").

McKerrow's charge is consonant with others who see the postmodern project as one of primarily questioning the taken-for-granted and in doing so destabilizing prevailing power relations. For example, following the work of Nietzsche, Foucault, and Heidegger, Scott describes the fundamental mode of postmodern thought as "a process of thinking that diagnoses, criticizes, clarifies by means of questions, destructures the components of meaning and power that silently shape our lives together, and also questions the values and concepts that have rule-governing and axiomatic power in our culture" (7-8). Similarly, Bauman asserts that the postmodern perspective "means above all tearing off of the mask of illusions; the recognition of certain pretenses as false and certain objectives as neither attainable nor, for that matter desirable" (3). Critical rhetoric thus exemplifies what Brown has termed "a hermeneutic of suspicion."

Objections that critical rhetoric is nihilistic, relativistic, and undercuts any legitimate stance from which to conduct critique mirror objections to postmodern thought generally. Probably the most persistent objection is that the emphasis on critique leaves little room for creative and productive action. Charland observes that "McKerrow does not guide us out of the infinite regress of critique" (71). Ono and Sloop explain: "For McKerrow, there is no possible end to domination, no right action for the critic outside of ceaseless critique" (49). In a metaphorical flourish that compares critical rhetoric to playing a game of "the emperor has no clothes," Brown observes that "the epistemological undressing of emperors and absolutes might also be politically prudish, for it keeps us from asking the more messy practical question of how, literally, to clothe the masses" (33). To correct for the problem of ceaseless critique, scholars have suggested "relinquishing skepticism from time to time in the critical process" in favor of "contingent *telos*" (Ono and Sloop 50), balancing the hermeneutic of suspicion with "a hermeneutic of affirmation" (Brown 33), and coupling critical rhetoric with an Isocratean imperative to "serve the community" (Clark 121). To these suggestions I wish to add a feminist perspective on critical rhetoric.

In perhaps the most pointed challenge to critical rhetoric, Biesecker charges that the "perpetual critique" advocated by McKerrow merely creates an illusion of transgression while overlooking "the conditions of possibility for resistance and social change" that are embedded in the Foucault's "non-monumentalized conception of power" on which McKerrow's critical rhetoric is based ("Michel Foucault" 352-54). By persistently focusing our attention on the repressive effects of power (either in terms of the domination of large systems or the normalization of everyday practices), critical rhetoric thus diverts us from investigation of communication practices that lead us out of the labrynth of confusion and alienation common to the postmodern condition. In contrast, investigating the creative possibilities of power yields a rhetorical stance that can cope with the postmodern condition. It is precisely on this point that I think feminist investigations of communication practices that engender social change may have something to offer the critical rhetoric project.

As Nicholson observed, "most feminists are not satisfied with a merely negative struggle" (203). Hence, feminist approaches to what might be termed the "rhetoric of resistance and renewal" can contribute to ameliorating the problem of perpetual critique outlined by those who have challenged the utility of critical rhetoric and, in doing so, perhaps lead us across the postmodern divide. Starhawk argues that a viable approach to social change requires both resistance and renewal. She writes:

> Our way out will involve both resistance and renewal: saying no to what is, so that we can reshape and recreate the world. Our challenge is communal, but to face it we must be empowered as individuals and create structures of support and celebration that can teach us freedom. Creation is the ultimate resistance, the ultimate refusal to accept things as they are. (26)

Feminist perspectives on the rhetoric of resistance provide a helpful complement to the project of critical rhetoric by identifying both critique and creation as essential components of a rhetorical stance. This is so in three ways.

First, feminist scholarship in rhetoric offers examples of critical rhetoric in practice. I was surprised to read a recent extension of the notion of critical rhetoric that lamented "while scholars sympathetic to the project of critical rhetoric have made significant theoretical advances, they still have not examined a practical application of the theory, i.e., a critical rhetor addressing an audience. The rhetor has remained a politically vacant form or face" (Clark 112). It seems to me that one quite viable face for the critical rhetorician is that of the feminist communication scholar who engages in ongoing struggle either to critique the grand narrative of patriarchy or to expose the operation of power in those smaller discourses that promise freedom. Among the first rhetorical critics to become a critical rhetorician is Karlyn Campbell, whose "two-volume study of women's rhetoric "call[ed] into question what has become the canon of public address in the United States, a canon that excludes virtually all works by women" (*Man* 9). While Campbell herself may embody a critical rhetorician, her investigations of countless women engaged in social and political struggle point to other critical rhetoricians.[2] In her earlier study of women's liberation rhetoric, Campbell emphasized the oxymoron of women's rhetoric that made such rhetoric inherently emancipatory ("Rhetoric"). In a more recent anthology that examines women's voices in literature from across the world, Lena Ross observed "the universality of disobedience in tales by and about women" (xi). From the perspectives of both Campbell and Ross, for most women in most places at most times simply to speak at all is an act of resistance that participates in the ongoing struggle to relieve women's oppression. Jamieson's discussion of how women break the cultural binds imposed on women's leadership supports this notion. Jamieson argues that suffragists, for example, broke the bind of the self-fulfilling prophecy by speaking and thus making a difference; she offers Hillary Clinton as a case in point of a contemporary woman breaking the no-choice/choice double bind.

But there is more to women's rhetoric than its critical function, for in the moment that the silenced finds her voice is an act of creation. Feminist investigations of women's rhetoric have investigated the discursive strategies that comprise such an act of creation, and herein lies the second way in which they contribute to the project of critical rhetoric. Feminist scholarship identifies specific rhetorical means through which critique is accomplished. In her early study of women's liberation, Campbell describes the movement's rhetoric as "characterized by rhetorical interactions that emphasize affective proofs and personal testimony, participation and dialogue, self-revelation and self-criticism, the goal of autonomous decision-making through self-persuasion, and the strategic use of techniques for 'violating the reality structure'" ("Rhetoric" 83). Later she rests her case for the inclusion of women and their voices in the study of rhetoric on precisely this point. She explains why "the omission of works by and about women [is] so damaging to our discipline" by noting that "to overcome unusually significant persuasive obstacles, such as prohibitions against speaking itself and stereotypes that reject them as credible or authoritative, [women] must be more inventive than their advantaged counterparts" ("Sound" 212). Campbell likens the inventive ability of a disadvantaged group such as women to the work of a crafter[3] and describes the rhetoric of women as a craft that is personal in tone, structured inductively, and invitational for audiences such that listeners are empowered (*Man* 13). Allen and Faigley examined feminist attempts at such empowerment and found eleven discursive strategies for social change that provide an alternative to the traditional rhetorical strategy of sound argument: new languages, new pronoun constructions, neologisms, redefinitions and reclamations, reversal, juxtaposition of languages, musical forms, perspective by incongruity, calling without naming, metaphor, and narrative. Such lists of rhetorical strategies provide hands to go with the face of the critical rhetorician and they do so by reference to lived-experience.

The discursive strategies that women craft to critique oppression point to a creative aspect of power. As Biesecker explains in her review of the nonmonumentalized view of power from which Foucault devised his theory of resistance: "[P]ower names not the imposition of a limit that constrains human thought and action but a being-able that is made possible by a grid of intelligibility . . . a 'can-do'-ness whose condition of existence is an orientation in time and space" ("Michel" 356). In the case of women's rhetoric, she calls the exercise of such a power-to "techne" and explains that it "establishes a degree of plurality and creativity" and "signifies a bringing about in the doing-of on the part of an agent that does not necessarily take herself to be anything like a subject of historical or cultural change" (Biesecker, "Coming" 156). The practices of informal kinship groups of welfare recipients described by Fraser come to mind as illustrative of such a power to make-do from a decentered and fragmented position within society (152-53). While Biesecker's description of *techné* follows closely the work of Foucault and thus avoids conferring autonomous agency on those who creatively resist oppression,[4] other feminist scholars point to more intentional yet temporal and self-reflexive acts that display the creative impulse in a rhetoric of resistance. Such work points to a third contribution of feminist practice and scholarship to the project of critical rhetoric.

By suggesting conditions of possibility for creation of a diverse yet common discursive space, feminist scholarship concerning women's rhetoric moves beyond the perpetual critique encouraged by critical rhetoric. Probably the most complete statement by feminist communication scholars about creating an alternative discursive space is Foss and Griffin's proposal for invitational rhetoric. In contrast to a tradition that defines rhetoric as persuasion, they define invitational rhetoric as "an invitation to understanding as a means to create a relationship rooted in equality, immanent value, and self-determination" (5). The mode of invitational rhetoric is "offering perspectives," inviting an audience to enter the rhetor's world by presenting a vision of the world and explaining how it works for the rhetor without advocating its support or insisting on its acceptance. According to Foss and Griffin, "if invitational rhetoric is to result in *mutual* understanding of perspectives," then an atmosphere of safety, value, and freedom must be created for the interaction (10-13). Although Foss and Griffin illustrate invitational rhetoric in public forums, probably the paradigm case of invitational rhetoric is that of the consciousness-raising group that encourages its members to share their stories in an atmosphere that confers value on their words through a norm of careful listening, protects them from interrogation or argument, and leaves open questions about what topics are acceptable and what choices will evolve from their sharing of perspectives.

By outlining the conditions necessary for diverse voices to be heard, invitational rhetoric epitomizes the creative and collective impulse that stands alongside the critical impulse of a rhetorical stance. The feminist practice of consciousness-raising "has been a crucial instrument for healing and for building grassroots feminist movements" as it invites people both to recreate individual identities and to find points of connection or affinity that create at least a temporary collective identity (Sawicki 307). Individual stories may require at least an illusion of a unified or authentic self, but when those stories are part of a larger dialogue of multiple voices, individual identities may be destabilized and reformulated. When stories are shared publicly under conditions of safety, value, and freedom, rhetoric empowers without necessarily conferring privilege. Following the work of Haraway, Sawicki explains that "narratives of oppressed groups are important insofar as they empower these groups by giving them a voice in the struggle over interpretations without claiming to be epistemically privileged or incontestable" (306). Once a variety of stories or perspectives are spoken, people are free to observe differences, to find points of commonality or affinity, to create alliances, to adopt new perspectives or to keep their own.

A critical rhetoric struggles against oppression by providing critiques of prevailing power/knowledge systems. Among the faces of the critical rhetorician are feminist rhetoricians and critics who participate in such struggles. Feminist investigations of the rhetoric of resistance identify particular communication strategies through which critique proceeds; those strategies are crafted from limited resources and point toward the creative nature of a rhetorical stance. While critical rhetoric risks perpetuating the postmodern condition by becoming stuck in perpetual critique, the feminist practice of invitational rhetoric offers one path through the postmodern condition by suggesting how to create a new discursive space that allows for both diversity and community. In this way feminist scholarship reminds us that rhetoric can be both critical and creative, both suspicious and affirming, both resistant and renewing.

Notes

[1] Nearly a decade ago, Balsamo raised an important but often neglected question: What is the specific relationship between postmodernism and feminism? (64). In her ensuing discussion, she observed that feminism had already encountered many aspects of the postmodern condition such as the lack of faith in master narratives and the problems associated with theoretical universality, noted the work of especially Haraway and Jardine in attempting to grapple with that postmodern condition, and concluded by wondering if the postmodern project would be open, flexible, and self-reflexive enough to engage relevant feminist thought (70). Any serious attempt to foresee the prospect of rhetoric in an age of postmodernity must, I believe, ask a similar question. While I am aware of the risk of essentializing, I concentrate on feminist investigations of women's rhetoric. I do not mean to suggest that *all* women engage in *all* the communication practices that are reviewed later in this essay. Instead, I take my cue from standpoint theory (Wood) and identify women because *some* women have engaged in coping practices and *some* have theorized about those practices because they have experienced oppression because they are women. Their experience of oppression is analogous if not identical to the postmodern condition. As Tanno observes: All the characteristics of postmodernism have been reality for the oppressed throughout history. All oppressed groups have intimately known fragmentation and anomie. All oppressed groups have continually experienced what it means to have nothing to hold on to. All oppressed groups have historically recognized the irrationality of a 'rational' stance that has been curiously selective in determining how far its 'humanizing force' should extend, which groups it would embrace, and which behaviors it would endorse (318). Although I could examine the communication practices of any oppressed group to find coping techniques, (probably) because I am a woman, I choose to turn to women.

[2] Note that I am blurring the distinction between metalanguage and object language such that a critical rhetorician may be a critic performing critique and/or a rhetor whose rhetoric functions as critique. Gaonkar argues that the dissolution of a distinction between critic and rhetor may be the most innovative thread within the project of critical rhetoric.

[3] Charland suggested that the critical rhetorician be considered a bicoleur, a kind of cultural tinkerer, rather than as a guerrilla, constantly undermining the foundations of any power/knowledge structure in a continued process of negative critique (74). While McKerrow objected to the image of bricoleur, he approved the notion of tinkering ("Critical" 77). Certainly a crafter tinkers, but she also makes something (probably something softer than a brick wall).

[4] Campbell questions the political and ethical impact of dismissing agency from the concept of *technê* ("Biesecker"). However, Biesecker maintains that making *technê* a function of a system of power/knowledge rather than a function of individual agency still preserves the possibility of resistance as described by Campbell while adding a self-reflexive concern the fragmented and decentered subject ("Negotiating").

Works Cited

Balsamo, Anne. "Un-Wrapping the Postmodern: A Feminist Glance." *The Journal of Communication Inquiry* 11 (1987): 64-72.

Bauman, Zygmunt. *Postmodern Ethics.* Oxford: Blackwell, 1993.

Biesecker, Barbara. "Coming to Terms with Recent Attempts to Write Women into the History of Rhetoric." *Philosophy and Rhetoric* 25 (1992): 140-61.

——. "Michel Foucault and the Question of Rhetoric." *Philosophy and Rhetoric* 25 (1992): 351-64.

——. "Negotiating with our Tradition: Reflecting Again (without Apologies) on the Feminization of Rhetoric." *Philosophy and Rhetoric* 26 (1993): 236-41.

Borgmann, Albert. *Crossing the Postmodern Divide.* Chicago: U Chicago P, 1992.

Bitzer, Lloyd F., and Edwin Black, eds. *The Prospect of Rhetoric.* Englewood Cliffs, NJ: Prentice, 1971.

Brown, Richard Harvey. "Reconstructing Social Theory after the Postmodern Critique." *After Postmodernism: Reconstructing Ideology Critique.* Ed. Herbert W. Simons and Michael Billig. London: Sage, 1994. 12-37.

Campbell, Karlyn Kohrs. "Biesecker Cannot Speak for Her Either." *Philosophy and Rhetoric* 26 (1993): 153-59.

——. *Man Cannot Speak for Her: A Critical Study of Early Feminist Rhetoric.* New York: Praeger, 1989.

——. "The Rhetoric of Women's Liberation: An Oxymoron." *Quarterly Journal of Speech* 59 (1973): 74-86.

——. "The Sound of Women's Voices." *Quarterly Journal of Speech* 75 (1989): 212-20.

Charland, Maurice. "Finding a Horizon and *Telos*: The Challenge to Critical Rhetoric." *Quarterly Journal of Speech* 77 (1991): 71-74.

Clark, Norman. "The Critical Servant: An Isocratean Contribution to Critical Rhetoric." *Quarterly Journal of Speech* 82 (1996): 111-24.

Ehninger, Douglas, et al. "Report of the Committee on the Scope of Rhetoric and the Place of Rhetorical Studies in Higher Education." *The Prospect of Rhetoric.* Ed. Lloyd F. Bitzer and Edwin Black. Englewood Cliffs, NJ: Prentice, 1971. 208-19.

Foss, Sonja K., and Cindy L. Griffin. "Beyond Persuasion: A Proposal for an Invitational Rhetoric." *Communication Monographs* 62 (1995): 2-18.

Fraser, Nancy. *Unruly Practices: Power, Discourse and Gender in Contemporary Social Theory.* Minneapolis: U of Minneapolis P, 1989.

Gaonkar, Dilip Parameshwar. "Performing with Fragments: Reflections on Critical Rhetoric." *Argument and the Postmodern Challenge.* Ed. Raymie E. McKerrow. Annandale, VA: SCA, 1993. 149-55.

Haraway, Donna. "A Manifesto for Cyborgs: Science, Technology, and Socialist Feminism in the 1980's." *Socialist Review* 80 (1985): 65-101.

Hariman, Robert. "Critical Rhetoric and Postmodern Theory." *Quarterly Journal of Speech* 77 (1991): 67-70.

Jamieson, Kathleen. *Beyond the Double Bind: Women and Leadership.* New York: Oxford UP, 1995.

Jardine, Alice A. *Gynesis: Configurations of Women and Modernity.* Ithaca: Cornell UP, 1985.

McKerrow, Raymie E. "Critical Rhetoric in a Postmodern World." *Quarterly Journal of Speech* 77 (1991): 75-78.

——. "Critical Rhetoric: Theory and Praxis." *Communication Monographs* 56 (1989): 91-111.

——, ed. *Argument and the Postmodern Challenge: Proceedings of the Eighth SCA/AFA Conference on Argumentation.* Annandale, VA: SCA, 1993.

Nicholson, Carol. "Postmodernism, Feminism, and Education: The Need for Solidarity." *Educational Theory* 39 (1989): 197-205.

Ono, Kent A., and John M. Sloop. "Commitment to *Telos*—A Sustained Critical Rhetoric." *Communication Monographs* 59 (1992): 48-60.

Ross, Lena B., ed. *To Speak or be Silent: The Paradox of Disobedience in the Lives of Women.* Wilmette, IL: Chiron, 1993.

Sawicki, Jana. "Foucault, Feminism, and Questions of Identity." *The Cambridge Companion to Foucault.* Ed. Gary Gutting. New York: Cambridge UP, 1994. 286-313.

Scott, Charles E. *The Question of Ethics: Nietzsche, Foucault, Heidegger.* Bloomington: Indiana UP, 1990.

Starhawk. *Truth or Dare: Encounters with Power, Authority, and Mystery.* New York: HarperCollins, 1987.

Tanno, Dolores. "The Meaning of Morality." Conference Proceedings of the Third National Communication Ethics Conference. Ed. James A. Jaksa. Annandale, VA: SCA, 1994. 317-19.

Wood, Julia T. "Gender and Moral Voice: Moving from Woman's Nature to Standpoint Epistemology." *Women's Studies in Communication* (1992): 1-24.

Part III

The Prospects of Rhetoric:
New Perspectives

SUSAN KATES

University of Oklahoma

The History of Language Conventions in Mary Augusta Jordan's Rhetoric Text, *Correct Writing and Speaking* (1904)

This essay grows out of a larger work, a case study of rhetorical instruction developed for disenfranchised students in the US. My archival research has allowed me to isolate particular features of rhetorical instruction for women, African-Americans, and labor workers in America between 1889-1937 in three specific institutions. Through what I would describe as "activist" writing and speaking instruction, rhetoric teachers at Smith College, Wilberforce University, and Brookwood Labor College offered students a distinctly politicized kind of rhetoric course at institutions designed for women, African-Americans, and labor workers. I would argue that teachers at these institutions enacted a prototype of what we now describe as critical pedagogy—a form of education most commonly associated with educators such as Paulo Freire, Henry Giroux, bell hooks, and Ira Shor, to name a few. One feature of critical pedagogy, as many of you know, is that educators help students to interrogate their marginalized position in society and to enact social change as a result of this understanding—an act that occurs through reading, writing, and speaking about oppression. This is the kind of education that took place at the sites of my study, particularly in the rhetoric classroom where the brand of rhetorical instruction, I would argue, was distinctively activist.

Three specific features characterize what I would call activist writing and speaking instruction: (1) a celebration of the language conventions students carried to the rhetoric classroom, (2) politicized writing and speaking assignments designed to help students to interrogate their marginalized standing, and (3) an emphasis on education for social responsibility. It is, however, the attention given to language conventions in rhetoric courses that I want to focus on today. I am interested in the fact that the rhetoric teachers in my study appear to have understood so much about the relationship between language and identity that they were quite respectful indeed of the language conventions that women, African-Americans, and labor workers carried with them to the rhetoric classroom. In every instance, the pedagogies of these teachers not only allowed for various language conventions but in fact celebrated them, and sought to make students aware of the strategic function of forms of discourse that were perhaps considered "incorrect" or "unauthorized" in other sites. What I'd like to do here, then, is to examine the pedagogical materials of one of the educators in my study, Mary Augusta Jordan, who taught rhetoric at Smith College from 1884 to 1921, and to illustrate how this particular feature of rhetorical instruction served the women she taught at this institution.

First, though, it would perhaps be helpful to have some kind of background information on Jordan and the nature of her remarkable career at Smith. From 1884 to 1921, she headed an English department that emphasized intensive instruction in rhetoric and composition. During her thirty-seven years at one of the first women's colleges in the United States, Jordan published not only a rhetoric textbook but a vast number of essays on rhetorical theory and women's education in *The Atlantic Monthly* and numerous scholarly journals. In many of her educational treatises, Jordan voiced her fear that women's colleges would not rise to a high academic standard and might, unfortunately, acquire the reputation of mere finishing schools. Interestingly enough, however, she felt strongly that higher education for women should not be modeled on a male precedent and that women's colleges ought to offer women a course of study from an alternative tradition. In an essay called "The College for Women" (written in 1892), Jordan writes:

> The college for women must solve the problem of education first hand. To that end, it must cut loose from the traditions of men, not because they are men's nor indeed because they are traditions, but because the best men have no saving faith in them. . . . Why insist upon sharing the wreck of educational dogma? Why insist upon ranking as "advantages" the under-inspiration of our over-examined young men . . . the student's mind is a republic of powers, not a receiving vault. (544)

I want to suggest that in writing rhetorical theory for female audiences, Jordan seeks indeed to cut loose from the traditions of men, such as John Franklin Genung and Adams Sherman Hill by treating a number of issues in regard to speaking and writing that seek to demystify the idea of standard English. Her treatment of language conventions certainly suggests that Jordan may have been attentive to the possibility that women's lack of formal education may have caused them a sense of inadequacy and inferiority in certain rhetorical situations. This is a problem that Jordan sought to remedy through her rhetoric text, *Correct Writing and Speaking*. This text was published in 1904 as part of a series edited by Margaret Sangster called "The Women's Home Library." In chapters titled "The Standard," "The Spoken and the Written Word," "The Office of Criticism," "Speaking and Singing," "Prose and

Poetry," "The Speller and the Copy Book," and "Bad Grammar," Jordan treats topics such as the history of the English language, the relationship between orality and literacy, and literary criticism. Although there is no indication that this text was used in her rhetoric courses at Smith, it does help to demonstrate her adaptation of rhetorical theory for another women's audience, most likely the women's club movement and others who studied rhetoric outside of the academy. Moreover, it provides a way to speculate about her classroom practice at Smith College during her tenure there.

As I said before, I am particularly interested in the ways in which Jordan examines the nature of language conventions and their history. While she certainly does not deter women from adopting certain language conventions in speaking or in writing, Jordan asks, however, that women students understand that the English language is comprised of conventions that could be better learned without a blind regard for them. The degree to which Jordan emphasizes this idea throughout her text is worth noting, for it seems to suggest that she had a particular mission in generating another kind of rhetorical instruction for women.

I would like to focus on a number of the passages from her rhetoric text that treat this issue and then explain how Jordan uses the history of the English language to help women to achieve a particular understanding in regard to the study of rhetoric. From the earliest moments of her book, she challenges the notion of language standards and the forces that create them. Consider, for example, this meditation on the issue of "correctness" in the first chapter of *Correct Writing and Speaking* where Jordan writes: "There certainly is at present, then, no standard English, either in writing or speaking that is easily and cheaply available. There is no one correct way of writing or of speaking English. Within certain limits there are many ways of attaining correctness" (36). In light of this sentiment, the title *Correct Writing and Speaking* seems an odd choice for this book indeed. Jane Donawerth suggests that Jordan asks women to revise their understanding of "correctness" out of her respect for her female audience, noting that readers of *Correct Writing and Speaking* were expected to speak "correctly" as if they belonged to a class of educated men even though they had not been provided the same educational opportunities. Jordan's insistence that there is no correct or standard English could be viewed as a liberating gesture to help women communicate more confidently despite their lack of formal education (Donawerth 18).

One of the ways that Jordan helps women to revise their idea of correctness is by taking up an historical examination of language conventions. She begins by framing her project differently than others who have written similar texts in the past. Often sarcastic in regard to the many rhetoricians who have appeared at various historical junctures to set society straight in regard to the rules of grammar, Jordan explains that "Once in a while an avowed or disguised pedagogue deplores the variety of dialects and sets forth some scheme for reforming human nature, speech, and spelling at once" (*Correct Writing and Speaking* 18). In Jordan's estimation this is an unrealistic goal for anyone and much more of an endeavor than she would ever attempt herself. Indeed, while she offers rhetorical and grammatical suggestions similar to those of many of her contemporaries such as John Franklin Genung and Adams Sherman Hill, Jordan is unique in her lengthy attention to the history of language conventions, which she includes, I think, to strategically demystify the notion of standard English. By invoking the history of the English language, Jordan explains in detail how conventions of communication have come to exert so much influence on a nation of writers and speakers craving direction at various historical moments. She writes:

> Most speakers naturally incline to agree with Ben Johnson's morose: "All discourses but my own afflict me: they seem harsh, impertinent, and irksome." . . . So the theory of a standard pronunciation is kept for the most part in reserve for use when we wish to silence opposition or to confirm our own judgment in our own behalf. (25)

Drawing upon the work of T. R. Lounsbury, a Professor of English at Yale during the nineteenth century, Jordan looks to the middle of the eighteenth century when "the craving for a pure and perfect orthoepic guide began to manifest itself in a way that required relief" (*Correct Writing and Speaking* 29). Lounsbury, as she notes, gives extensive treatment to the yearning of the British for a standard of English language usage. Jordan adds to Lounsbury's observations that those outside the linguistic majority always pay a price whenever a standard is set by that majority, and she illustrates that this has been the case in England: "It has always been a trait of English character," she writes, "to disregard any estimates of value except its own and to pass over others in silent indifference" (32). In moments such as this one, Jordan appears to empathize with those who have been denied entrance to a dominant discourse community on the basis of their background or lack of education.

Jordan's emphasis on the history of language conventions is worth noting in light of the fact that none of the major male rhetoricians who wrote texts that were used in men's colleges at this time consider the history of the English language as extensively as Jordan does, nor do they use history in the same way. John Franklin Genung, for example, gives no attention to the history of English whatsoever in his text, *The Practical Elements of Rhetoric*. And Adams Sherman Hill calls upon history, not to demystify language conventions, but to enforce them. In chapter two of *The Principles of Rhetoric*, "Violations of Good Use," Hill defines "Barbarisms" as offenses against the good use of language, "words which, though formerly in good use, are now obsolete" (24). He sees the evolution and changing nature of language as an annoying inconvenience—a challenge to those like him, whose job it is to define the appropriate modes of communication. In this respect he stands in opposition to Jordan, who uses history in order to liberate women from the debilitating rules of grammarians.

I focus on this treatment of the history of language conventions in Jordan's rhetoric text not to suggest that she believed that women possessed another language entirely or that she denounced the purpose served by a wide variety of language conventions. This feature of her pedagogy seems to me, however, useful for examining the ways in which pedagogies for marginalized students may have been developed in other historical moments. It is only one of the ways that Jordan suggests that women might have ways of communicating that were rewarded less in the larger culture. (I should add that a good bit of her text deals with conversation and letter-writing and the various rhetorical situations requiring these more private forms of discourse.)

As rhetoric historians begin to examine the history of rhetoric instruction in increasingly local and specific sites, pedagogical features such as those that I describe here appear to be important to trace, for though situated in a different historical moment, they suggest that rhetorical instruction in the US has always been informed by ideological concerns. Demonstrating but one of the ways that educators have historically chosen to acknowledge the political dimensions of rhetorical instruction, Jordan's work emphasizes that educators have often tried to respect the conventions of communication students bring to the rhetoric classroom and that pedagogical challenges arise from doing so. Whatever else might be said of Mary Augusta Jordan and the rhetorical theory she wrote and taught over a thirty-seven-year career at Smith, it appears that one of her primary purposes was to teach women how to write and speak what was on their minds and in their hearts by demystifying the very language conventions she hoped they might learn at the same time. This was a bold pedagogical step at a time when most of society encouraged women to doubt the powers of their own intellects. Thus, as Jordan crafted a rhetoric curriculum that slightly altered the prescriptive eighteenth-century rhetorics of male colleges, she enacted a pedagogy on the borderlands of more traditional institutions that allowed women to see the importance of rhetoric for reading and revising the world.

Works Cited

Donawerth, Jane. "Textbooks for New Audiences: Women's Revisions of Rhetorical Theory at the Turn of the Century." *Women and the History of Rhetoric.* Ed. Molly Wertheimer. Columbia: U of South Carolina P, forthcoming.

Freire, Paulo. *Pedagogy of the Oppressed.* New York: Seabury, 1973.

Genung, John Franklin. *The Practical Elements of Rhetoric.* Boston: Ginn, 1886.

Giroux, Henry. *Theory and Resistance in Education: A Pedagogy for the Opposition.* South Hadley, MA: Bergin, 1983.

Hill, Adams Sherman. *The Principles of Rhetoric.* New York: American, 1895.

hooks, bell. *Teaching to Transgress: Education as the Practice of Freedom.* New York: Routledge, 1994.

Jordan, Mary Augusta. *Correct Writing and Speaking.* New York: Barnes, 1904.

——. "The College for Women." *Atlantic Monthly*, October 1892. Box 3, Folder 96. Sophia Smith Collection, Smith College, Northampton, MA.

Lounsbury, T. R. *History of the English Language.* New York: Holt, 1897.

Shor, Ira. *Critical Teaching and Everyday Life.* Boston: South End, 1980.

HIU WU

Texas Christian University

The Enthymeme Examined from the Chinese Value System

Contemporary studies of the enthymeme have made scholars of rhetoric aware that the fundamentals of the enthymeme are much less established than they thought (Poster 4). Generally accepted definitions of the enthymeme lay more emphasis on the suppressed syllogistic reasoning than the probable nature of the premise on which the enthymeme is built (Horner 151-52; Corbett 77). Although almost every scholar of rhetoric now agrees with Lloyd Bitzer that the enthymeme is based on probabilities, signs, and examples (408), many studies continue to overlook the key role of probabilities in establishing the premise for the enthymematic development of proofs. The argument of this paper is based on my belief that the probabilistic nature of the enthymeme resides in its probable premise. Aristotle's notion of "commonly held opinions" (*On Rhetoric* I.11. [1354b]) indicates the relation between the probable truth in rhetoric and the probabilistic nature of the enthymeme. The enthymeme must begin with the premise that the audience correlates with the conclusion. Only when the premise agrees with the commonly held opinions of the audience can persuasion take place. The premises of the enthymeme are chosen from prescribed social values, and the conclusions that the enthymeme demonstrates are only valid within the beliefs that both the audience and the speaker esteem in the same culture.

Different value systems constitute varied forms of enthymematic reasoning in persuasion. This essay, by describing Chinese social structure and Chinese perspectives on individualism, will examine how the Chinese social-value system prescribes the premise of the enthymeme and affects the speaker's rhetorical strategies. Guided by Aristotelian assumption that reasoning is the intuition of the human being (*On Rhetoric* I.1.1. [1354a]), I posit that the enthymematic demonstration of proofs is rhetorical universals in argumentative discourse regardless of cultures. If we admit the existence of Chinese rhetoric, we must accommodate enthymematic reasoning in Chinese rhetoric.

Reversing the traditional Western belief that China lacks argumentation (Becker "Reasons"; Murphy "Origins"), recent literature on rhetoric has confirmed that China has a rhetoric in its own tradition, though its underlying values and applications vary from those in the Euro-American tradition (Garrett "Asian Challenge," "Chinese Conceptions," "Pathos"; Jensen "Asian

Argumentation"; Lu and Frank "*Bian*"; Zhao "*Wen Xin Diao Long*"). Many scholars rightly observe that Chinese rhetoric in most cases is applied to protect social harmony and stability and save face of both the speaker and the audience (Oliver 96-99; Becker 76-84; Jensen 154-56). But the common belief that Chinese society tends to suppress individualism does not completely agree with Chinese understanding of individualism. Unlike Americans, the Chinese do not declare a pursuit of individualism but contrive it through the fulfillment of social and familial responsibilities. Individuals exist not as autonomous beings but as social beings. In the Chinese mind, there is much emphasis on obligations rather than rights and prerogatives of the individual in relation to society. Individuals put their duties for the family and the community above themselves, and they believe that the fulfillment of duties will be rewarded by the society someday through consolidated upward mobility in the society.

This sense of social obligations extends from the core of the "family system" (Lin 172). The relation of the individual to society is envisaged in terms of a collection of a continuing permeation of the individual throughout the ever-broadening circles of family.[1] The celebrated passage of Confucius (551-479 BCE) in *The Great Learning* has categorized the relationship among the individual, the family and the state: "The ancients who wished clearly to exemplify illustrious virtue throughout the world would first set up good government in their states. Wishing to govern their states well, they would first regulate their families. Wishing to cultivate their persons, they would first rectify their minds" (129). Confucius necessitates a direct transition from the family to the state as successive stages of human organization (Lin 172). Y. P. Mei also observes, "The term for emperor in Chinese is 'Son-of-Heaven,' the local magistrate is addressed by his charges as 'parent-official,' and good friends become sworn brothers" (331). Thus society in Chinese eyes is hierarchically built in an enlarged circle of the family.

Consequently, the Chinese concept of family is more diverse and extensive than that of the West. Friends of parents are addressed as uncles and aunts. Even the remotest relatives are still called brothers, sisters, nephews, cousins, nieces, brothers-in-law, or sisters-in-law. Chinese has distinctive terms for patriarchal and matriarchal relatives. People with the same last names may identify themselves as members of the same family. They may say that "Three hundred years ago we were of the same family." People from the same home town or home province, if they meet in other areas, would regard each other as kinfolks and may soon strike up a friendship. In terms of social and personal relations, the individuality is not realized by one's strikingly different behaviors or thoughts but through a reflection of one's title of position or connections in a larger circle of "family," and one is only responsible for the interests of those within the "family."

In addition to a family-oriented social system, the stable and nonchangeable life patterns of the Chinese people have further strengthened this "familiocratic" relationship between the individual and the society. The tightly knitted personal network does not allow direct disagreements that tend to generate strifes and conflicts and that are thought to be detrimental to social and interpersonal harmony. Unlike their American counterparts whose life is more fluid, mobile, and changing, more often than not the Chinese have to work in the same institution or live in the same town for the most part of their lives, if not for their whole lives. In contemporary China most people identify themselves with their institutions because their residence statuses, medical care, housing, even marriage registration and childbirth certificates are superintended by their institutions. Career promotion is achieved not only through one's capability but also through personal connections. Therefore, interpersonal relationship with their bosses, coworkers, or colleagues is Chinese people's primary concern. They cannot afford having disagreements that would put relationships at risk. While American social values and Euro-American rhetorical tradition hold that disagreements among human beings are inevitable and that "rhetoric originates in disagreements is ultimately a good thing" (Crowley 2), the Chinese think that arguing openly and directly with one's boss or colleagues may be understood as personal conflict and even rivalry, and both parties lose face. Once people lose face, there is no possibility for conversation.

As a result, the primary means of persuasion in Chinese rhetoric is not frank and direct argumentation but skillful insinuation into the favor of the audience first and then a very cautious face-saving way to venture opinions. In order to persuade, it is important "to learn how to play up the aspects that the person you are talking to is proud of, and play down the aspects he is ashamed of" (Han Fei Tzu 75). Although Han Fei Tzu intended this skill to be applied when the audience is the ruler, the techniques he recommended have been and are being practiced universally in China. Before the conversation the speaker has to know the likes and dislikes of the audience, and then insinuates into their favor by flattering them on self-pride and appealing to their likes.

Persuasive techniques thus perceived, the Chinese usually do not respect an eloquent speaker who makes direct statements. Instead, they admire those who can bring their ideas home to the audience by applying their profound knowledge of history, using a special personal style, and at the same time, preserving the audience's dignity. In Chinese rhetoric reasoning alone cannot persuade the audience. First, the audience usually does not accept persuasion, for truth can never be proved by an individual; second, no addressee would admit the superior convincing power of the addresser. The admission implies the inferiority of the addressee to the addressor and lets the former lose face. Chuang-tse pointed out:

> In an argument between you and me, you think you have got the better of me, and I will not admit your superiority. Then are you really right, and I really wrong? I think I have got the better of you and you will not admit my superiority—then am I really right and you really wrong? Or perhaps are we both right, or perhaps are we both wrong? This you and I cannot know. Thus we are encircled in darkness. . . . (qtd. in Lin 88)

Because no individual can prove truth, the Chinese has to resort to historical sayings and facts (*ying jing jüdian* citing canonical texts and basing arguments on historical facts) to demonstrate their proofs. What the speaker says is never persuasive unless it is based on history, authority, or ancient Chinese philosophy. Therefore to Western scholars, Chinese reasoning features "the appeal to history, the delayed argument followed by a turn, and the final unconnected assertions" (Matalene 265).

This rhetorical practice must also be examined under Chinese political tradition. For more than five thousand years, China was devoid of democracy. Announcing truth based on a knowledge of the tradition and authoritative sayings is a safe rhetorical measure for persuasion. Throughout their history the Chinese are instructed to make ideologically "correct" claims. Writers are encouraged to resort to historical facts, authoritative or classical sayings, and statistical numbers to demonstrate proofs (*Chinese Language* 47-48). In today's China arguments must be based on "correct ideologies," e.g., Marxism and Mao Zedong thought or whatever the government thinks acceptable. As I discussed above, resorting to authority is a skill to avoid confrontation of disagreements. Individuality in rhetoric is displayed through appropriate application of style, language, and knowledge of Classics. Chinese are "strongly individualized as those of other countries. If gifted with original genius, they form a style of their own; if not, they produce in new and undesigned combinations the traits of earlier authors by whom they have been most deeply impressed" (Martin 125). A declaration of truths based on the authority of the past or of today enables the speakers to exhibit their knowledge of tradition and culture, thus establishing their ethos—intelligent and wise members of the audience's community. The audience would in turn respect speakers as their friends because the Chinese trust only those friends whom they regard as family members. In rhetorical practice writers and speakers usually use *we* to state their personal opinions instead of *I*. In written discourse *I* is substituted by *the writer* or *my humble self*. At the same time, the speakers must demonstrate modesty—personal ideas are considered to be generated from history or inspired by the audience. On most occasions of persuasion, when expressing personal opinions, speakers must begin with a cliché—"throw out a brick to get jade," meaning that their opinions, like bricks, are nothing, and the audience's opinions to them are valuable like jade. Distressing conclusions must be expressed indirectly. If it is not a distressing conclusion, it should be, in most cases, positive. If the audience is persuaded, it is not moved by an individual but accepts the "truth" proved by the tradition.

The fact that the premise is usually a declared truth indicates another contrastive feature in the Chinese enthymeme—"the Chinese do not judge the correctness of a proposition by the appeal to reason alone, but by the double appeal to reason *and* to human nature " (Lin 90). Aristotle believed that human beings have a nature for reasoning. Chinese philosophy admits this but adds that "Man should try to be a reasonable, and not a merely reasoning, being" (Lin 92). Speakers, while flattering the audience on self-pride, must trust the audience's reasonableness to see the good point in their persuasion, and by this they give face to the audience and preserve their dignity. In a word, esteemed interpersonal harmony, respect for authority and tradition, and individuality realized through fulfillment of social and familial duties have prescribed the practice of rhetorical tradition in China and accordingly have predetermined the Chinese reasoning pattern of argumentation.

The Chinese argumentative mode thus prescribed is puzzling and impenetrable to many Western scholars. Some of them think that there is no logic in Chinese argumentation and suggest that Chinese writings lack specific examples (e.g., Becker 83-84; Matalene 800). Some assume that "Asian rhetorics, specially in China, have relied far less on deductive reasoning than on other modes" (Jensen 161). At the same time, even though many scholars recognize the aspects of social values underlying Chinese discourse, most of them cannot see the correlations between those values and Chinese reasoning structures. I think an enthymematic analysis of Chinese written discourse can eliminate the confusion. The following part of this paper will show that Chinese rhetoric relies on logic for reasoning and that the enthymeme is also applied in Chinese argumentative discourse. Only the reasoning conventions vary because choices of premises are different.

When Aristotle said that the enthymeme is the substance of rhetoric, he envisioned the enthymeme more than just a group of clauses connected by *if*, *therefore*, *because*, etc. When the premise in the enthymematic process is taken into account, we will discover that the enthymeme can be regarded as a larger hierarchical structure of arguments that contains a macroenthymeme or thesis statement, and a number of m or supportive points of proofs.[2] The enthymemes formulated in the process of argument are not separated but logically interrelated. Vertically, the whole piece of argument is hierarchically built; horizontally, microenthymemes sometimes parallel each other, sometimes linearly progress and logically intertwine for strategic purposes. When we apply this notion of the enthymeme to Chinese discourse, we will also detect the

presences of the macroenthymeme and microenthymemes. Only their
constituents are different from those in the Western discourse. First, the
probable premise in the Chinese enthymeme is built on Chinese values. Second,
there is background information about the thesis to define or classify concepts
involved in the argument, to prepare the audience for the claim, and to show
the writer's knowledge about the subject matter. Third, the microenthymemes
consist of examples, analogies, or sayings from the Classics or from current
authoritative assertions, which Chinese writers believe are strong proofs for
their claims; this also is an approach that Chinese textbooks of composition
recommend. If the thesis statement is to conclude the essay, microenthymemes
appear before the claim.

Structurally, the Chinese argumentative essay does not necessarily place
the thesis statement near the beginning. One middle-school Chinese textbook
teaches students that writers can make the main claim at the beginning, in the
middle, or at the end, depending on the issue being discussed (*Chinese
Language* 46). Students are encouraged to apply logical reasoning in their
essays; and Chinese reasoning does contain logic, but it differs from the West
in development and structure. In her comparison of English to Chinese writing,
a Chinese student in my composition class observed that Chinese writing
requires strict organization and exact conjunctive words to make the essay
smooth but that English writing requires writers to describe their thoughts
randomly—just needs coherent sentences. She also observed that Chinese
essays use beautiful words to express one point at one time but that English
uses concise and easily understandable words to express the point. We may
think that her generalization is one-sided or even "ridiculous," yet her intuitive
response to English writing resembles what Westerners feel about Chinese
writing.

David Jolliffe, after citing a paragraph in his Chinese student's essay,
imagines an American composition teacher directing a student writer of the
prose to "cut the dead wood" or "make your point more succinctly" (269). The
paragraph is typical Chinese reasoning, beginning with background
information:

> China, as we know, is a very large country with mountains and
> plains, plateaus and basins, coastal and inland areas, cities and
> villages. Some areas have convenient transportation; some
> inconvenient. Some have advanced culture; some backward. City
> people travel a lot by train, ship, or plane, while some village
> children, even adults in remote areas don't know what the train,
> ship, and plane are like. In cities there are many universities,
> colleges, and all kinds of schools, but in some backward villages it

is very difficult to find a person to teach children to read and write.
(269)

This "dead wood" to a Chinese writer is necessary for preparing the audience
for the thesis of the essay: "All these differences, no doubt, will leave a great
influence on the educational standard for the people in different areas" (269).
Liu, the student writer, is practicing the method of placing the thesis at the end
of the paragraph. Chinese audiences can see the logic in his reasoning because
cities and rural areas vary in conveniences and educational means; people in
different areas receive unequal opportunities for education. The unstated
premise is that means of transportation and other conveniences are facilitators
of education. The minor premise is that less-developed areas lack transportation
means and other conveniences, and consequently, accesses to universities and
schools are difficult (conclusion). Liu trusts his audience's reasonableness and
their familiarity with the social context to make connections between
conveniences and education. To an audience who is devoid of a cultural
background, Liu's argument appears haphazard.

The above case study of Chinese argumentative discourse suggests that it is
a universal phenomenon that all human beings have an inborn disposition for
logical reasoning, though differing in patterns. Since the substance of rhetoric,
enthymematic demonstration of proofs, involves not only logical reasoning but
also rational reasoning, the reasoning process is quasi-logical. The logic in the
enthymeme is a chain of inference based on the beliefs of the human being that
vary in different social milieux. This is why Chinese argumentation appears so
puzzling and even illogical to many Westerners.

Having examined a mode of logical and rhetorical reasoning that differs
from Euro-American practices, we can conclude that the study of the
enthymeme can by no means depart from specific value system studies.
Whether the development of arguments is regarded as logical or illogical, or
even fallacious in another culture, it is arbitrarily constructed in a particular
culture. Rhetoric as a field of research is defined as discovering available means
of persuasion. To reach this goal and to facilitate global communications, we
ought to understand the beliefs of others and learn about their enthymematic
reasoning.

Notes

[1] Y. P. Mei thinks that the individual permeation is throughout the ever-broadening circle of the
society. But I hold that the Chinese sense of society is rooted in the family system, in which an
individual is identified as the core of the permeation.

[2] My interpretation of the enthymeme originates from Winifred Horner's analysis of Mark Twain's
"Fenimore Cooper's Literary Offenses." She examines the enthymeme as an equivalent to a complete
argumentative essay. See *Rhetoric in the Classical Tradition* 161.

Works Cited

Aristotle. *On Rhetoric*. Trans. George A. Kennedy. New York: Oxford UP, 1991.

Bitzer, Lloyd F. "Aristotle's Enthymeme Revisited." *Quarterly Journal of Speech* 45 (1959): 399-408.

Confucius. *Ta Hsüe (The Great Learning)*. Trans. Y. P. Mei. *Sources of Chinese Tradition*. Ed. William T. de Bary. New York: Columbia UP, 1960.

Corbett, Edward P. J. *Classical Rhetoric for the Modern Student*. 2nd ed. New York: Oxford UP, 1971.

Crowley, Sharon. *Ancient Rhetorics for Contemporary Students*. New York: Macmillan, 1994.

Becker, Carl B. "Reasons for the Lack of Argumentation and Debate in the Far East." *International Journal of Intercultural Relations* 10 (1986): 75-91.

Garrett, Mary M. "Classical Chinese Conceptions of Argumentation and Persuasion." *Argumentation and Advocacy* 29 (1993): 105-15.

——. "Pathos Reconstructed from the Perspective of Classical Chinese Rhetorical Theories." *Quarterly Journal of Speech* 79 (1993): 19-39.

——. "Asian Challenge." *Contemporary Perspectives on Rhetoric*. Ed. Sonja K. Foss, Karen A. Foss, and Robert Trapp. 2nd ed. Prospect Heights, IL: Waveland, 1991. 295-314.

——. "The 'Mo-Tzu' and the 'Lu-Shih Ch'un-Ch'iu': A Case Study of Classical Chinese Theory and Practice of Argument." Diss. University of California, Berkeley, 1983.

Han, Fei Tzu. *Basic Writings of Mo Tzu, Hsun Tzu, and Han Fei Tzu*. Trans. Burton Watson. New York: Columbia UP, 1967.

Horner, Winifred Bryan. *Rhetoric in the Classical Tradition*. New York: St. Martin's, 1988.

Jensen, Vernon J. "Values and Practices in Asian Argumentation." *Argumentation and Advocacy* 28 (1992): 153-66.

Jolliffe, David A. "Writers and Their Subjects: Ethnologic and Chinese Composition." *A Rhetoric of Doing: Essays on Written Discourse in Honor of James L.Kinneavy*. Ed. Stephen P. Witte et al. Carbondale: Southern Illinois UP, 1992. 261-75.

Lin, Yutang. *My Country and My people*. 2nd ed. New York: Day, 1939.

Lu, Xing, and David A. Frank. "On the Study of Ancient Chinese Rhetoric/Bian." *Western Journal of Communication* 57 (1993): 445-63.

"Lun dian he lun jü" ("Arguments and Proofs"). *Chinese Language*. Book 5. Rev. ed. Beijing: People's Education P, 1987. 45-48.

Martin, W. A. P. *The Lore of Cathay*. New York: Revell, 1901.

Matalene, Carolyn. "Contrastive Rhetoric: An American Writing Teacher in China." *College English* 47 (1985): 789-808.

Mei, Y. P. "Status of the Individual in Social Thought and Practice." *The Chinese Mind*. Ed. Charles Moore. Honolulu: U of Hawaii P, 1967. 323-39.

Murphy, James J. "The Origins and Early Development of Rhetoric." *A Synoptic History of Classical Rhetoric*. Ed. James J Murphy. New York: Random, 1983. 3-18.

Nakamura, Hajime. *Ways of Thinking of Eastern Peoples: India-China-Tibet-Japan*. Trans. Philip P. Wiener. Honolulu: East-West Center, 1964.

Oliver, Robert T. *Communication and Culture in Ancient China and India*. Syracuse: Syracuse UP, 1971.

Poster, Carol. "A Historicist Recontexualization of the Enthymeme." *Rhetoric Society Quarterly* 22 (1992): 1-24.

Zhao, H. "Rhetoric Invention in *Wen Xin Diao Long*." *Rhetoric Society Quarterly* 24 (1994): 1-15.

SCOTT LYONS

Miami University, Ohio

Crying for Revision: Postmodern Indians and Rhetorics of Tradition

This presentation is a mixed-blood attempt to make sense of what I think are indigenous rhetorics in development—and in conflict. Specifically, I want to examine the production of conflicting discourses of survivance (survival + resistance), Indian-to-Indian arguments over the deployment of ethnicity and the uses of what is commonly referred to in Indian country as simply "tradition": cultural practices, ceremonies, modes of discourse, expressions, looks, and poses. I will argue that American Indian uses of tradition and ethnicity are indeed in a sort of postmodern crisis right now, one made tangible in various discursive forms, producing emergent mixed-blood rhetorics marked by temporal and cultural play, new ways of looking, and communal critical poses. By comparing recent calls to tradition made in writing by well-known Indian activists to the more subtle oral pronouncements of Indian young people and elders at an all-Indian language retreat, I hope to complicate the ways we speak of Indian tradition and ethnicity and consider emergent mixed-blood rhetorics.

Rhetorics of tradition have long been in play in Indian country and beyond. On the one hand, Indian intellectuals and activists have worked hard to combat mainstream stereotypes of "traditional" Indians and cultures like the cigar-store Kaw-Liga or Hollywood Indians wearing beadwork and braids. On the other hand, and at the same time, Indian people have also worked to enhance and promote tradition to their young people as a means of survival. This enterprise received a real boost during the American Indian Movement (AIM) of the 1970s, which spawned not only a renewed interest in tradition but also a surge of Indian nationalism as well. One of AIM's leaders, the beaded, braided Russell Means, writes in his recent autobiography of his continuing tradition-based resistance to what he simply calls "Europe," suggesting that "[t]he strength for this effort can only come from the traditional ways, the traditional values that our elders retain." Furthermore, "it cannot come from the pages of a book or a thousand books" because white institutions like literacy or schooling "cannot make a person into a human being or provide knowledge into the traditional ways" (546). And yet there are Native professionals from the fields of Indian education who advocate a return to tradition *through* schooling (albeit in transformed ways). The Indian Nations At Risk (INAR) Task Force's educational manifesto, "A Treaty of 1992," calls for a national rejection of status quo Native educational models and for an implementation of what they call "true" Indian education, a "new Ghost Dance" that would put at the forefront Native languages, cultures, pedagogies, and traditions. Where does the INAR report locate the origins of tradition? From within the "Indian" recesses of the unconsciousness:

> For those Native people who have trouble understanding and hearing the message of the new Ghost Dance, take time, in a quiet place, dig deep into your hearts and minds; go past the years of indoctrination, past all the rationale for assimilation, go to the very center of the circle, seek your tribal identity. Keep looking; it is still there. When you find it, ask yourself, *Why was it so hard to find; why is it so buried, repressed and hidden?* Bring that tribal identity back to the surface, to the present, to co-exist in harmony with all other realities of your life. (Charleston 28)

Here the "discovery" of traditions within requires a sort of meditative therapy to recover repressed memories, a notion of tradition that posits ethnicity as prior to subjectivity: interior, dormant, repressed. While for Means, tradition is something to be mystically recovered via proximity to Native land, elders, and spirits, the INAR Task Force sees tradition as recoverable first through individual psychic work, then through social institutions. While the positions taken by both Means and the INAR Task Force are more complicated and intriguing than I'm allowing for here (and particularly the INAR report, which I find interesting and valuable in many ways), both are ultimately rhetorics of separatism and essentialism: Tradition is already inside, they suggest, and all we need to do is get away from whites, gaze inward, and re-member our Indian ways.

But getting away from whites is a difficult request these days, neither possible nor I would suggest desirable (but then again I'm pretty white), which is not to say that living with whites is working; on the contrary, the imperialism and then paternalism of federal Indian policy, racism, and poverty have created living conditions on reservations that are, as HUD secretary Henry Cisneros recently noted, the worst in the country. As the INAR report points out, "If Native conditions existed throughout the total population of our country, 150,000 more American people would die *each year*" (17, emphasis theirs). It is within a context such as this that Means, the INAR Task Force, and many others are reclaiming tradition as a strategy of survival. On local levels, too, traditional practices are making comebacks for their abilities to help people cope with their often violent, turbulent lives—alcoholics, for example, who use sweat lodge ceremonies and not 12-step programs as a means to sobriety. But it must be noted that separatist-essentialist rhetorics of tradition professed by leaders are by no means unanimously received in Indian country. Instead, there is dissent in the woods propagated by mixed-bloods who occupy multiple spheres in a post-AIM, post-*Pocahontas* world. These postmodern Indians are also interested in tradition, not of a separatist, essentialist order, but of a transculturated sort marked by play, biculturalism, and a critical pose. How they invoke and define tradition, and the reservations rhetorics they employ, will be my focus from here on.

Last summer I attended an all-Indian Anishinabe language retreat on the White Earth reservation in Minnesota. A four-day affair for families and individuals, the retreat was a combination of language-instruction, games, ceremonies, and socializing. Native-speaking elders, tribal college language instructors, adults, and children all collaborated on a collective project of language-enhancement, and since you couldn't eat unless you asked for your food in the Anishinabe language, the humor was pervasive: "*Gi wi* . . . uh, commodity stew-*ineg.*" It was also a very conscious communal attempt at cultural survival funded by tribal councils, corporate sponsors, casino revenues, and colleges, specifically designed to promote tradition.

On the final night there happened an event I had not seen—or noticed—before, something anathematic to most Indians: The elders were dishonored by their grandchildren. Early in the evening, the elders were asked to sing some songs for us. They replied by suggesting that we would all sing together; after all, the Anishinabe words would be good to learn, the tunes were familiar, and most importantly, we would be singing as a *group*. The songs they had in mind were Christian hymns translated into the Anishinabe language: "Bringing in the Sheaves," "Just a Closer Walk with Thee," "Amazing Grace"—important songs to the elders, as it turned out. Songbooks were passed out and the elders closed their eyes and started singing, but a significant number of young people, men in particular, laughed and walked away, a noticeable and meaningful slight.

After two or three hymns, the young men returned, and one made an honoring speech to the elders. An honoring speech is typically made by an adult at a tribal gathering—a powwow, a giveaway, a family celebration, a wake—in praise of one or more individuals for their accomplishments or character and almost always with a commentary about the community: who "we" are, where we appear to be going, and what we need to do. The young man commented on the "crucial importance" of the elders in Indian culture "both historically and today." Emphasizing the need for a "community effort" united against a world marked by white intrusion, racism, and social problems, he called the elders the cement" of our society and culture. "Whites put their elders in nursing homes when they are no longer useful," he said. "We, however, honor you, exalt you, and follow your lead. You are our models as we *return to our traditional ways."*

He was then joined by three other young men in a drum group to sing a traditional Anishinabe song for the elders. A drum group usually consists of young men who sing traditional songs at powwows, parties, and other social events, and among their functions is to provide music for communal dancing. On this night, however, we did not dance; rather, we listened. We were spectators to a rather impressive, loud, and exhilarating performance. The first two songs they performed were Anishinabe honoring songs in Ojibway. The third was a parody of a popular TV commercial sung "Indian style": *You got the right one, ba-by, uh huh huh huh.* . . . They finished to rousing applause and a group of children sitting in adulation at their feet as if it were a rock concert.

Afterward, an elder stood up and thanked the drum group briefly and with little enthusiasm, adding that while he and the others appreciated the "return to tradition" the young men represented, he had some worries. "We want you to sing *our* songs," he said. "Your songs are fine, but we can't sing like that." Suggesting that we should sing songs together, as a *community*, he then led his group in another Ojibway hymn. The young men and children, meanwhile, paid little attention to his words and ran off to go swimming. Those of us who remained, barely a handful, continued to plod through the difficult and confusing translations of Anishinabe Christian hymns.

For the sake of flagrant reduction, there were two groups here: "new elders" and "young traditionalists." New elders are indigenous survivors of European imperialism, the last generation of "natural" native speakers of Anishinabe. They, like my own grandparents, were sent to boarding schools and returned (sometimes with bruises and broken bones) to tribal lands sold off piece by piece by their desperate forebears. Many of the men worked as loggers on tribal lands, felling ancient pines and dragging them out of their forests with a team of horses for processing and eventual shipping, while the women worked to provide physical and psychical sustenance to children and adults who often suffered. Today they live off the land: ricing, tapping maple trees, picking blueberries, doing beadwork and birchbark, and supplementing their poverty by drawing welfare. This generation of new elders is uniquely situated in time. My grandfather's grandparents were Nay-tah-wish-kung and Pah-gwah-bin-dig-equay; my grandfather's grandson is Scott Lyons. The body of a new elder—brown, wrinkled, tough, wizened—is a direct locus of the collision of worlds: one "old," one "new." Hailing from small Indian communities on the White Earth and Leech Lake reservations, these elders are fluent speakers of the Anishinabe language, very traditional in their demeanor and presence ("Indianish" on the rez), and well aware of traditional Anishinabe lifestyles and customs from ricing to beading. They were also all Christians.

Young traditionalists are students, professionals, and high-school dropouts who advocate a return to "tradition" on a variety of fronts: religious, aesthetic, epistemic, political, and linguistic. Activists pursue their language at retreats, enroll in Indian studies courses, Sun Dance at Pine Ridge (and proudly display their scars), and wear the vestments of what they would call "traditional" culture: beadwork and buckskin, in addition to reservation baseball caps with eagle feathers attached. Many young traditionalists have done their share of ricing and beading, but most don't—can't—plan to live on that work. The bodies of young traditionalists—light-to-dark skinned, pierced, sometimes abused, ambiguous—are angry bodies. Sometimes read as "assimilated," young traditionalists are de facto resistors of imperialism; as they see it, they are the first generation to actually "go back" and retrieve Indian culture. They want to (re)introduce tradition.

The elders have not possessed that kind of agency; for them, life has been a series of forced adaptations: We're Christians now, but still communal in our worship. For young traditionalists, Christianity is white and ineffective: We're Indians now, and that means recovering traditions. Two groups, different but connected and multiply interpolated by contradictory discourses, are united in the production of resistance to white domination and cultural annihilation yet divide in apparent conflict with each other. New elders, it would seem, pursue tradition by participating in a communal retreat that promotes their language, sense of community, and the spiritual emphasis of life and culture, an Indian-Christian form of tradition as it is lived out and felt in reservation woodlands. Young traditionalists seem to share these concerns and motivations but object to the "white" Christianity of the elders in the form of a slight, which, to the elders surely, was anything but "Indian" in nature. This contest, then, can be said to be over the strategic deployment of ethnicity: the inscription of tradition and the practice and selection of aesthetic forms.

It was a tangible conflict, and we all saw it. In fact, at one point a young language instructor turned to me and actually rolled his eyes when the elders jumped out of their seats to honor an eagle they saw flying overhead. "Good god," he snickered, "that's not an eagle, it's a vulture." And it was. So what does it mean when traditional elders see an eagle when in fact a vulture circles our camp? What do I do when a young traditionalist rolls his eyes at the old ones? What kinds of seeing—or unseeing—are going on in this particular location? Are the elders blind? Are the young people refusing to look? And what of my scholarly gaze: How do I interpret what I think I see, what do I want to see, and why? Clearly, a lot of looking is going on here: looking, seeing, being gazed upon—visionary pursuits of a bird's eye perspective.

In recounting Anishinabe creation stories, Gerald Vizenor writes of the powerful "trickster stare," a particular form of looking that would inflict a "mortal wound to humans" while at the same time setting the creation of the world into motion (3)—a gaze that at once destroys and creates, inscribes and erases, kills and begets life. In a different visual spectrum, anthropologist Michael M. J. Fischer suggests "Ethnicity and the Post-Modern Arts of Memory" that "ethnic search is a mirror of . . . bifocality . . . seeing others against a background of ourselves, and ourselves against a background of others" (199). Fischer's bifocality or "reciprocity of perspectives" is a form of looking that he finds in contemporary ethnic autobiography and advocates for ethnographic writing. Bifocal looking requires (and automatically creates) a third vantage point, as does the trickster stare, which collapses the binary between life and death. These are new ways of seeing that I believe guide the visions of not one or the other, but *both* new elders and young traditionalists. Both groups are mixed-bloods, differently situated from each other in time and space yet joined in forms of mixed-blood seeing, expression, and rhetoric.

In contradistinction to essentialist-separatist rhetorics of Indianness, Vizenor posits the mixed-blood as "a new metaphor" of Indian ethnicity, "a transitive contradancer between communal tribal cultures and those material and urban pretensions that counter conservative traditions" (263). Simultaneously living in multiple mythic times and places, the mixed-blood "contradances" between the city and the rez with a "trickster signature." The trickster—the sustaining, contradictory union of human and animal, flesh and spirit, male and female, humor and sorrow, good and evil—can be either friend or foe to the individual but is always a boon to the collective community. Like Gloria Anzaldúa's *mestiza*, the mixed-blood trickster embodies a consciousness that "straddles cultures," develops "a tolerance for ambiguity," and works to break down subject-object duality in the development of a "new mythos" (Anzaldúa 51). The trickster is at once ancient and postmodern and, as Vizenor shows, plays discursively and refuses to be constrained by time.

A fragmented relationship to time is something Indian mixed-bloods share with other "new ethnics" in contemporary America. Fischer suggests that contemporary ethnic writers who work with traditional themes engage in "retrospection to gain a vision for the future." Writing in an often hostile society with the constant fear of "being leveled into identical industrial hominids," these writers invoke tradition in ways which "seem to be ironic, reflecting good natured nonbelief, skeptical, hedonistic, and commercial in overtone" (197). Fischer reads these new visionary rhetorics of ethnicity as thematically "paradoxical" in three principal ways. First, "ethnicity is something reinvented and reinterpreted in each generation" in ways "quite puzzling to the individual." Second, with "no role model" to follow, the postmodern ethnic subject searches for a "voice or style that does not violate one's several components of identity." And third, "the search or struggle for a sense of ethnic identity is a (re-)invention and discovery of a vision, both ethical and future-oriented" (195-96). Furthermore, these deployments of ethnicity "turn out to be powerful critiques of several contemporary rhetorics of domination" (198).

What, then, of tradition in a postmodern ethnic rhetoric or trickster cosmology? I want to suggest that the mixed-bloods at the retreat invoke competing notions of tradition oriented toward the future, not the past, and that this invocation is constituted by a mixed-blood rhetoric that, trickster-fashion, both annoys individuals and benefits a community, that straddles both Indian and non-Indian cultures, that both laughs and cries. Differences abound, but both groups at the retreat are engaged in a new form of what the Lakota call *hanbleciya,* or "crying for a vision." Both cry for visions "both ethical and future-oriented"—how we should live, what we should do—as bifocal seekers, looking at worlds both "white" and "Indian" in an effort to redefine tradition against a context both interior and exterior to their bodies, land, and histories. This mixed-blood rhetoric—future oriented while invoking the past, bifocal, and communal—was in full force at the Anishinabe language retreat, played out as a contest of forms and appropriations.

Forms: the young traditionalists openly rejected Christian hymns even though sung by respected elders in the Anishinabe language, while the elders rejected traditional honoring songs and an Indianized Pepsi jingle. For the former, Christian songs are "white"; for the latter, drum groups are for spectators, not a community. The elders' songs took a communal form—that is, we sang together sitting in a circle outside—that belies simple categorization as "white." On the other hand, the performativity of the drum group attracted the attention of previously disengaged children who came running to the sound of the drum, a communal act in itself that belies categorization as a form in which "we" cannot participate together. Both forms here are future-oriented, bifocal, and communal, and while they did create a moment of what I've been calling a conflict or contest (which, clearly, it is), the point is *they both happened.* This contest of forms, then, did not produce a "winner" or "loser"—that's no longer the question—but rather created *new* forms of *traditional* Indian culture.

Appropriations: the elders sang Christian hymns in Ojibway, while the young people sang recently composed drum songs and an Indianized TV jingle—both, remember, in the name of restoring tradition. Can Indians appropriate white culture—and then call it "traditional"? While people usually speak of Christianity or other forms of white culture as things imposed upon Native people that are then measured in terms of "assimilation" or "resistance," Richard Rodriguez has recently discussed Native cultural appropriation in terms of Indian desire, "not only to move the Indian away from the role of victim" but to see "something aggressive about the Indian interest in the Other" (qtd. in Postrel and Gillespie 79). Indian desire for the Other leads not to selling out but to acts of "transculturation," as Mary Louise Pratt points out, an alternative term to "overly reductive concepts of acculturation and assimilation," and a major "phenomenon of the contact zone" (36). New elders love their Christianity, a fact unmarred by the critical objections and rolled eyes of young traditionalists (and others). The Indian country commonplace that one never meets an Indian who doesn't believe in God—of whatever form—is complicated by a more recent expression: "born-again Indian," signifying people who return to traditional religion. These born-again young traditionalists can be distinguished from white fundamentalists in that instead of occupying themselves with questions of Truth—who will or will not burn in hell or whether or not women and men should sweat together—they are primarily concerned with ethnicity and appropriation: Whose traditions will we practice?

Occupying different worlds than their elders, young traditionalists also have to contend with the Pepsi generation. What does it mean to parody a Pepsi jingle—symbol par excellence of white, late capitalist culture—in a drum group? In this particular context, a reservation with televisions everywhere and capital hard to find, where consumptive desire is high and commodity production low (and not reified in the Lukacsean sense), where teenagers come home to tribal housing projects wearing the latest Starter jackets and Nikes and then work on their own dance regalia, parody is a form of critique of the dominant culture. I make this claim tentatively, but the contradictions here are many, and a parodic response that laughs at the ironies of Indian life in the face of global (white) capital while subsuming a commercial jingle and calling it tradition resists accusations of reinforcing the dominant or serving global capital. Certainly, the elders didn't get the joke. But their appropriation and Indianization of Christianity, forms of which are not only communal but emphasizing of the oft-neglected Christian virtues of charity, justice, and valorization of the poor, also offer a critique of commodity culture on reservations by marking itself as traditional Indian culture, thus positing an attractive reservation alternative to rampant consumerism. Drum-group parodies of commercialism update the critique to appeal to the young and deal with contemporary situations. Taken together, both of these Indian appropriations, the forms they employ, and their designations as tradition, offer strong critiques of dominant rhetorics of consumption, commercialization, and domination.

And so a mixed-blood rhetoric of tradition is at play in the fields of our Lord and Trickster, eagles and vultures, wild rice, and Pepsi. Rather than producing winners and losers, and resisting a retreat into rhetorics of separatism and essentialism, this oral mixed-blood rhetoric provides space and time to collectively forge new ethnic strategies and seek traditional (re)visions. A retreat from assimilation into tradition is not a retreat from the world, and postmodern Indians who retreat from retreat offer powerful and compelling alternatives to domination on the one hand, separatism on the other and, like

Nanabozho the Anishinabe Trickster, forge new worlds out of water and soil with the help of unlikely companions: beaver, muskrat, otter, elder, youth, Indian, white.

Note

In memory of Aubrey A. Lyons, grandfather and new elder, 1913-1996.

Works Cited

Anzaldúa, Gloria. "*La conciencia de la mestiza*/Towards a New Consciousness." *Ways of Reading*. Ed. David Bartholomae and Anthony Petrosky. 3rd ed. Boston: Bedford, 1993. 49-61.

Charleston, G. Mike. "Toward True Native Education: A Treaty of 1992." *Journal of American Indian Education* 33 (1994): 7-57.

Fischer, Michael M. J. "Ethnicity and the Post-Modern Arts of Memory." *Writing Culture: The Poetics and Politics of Ethnography*. Berkeley: U of California P, 1987. 194-233.

Means, Russell, with Marvin J. Wolf. *Where White Men Fear to Tread: The Autobiography of Russell Means*. New York: St. Martin's, 1995.

Postrel, Virginia, and Nick Gillespie. "On Borders and Belonging: A Conversation with Richard Rodriguez." *Utne Reader* 68 (1995): 76-79.

Pratt, Mary Louise. "Arts of the Contact Zone." *Profession* 91 (1991): 33-39.

Vizenor, Gerald. *Interior Landscapes: Autobiographical Myths and Memories*. Minneapolis: U of Minnesota P, 1990.

St. Cloud State University

Rhetorical Study and Practice in the Zone: Chicano/as, Sky Rhetoric, and Earth Rhetoric

The Rhetorical Situation in a Polyculture

We have moved from a monocultural perspective to a polycultural one. I like Michael Halloran's thoughtful rereading of his article, "On the Ends of Rhetoric," because it pretty well defines what the rhetorical situation is in a polyculture:

> What "O. E. R." ignored was the possibility that we live in multiple and fragmentary worlds, worlds that overlap, compete, and transform themselves continuously, worlds provided by family, ethnic community, neighborhood, profession, political affiliation, and so on. A more accurate portrayal of the modern condition, and perhaps of the postmodern and premodern conditions as well, would have emphasized the way identity is shaped by the voices of these multiple worlds in which we live, each of us an unstable, occasionally harmonious but more often cacophonous chorus of these voices or—to return to the spatial metaphor—a mosaic or quilt, made up of bits and pieces of past identities that were themselves assemblages of fragments. (114)

Halloran's description of the modern condition describes a situation needing a different kind of rhetoric. As one of my students, William Spath, puts it, "To adequately function in a diverse, polymorphous, postmodern setting, rhetorical theory must posit itself within a site . . . between diverse discourse groups" (2).

Studying rhetoric in a polyculture has provided us with exciting knowledge and approaches to living and learning. We have learned to direct our attention to the injustices done to minorities and have discovered rhetorics we have not studied well enough. We have a start. What we have not yet done is articulate a way to bring diverse views together through a philosophy, theory, and practice of rhetoric, and part of our work as rhetoricians is to find a place among competing rhetorics where we can act as translators. We need to practice a rhetoric in the cracks between cultures, a rhetoric that allows people to be bicultural or multicultural, a rhetoric that facilitates cross-cultural exchanges. I call this kind of rhetoric a "zone rhetoric."

Zone Rhetorics

We are familiar with the idea of contact zones. Mary Louise Pratt explains that contact zones are historical and geographical; they are places where groups contend and negotiate for power while recognizing their cultural differences. Each group, she suggests, must develop a rhetoric for communicating not only within the group but for communicating across cultural boundaries as well (*Toward a Speech Act Theory of Literary Discourse*; see also Bizzell and Herzberg "Preface").

However, when I think of zone rhetoric, I think of something a bit more messy than a contact zone. I think of something more like Halloran's "unstable, occasionally harmonious but more often cacophonous chorus," that happens on the borderlands between cultures. Three writers help me understand more fully the nature of the border: Gloria Anzaldúa, Paula Gunn Allen, and Guillermo Gómez-Peña.

Anzaldúa says in *Borderlands*:

> Borderlands are physically present wherever two or more cultures edge each other, where people of different races occupy the same territory, where under, lower, middle and upper classes touch, where the space between two individuals shrinks with intimacy. ("Preface")

All of us, she says, "resemble the bordertowns."

Paula Gunn Allen in "'Border' Studies: The Intersection of Gender and Color" explains that border people are citizens of more than one community. Although border people may practice an oppositional rhetoric and therefore be seen as *desperadoes* and *desperadas*, Allen argues that to adopt subversive dissidence as a rhetorical strategy feeds the power of those already in power. She quotes Audre Lorde: "The master's tools will never dismantle the master's house" (312). She suggests border people learn to celebrate their cultures as a rhetorical strategy for social change.

Guillermo Gómez-Peña in "Documented/Undocumented" describes the zone as a place where everyone is detribalized and "deteritorialized." Border people, he says, are known for their "multiple repertories" and "walk amid the tower of Babel of our American postmodernity" to become a "tribe of fiery people" (128-30).

Considering these writers, the "contact zone," as we sometimes think of it in rhetorical studies and literary criticism, is too tidy a place. The zone described by border people is dangerous, dissenting, and dizzying. It is a place where multiple personalities and multiple languages contend in the society, in the individual, and in history. Border rhetoric is the rhetoric of Chicano/as and other tribal peoples.

One lesson suggested by the Chicanos and tribal peoples in both my readings and my work with them is that rhetoricians who settle in one culture or society will exercise the old rhetoric of power and coercion, but rhetoricians who place themselves on the borders of consciousness and society will practice the new rhetoric of reconciliation and celebration that Allen suggests is necessary for real change in our society.

An Example of Zone Rhetoric: Chicano/as and Their Indio Heritage

Understanding the position of Chicanos and Native Americans, their relationships among themselves, and their relationships with the other cultures is one way to begin to understand the dynamics of zone rhetoric. The three faces of the Chicano/a, the Spanish, the indio, and the mestizo, which is a mixture of the first two, represent a polymorphous heritage. Considering this, it is not surprising that one of the dominant themes in Chicano/a writings is the search of an identity, a search for unity, without which they cannot have a political or cultural identity. One single aspect that stands out in their search is an identification with Aztlan and indigenous peoples.

Chicanos are political and cultural activists, and their political agenda includes a point-by-point fulfillment of a plan for the reclaiming of Aztlan, proposed at the National Chicano Youth Liberation Conference in Denver in 1969: *El Plan Espiritual de Aztlan* (Anaya). The plan proposes political, cultural, and social reformation aimed at reclaiming their heritage, their pride, and their lands (Anaya). The story of Aztlan is the story of a people who left their place of origin but intend to return. Some say Aztlan is just north of Mexico City. Others say it is centered in the Southwestern United States. Whether Aztlan is a physical place, an attitude, a dream, a medicine story, or (in Western terms) a myth is unimportant because Aztlan is real for the Chicano/a. Aztlan's power is its power to unite la Raza in a common vision of the past and the promise of a future.

Aztlan brings Chicanos back into the world of indigenous peoples. They lost that world when the Spanish took it, and it isn't until we understand the role of rhetoric in Spanish conquest and something of the rhetoric it displaced that we come to comprehend the role that rhetoric played in the destruction of the Chicano/a's indigenous past or how rhetoric might facilitate their return to Aztlan.

Earth Rhetoric and Sky Rhetoric

Two scholarly reference points help us understand the dynamics of rhetorical history and Chicano/as. The first is Calvin Martin Luther's *In the Spirit of the Earth*, and the second is Don Paul Abbott's *Rhetoric in the New World: Rhetorical Theory and Practice in Colonial Spanish America.*

Martin, an historian, describes the mind set of preneolithic societies, and he inadvertently describes the rhetorical context for hunter gatherers. In order to live, preneolithic humans had to establish a dialogue with the animals and plants they depended upon and with the earth they lived on. He says:

> [T]he universal image of such oral and manual discourse was one of intimate identification, indeed kinship, in a mythically literal sense, with the rest of earth's society—a speech and technology of power, though not so much a power *over* other things as the power of these other sentient beings. Humans learned their *human* powers and abilities from these other-than-human beings. (18)

Martin points out that one distinctive feature of the culture was its belief that through their discourse with animals and plants, human beings learned to live. Language and artifice were the means by which humans established a relationship with the wild. He continues:

> "Once we were shape-shifters," hunters remind their children, in the language of myth, today we wear the skin of human people, but through language and art we continue to commune with the creatures into which our ancestors could be transformed . . . the power of that transformation can always be rekindled in speech and artifice. (19)

Martin's description allows us a glimpse of the cosmology and discourse practices of people before we gathered in villages and learned the arts of farming, deliberation, and legislation. If we imagine a rhetoric for such a world, it would be mostly a story rhetoric, a rhetoric of identification with the other, a rhetoric that sought to teach children how to live in close relations to the wild things and sought to explain how they might maintain those relations. It would be a rhetoric of place, where the rhetorician would attempt to describe the special relationships among a place, animals and plants, and humans. It was an earth rhetoric, dedicated to articulating relationships among earthly things. It was also mostly, I think, epideictic rhetoric—a rhetoric that told the stories of the ancients because, as Martin points out, nothing made sense unless related to an ancestral story. Power existed in the stories, Martin says, "scores, if not hundreds of them, each a packet of Power. These are the tales of the ancestors, the heroes, the spirit beings" (72). To remember and repeat the stories and speeches of the ancients was the purpose for rhetoric. Whatever debate or deliberation took place, the success of the rhetorician depended upon his or her ability to connect the argument to the stories about the ancient beings.

Of course, when the Spanish came to the Americas, the cities of the Maya and the Azteca were centers of commerce; they were not hunter gatherers. However, they had retained the rhetorical forms and strategies of the hunter gatherer, and through centuries of practice created highly complex and stylized forms of song, poetry, story telling, and epideictic rhetoric. It was inevitable that this ancient rhetoric and the rhetoric of civilized Europe, based mostly on legislative and deliberative models, would come into conflict. Don Paul Abbott's description of that conflict allows us to understand why Europe's rhetoric was destructive to the Mexica way of life, and why Chicanos who are exploring their indigenous past find anything European, including its rhetoric, as destructive as the diseases the Europeans brought with them.

Milan Kundera points out in *The Book of Laughter* that

> The first step in liquidating a people is to erase its memory. Destroy its books, its culture, its history. Then have somebody write new books, manufacture new culture, invent a new history. Before long the nation will begin to forget what it is and what it was. (159)

According to Abbott, rhetoricians in the new world were key figures in attempting to "liquidate a people." His *Rhetoric in the New World* is an impressive scholarly work, tracing the influence of classical rhetoric on Spanish clergy and their efforts to use rhetoric to convert New World peoples to Christianity and, with it, the culture of Spain and Europe. Their Christian rhetoric was mainly about sky people, the spiritual allegiance to heaven.

For the most part, Abbott points out, two forms of Christian sky rhetoric prevailed in the New World. Some held that the indios were human and subject to the same persuasive techniques as Europeans. Others viewed indios as subhuman, and it was therefore necessary to create a "compressed and simple" rhetoric for them (112). However, most conversion was forced and swift rather than persuasive and incremental—sky rhetoric was based on coercion. The basic technique was to read a "Requirement" to the indios, where they were required to accept Spain's rule and religion or die. As Martin points out, "the Spanish attitude was that the indios' submission was to the chosen people of a divinely calibrated history" (102).

Then, as the Spanish retreated from the countryside into the cities, the study of rhetoric went with them, and indigenous people, denied entry into the clergy, were also denied a rhetorical education. Abbott concludes: "Cloistered in European-like centers of learning, rhetoricians had no compelling incentive to understand the variety of audiences potentially available to the orator in the Americas" (113). What the Spanish also missed was an opportunity to find the means of communicating with the Amerindians and, perhaps, learning from them.

However, some early Franciscan friars were sensitive to the accomplishments of the Aztecas, and before the Church disallowed it, collected examples of Azteca speeches and ceremonies. One friar in particular, Sahagun, recognized the importance of Nahuatl speech and discourse and collected *huehuehtlahtolli*, a Nahuatl word formed by the compression of the words for "men of old" and "word" or "oration" (Abbott 25). These orations of men of old are, in fact, epideictic speeches: highly stylized orations based on other orations given by the ancients. Many of the newer examples were speeches where the orator used the ancient ideas and related them to a contemporary context. Sahagun explains that the speeches were "carefully crafted discourses delivered by men who had been formally trained in the art of public speaking, and the schooling was so rigorous that if a student made a mistake "they drew blood from him . . ." (Abbott 29).

Sahagun's careful collection of these speeches and his interest in the culture of the Azteca, leaves us with an understanding of the indigenous peoples and an understanding of how much the Spanish missed. Not only did they miss the rich rhetorical tradition of the Aztecas but they missed an opportunity to relate indigenous stories, and all their persuasive power, to their own stories. Ironically this happened anyway. The Amerindians adapted Christianity to their beliefs, transforming what was European into a version that suits them and that is perhaps uniquely Amerindian.[1]

It would be a shame if as rhetoricians we repeated the mistakes of the Spanish in the New World. First, as rhetoricians we need to learn more about tribal rhetorics and their place in the societies they served. As zone rhetoricians, it is necessary for us to recognize that as tribal peoples and Chicano/as rediscover their indigenous heritage, they will also rediscover the power of their stories and their speeches. This power will change their perception of the world and the way they view the rest of us.

Second, the Spanish failure to engage cultures and to communicate with them by retreating into their urban universities is another lesson. The rhetorician of the future, the zone rhetorician, will need to study, to act, and to reflect on actions. In order to do that, the rhetorician will need to get involved in our communities and the polyculture that offers us an opportunity to do something with the rhetorical tools we have learned—to celebrate earth as much as sky and practice the rhetoric of reconciliation. Thus a theory and practice of rhetoric for the future will be a zone rhetoric, aware of the rhetorics of the past, their power and their use of power, but conscious as well of the way rhetoric can help us all become polycultural through ceremony and celebration.

Note
[1] Guillermo Lux and Maurilio E. Vigil claim that "the gods of Aztlan must be Indian. . . . Today the *huelgas* (labor strikes), the processions, and other solemn occasions of the Chicanos are conducted under the sacred banner of the brown Virgen de Guadalupe, the patron saint of the Mexican campesino, who is the Christian counterpart of the gentle Indian goddess Tonantzin. Tonantizin was worshipped at the place where the Basilica of the Virgen de Guadalupe now stands in the Valley of Mexico" (100-01).

Works Cited

Abbott, Don Paul. *Rhetoric In The New World*. Columbia: U of South Carolina P, 1996.

Allen, Paula Gunn. "'Border' Studies: The Intersection of Gender and Color." *Introduction To Scholarship In Modern Languages and Literatures*. Ed. Joseph Giabaldi. New York: MLA, 1992. 303-19.

Anaya, Rudolfo, and Francisco Lomeli. *Aztlan: Essays On The Chicano Homeland*. Albuquerque: U of New Mexico P, 1989.

Anzaldúa, Gloria. *Borderlands/La Frontera: The New Mestiza*. San Francisco: Spinsters/Aunt Lute, 1987.

Bizzell, Patricia, and Bruce Herzberg. *Negotiating Difference*. New York: Bedford, 1996.

Gómez-Peña, Guillermo. "Documented/Undocumented." *The Graywolf Annual Five: Multicultural Literacy*. Ed. Rick Simonson and Scott Walker. Saint Paul: Graywolf, 1988. 127-34.

Halloran, Michael S. "Further Thoughts on the End of Rhetoric." *Defining The New Rhetorics*. Ed. Theresa Enos and Stuart C. Brown. Newbury Park, CA: Sage, 1993. 109-19.

Kundera, Milan. *The Book of Laughter and Forgetting*. Trans. Michael Henry Heim. New York: Knopf, 1980.

Lux, Guillermo, and Maurilio E. Virgil. "Return to Aztlan: The Chicano Rediscovers His Indian Past." *Aztlan: Essays on the Chicano Homeland*. Ed. Rudolfo A. Anaya and Francisco Lomelli. Albuquerque: U of New Mexico P, 1989. 93-110.

Martin, Calvin Luther. *In The Spirit of The Earth*. Baltimore: John Hopkins UP, 1992.

Pratt, Mary Louise. *Toward a Seech Act Theory Of Literary Discourse*. Bloomington: Indiana UP, 1977.

Spath, William. "Epideictic Discourse Theory: Methodology and Model." St. Cloud State University. Unpublished paper, 1996.

Timmerman, David M. " Epideictic Oratory." *The Encyclopedia Of Rhetoric*. Ed. Theresa Enos. New York: Garland, 1996. 228-31.

RICHARD JOHNSON-SHEEHAN

University of New Mexico

A Hermeneutic View of Scientific Metaphor: A Move Away from Assumptions of Causality in the Rhetoric of Science

I am much occupied with the investigation of the physical causes. My aim is to show that the celestial machine is to be likened not to a divine organism but rather to a clockwork . . . , insofar as nearly all the manifold movements are carried out by means of a single, quite simple magnetic force, as in the case of a clockwork all motions [are caused] by a simple weight. Moreover, I show how this physical conception is to be presented through calculation and geometry.
—*Johannes Kepler,* Letter to von Hohenburg *(1605)*

And I have been greatly helped by considering machines. The only difference I can see between machines and natural objects is that the workings of machines are mostly carried out by apparatus large enough to be readily perceptible by the senses . . . whereas natural processes almost always depend on parts so small that they utterly elude our senses.
—*Rene Descartes,* Principia Philosophiae *(1644)*

Are we not coming to see that the whole works of scientific research, even entire schools, are hardly more than the patient repetition, in all its ramifications, of a fertile metaphor?
—*Kenneth Burke,* Permanence and Change

My purpose in this essay is to explore an alternative view of metaphor that might prove useful toward understanding the role of metaphor in scientific discourse. Over the past thirty years—beginning with the work of Mary Hesse in *Models and Analogies in Science* (1966) and comments by Thomas Kuhn and Max Black, metaphor has taken on a much greater importance in studies of the rhetoric of science. In fact, several rhetoricians of science have recently argued that metaphors are the primary flashpoints from which scientific revolutions, even whole paradigms, in scientific thought originate.

With few exceptions, however, scholars who study scientific metaphors have employed what is typically called the "interaction view" of metaphor that was first developed by I. A. Richards and later enhanced by Black. In this essay I will argue that this "interaction view" does not adequately describe how metaphors are *used* in scientific discourse. Then I will suggest that a "hermeneutic" or "interpretive" view of metaphor better illustrates how scientists use metaphors to invent new scientific theories and beliefs. The thesis of this essay, therefore, is that metaphors are significant in scientific discourse because they form the *basis of invention* for scientific narratives. As such, scientific metaphors should be discussed according to how they are used, not how they work.

What Metaphors Do

First, let me point out that there is general consensus among scholars about what metaphors do. Metaphors, as Kenneth Burke points out in his *Grammar of Motives*, change one's perspective, one's point of view (503-04). They invite us to look at the world from a different angle, reconceptualizing reality in a different way. For example, the metaphor "time is money" urges us to talk about time as a quantifiable entity of value. In Western culture we can actually spend, lose, or save time. If we are efficient, we can gain or make time; but if we are not efficient, we can run out of time. As Lakoff and Johnson suggest, a metaphor such as "time is money" is so central to our understanding of time that it actually structures how we conceptualize and discourse about temporal issues (290).

Now here's what I want you to notice. When we change our metaphor, we change our perspective. Let's replace the metaphor "time is money" with another important metaphor, "time is a stream." It is common for people to speak of time flowing, slipping away, or moving at a slower or faster rate. The metaphor "time is a stream," like "time is money," defines how Western culture thinks and talks about temporal issues. Notice, however, that these two metaphors for time are not compatible. Rather, each invites us to adopt a different perspective from which we conceptualize and talk about temporal issues.

In scientific discourse, as Mary Hesse has pointed out, a change in root metaphors often leads to a change in the way scientists conceptualize natural phenomena. For example, Isaac Newton's "light is corpuscular" metaphor (i.e., "light is a particle"), introduced in the *Opticks* (1704), was the basis of almost all early Enlightenment theories of light. Using this metaphor as a basis for their theories, scientists described light in corpuscular terms through phrases like "the refraction of light," "the transmittal of light through rays or streams," and "the sorting of light particles into colors by a prism." In essence, the metaphor "light is corpuscular" provided the basis for a narrative that described the behavior of light as a stream of particles. Many scientists' perspectives on light, however, changed a century later when Thomas Young employed the metaphor "light is the undulation of an elastic medium" (i.e., "light is a wave") to explain interference patterns in light. This new metaphor shifted the perspective of scientists, inviting them to view light from a new angle, a new point of view. Essentially, the metaphor "light is a wave" invited Young and his followers to describe light through a wave narrative that included words like *reflection, amplitude, frequency,* and *wavelength*—terms that are associated with waves, not particles.

So what do metaphors do? They are linguistic devices for changing perspective. I have always found it interesting that the word *trope* in ancient Greek means *turn*. Greek rhetoricians seem to have recognized that metaphors turn perspective, inviting people to conceptualize and discourse differently about a particular topic or situation.

How Metaphors Work

The debate that has characterized discussions of metaphor in the twentieth century is *how* metaphors work their magic. Scholars of scientific metaphor have almost exclusively adopted the "interaction view" of metaphor—as developed by Richards and Black—to explain how metaphors work. The interaction view suggests that metaphors make meaning by bringing two different words and their associated meanings into contrast. For example, Richards and Black would suggest that the phrase "light is a wave" is a metaphor because the words *light* (the tenor) and *wave* (the vehicle) interact to create a new meaning. Black would say that the word *wave* projects its meanings onto the word *light*, imposing an extension of meaning of the word *light*. The word *wave*, meanwhile, serves as a filter through which we extend the meaning of *light* (73). It is important to note, however, that both Richards and Black believe that bringing words together causes an interaction that leads to new meaning.

When the interaction view is applied to metaphors in scientific discourse, as it has been by Hesse, Gerhardt and Russell, Rothbart, Peterfreund, MacCormac, among many others, it takes on some interesting characteristics. These scholars suggest that a particularly effective metaphor, like "light is a wave," causes an interaction in the minds of scientists. Gerhardt and Russell even suggest that the interaction of the words creates an "ontological flash" that changes the way the scientist conceptualizes reality (121). Others suggest that metaphors cause scientists to have new insights, eventually sparking a whole paradigm shift as described by Kuhn. To use Kuhn's terminology, as Hesse and others have done, a new metaphor causes scientists to enter a new world or reality, viewing the world from within the new paradigm.

The problem with this explanation of the role of scientific metaphor is that the history of science does not support it. First, some metaphors, like "light is a particle" and "light is a wave," have been in existence, even competed with one another, for centuries. If metaphors cause moments of insight, ontological flashes, or revolutions, then how do we explain the lack of insights, flashes, and revolutions over the centuries? Second, revolutions, despite what Kuhn and others may have said, are not sudden. Rather, they often take a good century or two to take hold. If metaphors *cause* people to enter new realities or new worlds, how do we explain the gradual change from one root metaphor to another? And finally, if new scientific metaphors create moments of insight, when do they stop being metaphorical and start being literal? In other words, is a metaphor like "light is a wave" still a metaphor? Or, at some point does it become a truth statement of some kind? When does it stop sparking insights or ontological flashes?

How Metaphors Are Used

I don't propose to answer these questions, because I think they are created by a misunderstanding of the role of metaphor in scientific discourse. The problem I see with using the interaction view of metaphor to study scientific discourse is that it puts the emphasis on the wrong place. The interaction view suggests that the meaning of a metaphor can be identified in one of two places: (1) the intention of the speaker or (2) the relationships among the words in the phrase. This account of metaphor, I believe, has the whole situation backwards. The responsibility for making meaning, as Donald Davidson points out, is not on the speaker or the phrase; rather, it is the interpreter's responsibility to *invent* the meaning of a metaphor out of his or her own beliefs and experiences (31-32). For example, consider once again the scientific metaphor "light is a wave" used by Young. I imagine most of us can readily see that this phrase is a metaphor. Or is it? You see, if I show this phrase to scientists in the late nineteenth century, they would say that this phrase is a literal truth statement, not a metaphor. Light *is* a wave. But, if I were to show this phrase to pre-Young scientists in the eighteenth century, they would be inclined to say that this statement is "false" or even "absurd."

So, what or who makes this phrase a metaphor? I suggest that it is the interpreter that makes a phrase a metaphor. Upon experiencing the phrase, the interpreter faces an important decision. He might reject the metaphor as false or absurd—rejection of new metaphors is quite common in scientific discourse. Or he might suspend judgment, using the metaphor to reconceptualize his beliefs about light. If the interpreter decides to accept the metaphor, then he will flesh out its meaning by inventing a narrative that is based on the metaphor. This is what Young and his followers did after employing the metaphor "light is a wave." Once they had accepted this metaphor, they began to reinvent their beliefs about light with terms like *amplitude, frequency, wavelength,* which are commonly associated with waves. In other words, the new perspective urged by the metaphor invited them to reinterpret the phenomenon of light from a new perspective, a new point of view. The metaphor then formed the basis of a new narrative, or theory, of light that Young and others used to invent their beliefs about this phenomena.

Indeed, in an 1801 lecture by Young to the Royal Society, we see the narrative developing. After setting out his main hypothesis that light is a wave, Young offers four further hypotheses that are based on the "light is a wave" metaphor:

1. A luminiferous ether pervades the universe, rare and elastic in high degree.
2. Undulations are excited in this ether whenever a body becomes luminous.
3. The Sensation of different Colours depends on the different frequency of Vibrations excited by Light in the Retina.
4. All material Bodies have an Attraction for the ethereal Medium, by means of which it is accumulated within their substance, and for a small Distance around them, in a state of greater Density, but not of greater Elasticity. (qtd. in Wood 160)

Of particular interest in this list of hypotheses is the invention of the luminiferous ether. Recognizing that waves always travel through a medium of some kind, Young's metaphor "light is a wave" invites him to invent that medium to preserve his theory, or narrative, of light. Young did not discover ether; rather, he invented it based on his guiding metaphor.

So here's my point. How a scientific metaphor works is really unimportant. What is important is how the metaphor is used. Scientific metaphors invite interpreters to reconceptualize their beliefs from a different point of view. Then, if accepted, these metaphors serve as invention tools that form the basis of a new scientific narrative.

An Interpretive View of Scientific Metaphor

Now let me return to the quotations by Kepler and Descartes with which I started this discussion. In Kepler's quotation I think we see the emergence of a new root metaphor for science. He suggests that he is going to view nature not as a divine organism, as Aristotle and Aquinas had, but as a clockwork or a machine. According to the interaction view of metaphor, what we are observing here is the moment at which a "paradigm shift" occurred. Proponents of the interaction view would say that the words in the metaphoric phrase "nature is a machine" caused a moment of insight, an ontological flash in the mind of Kepler, causing him to see the world differently. Moreover, other scientists, upon experiencing Kepler's new metaphor, also experienced a paradigm shift,

leading to an all-out revolution from Aristotelian science to Mechanistic/
Enlightenment science.

Unfortunately, history seems to deny this happened. Over two centuries
passed, even beyond Newton, before mechanism became the dominant narrative
of science. If there was any ontological flashing or revolutions going on, they
were quiet indeed. Instead, I believe a scientific metaphor, like art, is in the eye
of the beholder. For Kepler and his followers, the metaphor "nature is a
machine" opened a new way to interpret natural phenomena. It also opened
whole new paths of research. For other scientists, however, the suggestion that
"nature is a machine" was patently false. Why? The answer is quite simple.
Each scientist interprets the phrase from his or her previous beliefs. The
metaphor itself does not cause a cognitive flash or moment of insight. Rather it
is up to the interpreter to make meaning out of the phrase itself. In fact,
numerous scientific metaphors were rejected for years and then later accepted
as truth statements.

An interpretive view of metaphor, I believe, allows us to describe a more
evolutionary process in which one dominant metaphor in science gradually
overcomes another. It suggests that metaphors serve only as a basis for
invention. The scientist, upon adopting the metaphor (perhaps only
temporarily), uses the perspective it urges to create a new narrative that
describes natural phenomena. In fact, the scientist can return over and over to
the metaphor for guidance. I think this is what is happening in the quotation by
Descartes. He says, "And I have been greatly helped by considering machines."
The metaphor "nature is a machine" becomes an invention tool that Descartes
refers to over and over for guidance and insight. Using the metaphor for
invention, Descartes develops a narrative on which much of mechanistic
science was later based. Moreover, the metaphor "nature is a machine" becomes
the basis for invention of a whole scientific movement. I think this is what
Kenneth Burke is implying when he asks in *Permanence and Change,* "Are we
not coming to see that the whole works of scientific research, even entire
schools, are hardly more than the patient repetition, in all its ramifications, of a
fertile metaphor?" Indeed, what often joins schools of scientific research
together is the common acceptance of a particularly useful metaphor.

I conclude by pointing out what I believe is the greatest advantage to an
interpretive or hermeneutic view of metaphor. This view of metaphor, I believe,
does away with the need for causal explanations of scientific discourse. The
interaction view suggests that metaphors cause scientists to have insights. A
hermeneutic view, quite the opposite, suggests that it is up to the scientist to
make meaning out of the metaphor. This leads me to two conclusions about
metaphors. First, humans are responsible for inventing their scientific beliefs
about nature; or, to put it another way, scientific beliefs and theories aren't
discovered—they're invented. Second, scientific metaphors are merely sites

from which scientists can invent narratives that describe natural phenomena. They do not in themselves hold special insights into reality.

Works Cited

Arbib, Michael, and Mary Hesse. *The Construction of Reality*. Cambridge: Cambridge UP, 1986.

Black, Max. "Metaphor." *Philosophical Perspectives on Metaphor*. Ed. M. Johnson. Minneapolis: U of Minnesota P, 1981. 63-82.

Davidson, Donald. "What Metaphors Mean." *On Metaphor*. Ed. S. Sacks. Chicago: U of Chicago P, 1979. 29-45.

Gerhardt, Mary, and Allan Russell. *Metaphoric Process: The Creation of Scientific and Religious Understanding*. Fort Worth: Texas Christian UP, 1984.

Hesse, Mary. *Models and Analogies in Science*. Notre Dame: U of Notre Dame P, 1966.

Kuhn, Thomas. *The Structure of Scientific Revolutions*. 2nd ed. Chicago: U of Chicago P, 1970.

Lakoff, George, and Mark Johnson. "Conceptual Metaphor in Everyday Language." *Philosophical Perspectives on Metaphor*. Ed. M. Johnson. Minneapolis: U of Minnesota P, 1981. 286-325.

Richards, I. A. *The Philosophy of Rhetoric*. London: Oxford UP, 1936.

Wood, Alexander. *Thomas Young, Natural Philosopher 1773-1829*. Cambridge: Cambridge UP, 1954.

ROLF NORGAARD

University of Colorado, Boulder

The Prospect of Rhetoric in
Writing across the Curriculum

The Prospect of Rhetoric, the 1971 report on the National Development Project in Rhetoric edited by Lloyd Bitzer and Edwin Black, shares its historical moment with the beginnings of the writing-across-the-curriculum movement, arguably one of the more important developments in composition over the last quarter century. Twenty-five years after the report, and a quarter-century into the WAC movement, it is appropriate to take stock of this historical confluence and to consider how each might enrich the other in the years ahead.

In some respects both the report and the incipient WAC movement shared similar impulses. Seeking a "conception of rhetoric applicable to our own time," the scholars writing in *The Prospect of Rhetoric* argued that the "scope of rhetorical theory and practice should be greatly widened" (237-38). Indeed, the report calls for nothing less than "major cultural change," initiated by adopting a "'rhetorical stance' in humanistic and social affairs" (244). Writing-across-the-curriculum proponents voiced similar concerns for renewing the relevance of communication in and across disciplines, and for widening both the scope of and avenues for instruction.

I shall argue, however, that the prospect of rhetoric in writing across the curriculum remains largely that: a prospect. To be sure, WAC programs have proliferated, and research on the rhetoric of disciplinary communities has prospered. However, undergraduate classroom instruction in WAC programs has yet to adopt, for the most part, the "rhetorical stance" envisioned in *The Prospect of Rhetoric*. Specifically, WAC's inclination to accommodate disciplinary concepts of expertise and existing curricular structures—an inclination that has allowed WAC to develop, even prosper, over several "generations"—has also diminished its rhetorical prospects.

This paper inquires into these causes and briefly suggests possible remedies. The 1971 report provides a useful place to start, for in its pages we can uncover impulses for reform that WAC proponents shared, even as we identify different rhetorical stances and divergent attitudes on curricular issues and disciplinary expertise. Unlike many earlier reform movements, WAC programs have survived because of accommodations to a "culture of expertise." However, this accommodation has also narrowed students' rhetorical education.

By examining various instructional paradigms within the WAC movement, we come to learn that each labors under a tyranny of content. If the effort of the 1971 report is to "rhetoricize" our educational endeavors, even our social institutions, then we might ask in closing, some twenty-five years later, how we might rhetoricize WAC (244). In turn, we might reflect on how twenty-five years of WAC contribute to rhetoric's future prospects.

Twins Separated at Birth

Publication of the 1971 report and the nearly simultaneous emergence of the WAC movement might seem to be one of those accidents of history. After all, the intellectual origins of WAC are often linked to the British classroom research and theorizing of James Britton and thus seem far removed from the social tumult on American campuses that helped shape the rhetorical context of *The Prospect of Rhetoric* (Martin). But David Russell, among others, has alerted us to WAC's distinctively American origins, especially in the work of John Dewey and the progressive education movement. The first stirrings of the WAC movement in the early 1970s were shaped by some of the same social, educational, and institutional forces that influenced the 1971 report. Widely expanded access to higher education and the highly charged political environment of the day both helped focus attention on three concerns: the role of language in education, the need for renewing the relevance of the subject matter being taught, and interest in new ways of teaching that subject matter. Virtually every contribution to the 1971 report raises or echoes these concerns. The same concerns motivated many of the early experiments in writing across the curriculum, as faculty recognized writing as a tool for learning, sought to renew the relevance of both writing instruction and disciplinary subject matter, and explored new avenues of teaching afforded by a more sustained focus on writing.

If *The Prospect of Rhetoric* and the incipient WAC movement are in some respects intellectual twins, they are siblings who have been separated virtually from birth. The rhetoric adopted by each and divergent attitudes on curriculum and disciplinary expertise account in large part for their separate lives.

Writing in the immediate wake of student protests and the Kent State shootings, the scholars whose work is collected in *The Prospect of Rhetoric* seem to have adopted, in varying degrees, some of the same "manifesto rhetoric" already in the air. The report's recommendations seem charged with a rhetoric that might inspire a movement: "Were the judgments of our conference accepted, sweeping changes would be necessary throughout the educational establishment of the nation" (243). One of the reasons we can look back to the report some twenty-five years later is that its rhetoric announces itself as revolutionary. The early stirrings of the WAC movement couldn't be more different. Instead of one memorable manifesto, we witnessed various local, often inconspicuous attempts to encourage faculty in the disciplines to use and study writing in their own classrooms. Analyzing the first twenty-five years of WAC in light of the literature on social movements, Barbara Walvoord emphasizes the movement's local origins and variations, its bottom-up approach to change, and its loose network of committed faculty. Although Daniel Mahala and others have recognized WAC's potential for radical educational critique, the rhetoric of WAC proponents is largely that of accommodation. Whereas the 1971 report envisioned a lofty "prospect" of rhetoric, WAC's educational reforms appear modest by comparison, even pedestrian in the attention given to local contexts and practical innovation. If the 1971 report seems like a manifesto in search of a movement, WAC seems to have become a movement almost in spite of itself.

These differences in rhetoric reveal, in turn, divergent views on curriculum and expertise. *The Prospect of Rhetoric* explicitly challenges academic structures. In his essay Wayne Booth offers a naïve observer's tour of rhetoric's broad and ever-broadening domain. The purpose of this tour, says Booth, is to "startle us, once and for all and forever, out of any notion that 'rhetoric' is the special province of any one of our disciplines" (104). Like others, Edward Corbett embraces rhetoric's transdisciplinary status: "As far as I have been able to determine, this is the first national conference on rhetoric involving participants from such varied academic disciplines" (166). Citing a "separation of cultures" and a pervasive inability of groups to communicate with each other, the 1971 report points fingers: "Conventional curricula and patterns of academic organization are partly to blame for these difficulties" (211). Yet even as *The Prospect of Rhetoric* criticizes curricula and offers a manifesto for change, contributors to the report find strength in a shared rhetorical tradition. Looking back even as they look forward, they prize their own expertise. "If I had only one recommendation to make," writes Edward Corbett, "I would suggest that in our quest for a relevant rhetoric for the modern age we take a firsthand look at the classical rhetoricians" (170).

While sharing the impulse for educational reform, early WAC proponents tended to work within, not challenge, curricular patterns and to accommodate the disciplinary expertise of others without explicitly claiming a body of expertise as their own. Explaining WAC's success, David Russell notes that WAC "did not attempt to substitute some overarching educational or philosophical program or a millennial hope of doing away with disciplinary boundaries. . . . Instead, WAC acknowledged differences among disciplines and tried to understand them, without trying to dismiss or transcend them" (39).

Yet success exacts its own price. Although the long-term prospects of WAC are still in question, its willingness to accommodate disciplinary expertise has diminished, to my mind, the "prospects of rhetoric" within the undergraduate classroom. To uncover the reasons for the eclipse of rhetoric in WAC classroom instruction, we must take a closer look at WAC's view of expertise and the resulting tyranny of content in several WAC paradigms.

Accommodating Expertise: The Tyrannies of Content

The two paradigms that now govern writing-across-the-curriculum programs—writing-to-learn in whatever discipline, and learning-to-write in a particular discipline—are increasingly viewed in antagonistic terms. Writing in the February 1993 issue of *College Composition and Communication*, Robert Jones and Joseph Comprone regret that these two paradigms provide "either/or responses" (62) for teachers and writing program administrators. If anything, the dilemma seems to be getting worse. Writing in the same journal some eighteen months later, Judy Kirscht, Rhonda Levine, and John Reiff characterize the two paradigms as representing opposing "ideological positions" (372).

To my mind, the differences between these two paradigms, however real they may seem to be, mask a more fundamental problem that both paradigms share: an unthinking accommodation to what Cheryl Geisler and others have termed a "culture of expertise." Both approaches accommodate expertise without acknowledging what Geisler refers to as the "burden of rhetorical persuasion" that accompanies expertise (253). That is, both approaches tend to strip away the rhetorical dimension from inquiry and disciplinary knowledge. I prefer to seize this "burden of rhetorical persuasion" as a curricular opportunity—one central to the reform project announced in *The Prospect of Rhetoric*.

Writing to Learn

One of the two paradigms, "writing-to-learn," directs our attention to process, to the use of writing as a tool for active learning, to the humanistic impulse that lies behind this generalized, expressivist pedagogy: generalized in that this approach seeks to serve a wide variety of courses and course objectives and expressivist in that the approach often makes heavy use of informal writing, as in personal journals.

Yet the unasked question remains, "writing to learn" what? The content or expertise that writing is meant to serve rarely figures as an issue. Although this approach may facilitate learning, in the end the writing tends to accommodate prior notions of expertise. In so doing, "writing to learn" strips away the rhetorical dimension from inquiry and disciplinary knowledge. Nowhere is this more evident than in the informal writing the students produce or in the journals they keep. Issues of audience rarely come up, as the writing tends to serve the individual author or at best the professor, the keeper and dispenser of expertise. In the case of "writing to learn, "knowing one's subject has little to do with knowing one's audience.

Writing in the Disciplines

A second approach, "writing in the disciplines," with its emphasis on discourse communities and disciplinary cultures, would seem to address this concern. And yet, here too, writing all too often simply accommodates a culture of expertise. In its most reductive form, "writing in the disciplines" can simply become a matter of making students proficient writers in their field, usually through mastering prescriptive conventions and socializing students to its culture. More recently, research on "writing in the disciplines" has moved well beyond these simplistic notions, viewing disciplines as socially negotiated territory and conventions as motivated by processes of inquiry.

Yet this research all too rarely makes its way into curriculum design and the undergraduate classroom, for "writing in the disciplines" is most often taught in curricular structures whose boundaries have long since been negotiated and in courses whose focus lies less in pursuing lines of inquiry than in mastering areas of content. Like "writing to learn," "learning to write" in a particular discipline tends to accommodate, not problematize, prior notions of expertise. In so doing, "writing in the disciplines" can also strip away the rhetorical dimension from inquiry and disciplinary knowledge. Consider, once again, the matter of audience. Although professionals in the discipline may indeed share a real discourse community, that community is at best a virtual concept for students. If embodied at all, the discipline's discourse community becomes reduced to one member: the professor. "Learning to write in a discipline" thus becomes a matter of "writing to the learned," to the expert. The rhetorical context in which inquiry occurs becomes diminished to a point where persuasion becomes little more than convincing the expert that one has acquired some measure of his or her expertise. Here, knowing one's subject has become reduced to knowing but one particular audience.

WAC Approaches in Composition Courses

Given that "writing to learn" and "writing in the disciplines" work within existing curricular structures and adopt prevailing concepts of disciplinary expertise, both paradigms can easily suffer under the tyranny of content. Yet what of WAC approaches in our own composition courses? Surely in a course under our own purview, we can more readily adopt the "rhetorical stance" envisioned in *The Prospect of Rhetoric*.

When WAC anthologies started to have an impact on composition courses some fifteen years ago, those texts had a salutary effect. No longer would composition courses operate exclusively within the universe of literary criticism. Yet, oddly enough, this broader curricular perspective in a course of our own design did little to improve the prospects of rhetoric.

Research by Charles Bazerman, Herbert W. Simons, and others has drawn attention to the rhetorical construction of knowledge in the disciplines. Ironically, WAC classroom anthologies still labor under a tyranny of content surprisingly similar to the focus on topical coverage common in the disciplines themselves. Exceptions apart, WAC anthologies present decontextualized, belletristic set pieces on various topics. They adopt a field-coverage principle by organizing those essays according to broad curricular categories. They then overlay generic rhetorical patterns (often Bain's modes of discourse) on that organization, all the while relegating rhetorical concerns to introductory chapters. In so doing, WAC texts divorce rhetorical instruction from the readings, and the topically oriented readings are themselves divorced from genuine rhetorical issues in and across disciplinary communities.

The virtual banishment of rhetoric from WAC anthologies can be traced to at least three causes: (1) conventions of textbook publishing that do not square with WAC principles (or even, all too frequently, with rhetorical principles); (2) composition's curricular location and marginalized status; and (3) the often tenuous condition of WAC programs that makes disciplinary accommodation a means for survival. Whatever the instructional paradigm, such accommodation, while politically and institutionally expedient, can undermine rhetorical education.

Rhetoricizing WAC, Contextualizing Rhetoric

As we consider ways of fostering rhetorical education a quarter-century after *The Prospect of Rhetoric* and the beginnings of the WAC movement, we would do well to place both in closer connection to each other, linking their ostensibly separate lives. The challenge offered in the 1971 report is that we "rhetoricize" our educational endeavors (244). That challenge remains timely, given the tyranny of content so apparent in WAC instructional paradigms. Yet writing across the curriculum, given its persistence if not success, offers up its own challenge. As we consider rhetoric's future prospects, we can ill afford to dismiss what we have learned about writing in specific discourse communities or about the local contexts in which rhetoric operates.

The tension between these two intellectual siblings of the early 1970s is as inevitable as it can be productive. In its vision of rhetoric as a transdisciplinary endeavor, the 1971 report reenacts rhetoric's tendency to offer a generalized *technê*. As Charles Bazerman and David Russell note, "Rhetoric, as a general teaching, while preaching locality of action and guidelines for handling that locality, has tended from the beginning to a universality" (xi). Writing across the curriculum, on the other hand, has focused on those localities, ever attentive to the demands of specific discourse communities and specialized knowledge. But without meaningful connection to rhetoric as a generalized *technê*, writing across the curriculum can easily fall victim, as we have seen, to the tyranny of content. When isolated, each tendency—be it generalizing or localizing—diminishes its own prospects as well as the prospects of the other. Thus, as we look ahead to the next twenty-five years, a twin challenge presents itself: We must rhetoricize WAC even as we contextualize rhetoric.

To meet the challenge of rhetoricizing WAC, we might consider turning the "burden of rhetorical persuasion" accompanying expertise into a curricular opportunity (Geisler 253). Adapting the notion of contact zone introduced by Mary Louise Pratt, let us ask students to write in disciplinary "contact zones"—zones that challenge students to make their expertise relevant and accessible to well-trained readers in different but related disciplines. That is, we might position classroom communities, and indeed WAC programs, in ways that are not entirely congruent with the disciplinary communities in which expertise is first acquired. By repositioning ourselves to encourage what Charles Bazerman and David Russell call "interface discourse" (xvi) and what Debra Journet calls "boundary rhetoric," WAC programs might reconcile institutional survival and rhetorical success.

Let us also rhetoricize WAC-inspired classroom texts in our own composition courses. Instead of offering a steady diet of topical essays that cover various fields, why not have those classroom essays broach genuine rhetorical issues—disciplinary constructions of ethos, varieties of persuasion, social perspectives on genre—that help shape knowledge in disciplinary communities. If we hope to rhetoricize WAC, we can find no better place to start than in our own classrooms.

Not only is a rhetoricized WAC in keeping with the spirit of the 1971 report, it also would enrich rhetoric's prospects. The lessons we have learned from WAC—lessons of local context and community, lessons of particular circumstance—are those in which the contributors to the report were themselves interested. The desire for "a conception of rhetoric applicable to our own time" was chiefly a desire for a contextualized rhetoric, a rhetoric that would account, in the early 1970s, for new forms of social protest, new forms of media, new communities and avenues for discursive and symbolic action (237). If we were to rewrite *The Prospect of Rhetoric* today, we would surely have to account for the twenty-five years of WAC that have sharpened our awareness of rhetoric in context.

Interested that the efforts of the National Development Project on Rhetoric "bear fruit," Edward Corbett worried whether "the deliberations of this conference may come to be referred to as Murmurings from the Wax Museum" (167). He needn't have, for the challenge announced in *The Prospect of Rhetoric* some twenty-five years ago still endures. Indeed, it has been complicated and enriched by our experience in writing across the curriculum. If we are to improve the prospect of rhetoric in writing across the curriculum, if we are to "rhetoricize WAC," we ourselves must approach disciplinary expertise, curricular structures, and prevailing institutional arrangements in explicitly rhetorical terms. Likewise, the success of WAC offers its own challenge: that we contextualize the generalized *technê* of rhetoric, studying as we must rhetoric's role in specific circumstances and varied discourse communities. Rhetoricized WAC instruction can only enlarge and enrich the future prospects of rhetoric.

Works Cited

Bazerman, Charles, and David R. Russell, eds. *Landmark Essays on Writing across the Curriculum.* Davis, CA: Hermagoras, 1994.

Bitzer, Lloyd, and Edwin Black, eds. *The Prospect of Rhetoric: Report of the National Development Project.* Englewood Cliffs, NJ: Prentice, 1971.

Booth, Wayne. "The Scope of Rhetoric Today: A Polemical Excursion." T*he Prospect of Rhetoric: Report of the National Development Project.* Englewood Cliffs, NJ: Prentice, 1971. 93-114.

Corbett, Edward P. J. "Rhetoric in Search of a Past, Present, and Future." *The Prospect of Rhetoric: Report of the National Development Project.* Englewood Cliffs, NJ: Prentice, 1971. 166-78.

Geisler, Cheryl. *Academic Literacy and the Nature of Expertise: Reading, Writing, and Knowing in Academic Philosophy.* Hillsdale, NJ: Erlbaum, 1994.

Jones, Robert, and Joseph J. Comprone. "Where Do We Go Next in Writing across the Curriculum?" *College Composition and Communication* 44 (1993): 59-68.

Journet, Debra. "Interdisciplinary Discourse and 'Boundary Rhetoric': The Case of S. E. Jelliffe." *Written Communication* 10 (1993): 510-41.

Kirscht, Judy, Rhonda Levine, and John Reiff. "Evolving Paradigms: WAC and the Rhetoric of Inquiry." *College Composition and Communication* 45 (1994): 369-80.

Mahala, Daniel. "Writing Utopias: Writing across the Curriculum and the Promise of Reform." *College English* 53 (1991): 773-89.

Martin, Nancy. "Language across the Curriculum: Where It Began and What It Promises." *Writing, Teaching, and Learning in the Disciplines.* Ed. Anne Herrington and Charles Moran. New York: MLA, 1992. 6-21.

Pratt, Mary Louise. "Arts of the Contact Zone." *Profession 91.* New York: MLA, 1991. 33-40.

Russell, David R. "American Origins of the Writing-across-the-Curriculum Movement." *Writing, Teaching, and Learning in the Disciplines.* Ed. Anne Herrington and Charles Moran. New York: MLA, 1992. 22-42.

Simons, Herbert W., ed. *The Rhetorical Turn: Invention and Persuasion in the Conduct of Inquiry.* Chicago: U of Chicago P, 1990.

Walvoord, Barbara E. "The Future of WAC." *College English* 58 (1996): 58-79.

JANICE NORTON

University of Tennessee

Luce Irigaray and the Ethics of Sexual Difference: Toward a Twenty-First-Century Rhetoric

In practice feminist rhetorical studies scholars are still likely to engage in the same scholarly projects that nonfeminists do, that is, criticism and critical studies. They may focus on texts of or about women as their content, but their assumptions about *what* to do as scholars are usually no different. In fact, perhaps the most prominent feminist in rhetorical studies, Karlyn Kohrs Campbell, has advised young women entering the field to focus on criticism in the interest of their being "taken seriously" by the male scholars who dominate rhetorical studies. That is, if feminists hope to be successful scholars, they must "walk the walk," "talk the talk," "be a man" about their work. Practically, Campbell accurately if dismayingly describes "the prospect of rhetoric" for women.

But a difficulty arises here directly out of rhetoric's traditional commitments to the timely and the appropriate: It is not necessarily a straight line from taking oneself to be "equal" to it being appropriate to *act* as if it were so. Indeed, I argue that it may be neither timely for all women-scholars to pursue the same scholarly projects nor appropriate for them to act as if they have the same status—the same access to culture—as do men in rhetorical studies.

The best brief elaboration I can make of this claim starts with a confluence of absences. First, while "the body" ranks among the more hotly contested issues in the larger academy, rhetoric has hardly noticed that it continues to theorize without reference to bodies marked by sexual difference. Second, while other disciplines have been investigating the operations of binary logic—nature/culture, masculine/feminine, reason/emotion, etc.—for two decades and more, rhetorical studies remains conspicuously absent at those forums. Third, while ever-increasing numbers of scholars are preoccupied by what the French philosopher and psychoanalyst Luce Irigaray calls "the burning question of our age," sexual difference, rhetoric has yet to notice either this development or its significance (Whitford, *Reader* 165).

These absences foreground a peculiarity: While the level of scholarly production in the larger academy suggests that what *constitutes* the speaking subject is perhaps the single most disputed contemporary intellectual issue, the topic barely has been broached in a discipline still claiming to "know" *how* the speaking subject persuades other speaking subjects. Indeed, not only does rhetorical studies go on as if subjectivity were a settled issue, there is little scholarly evidence that it has ever been contested at all. As a party to that contest, I want to take up here the stakes of maintaining ignorance of its conversation.

Kenneth Burke is the only twentieth-century rhetorician who attempts to think rhetoric through material bodies. Indeed, his theory of identification depends upon it: Identification takes place when body A is consubstantial with ("one with") body B, or within an economy of interest:

> A is not identical with his colleague, B. But insofar as their interests are joined, A is *identified* with B. Or he may *identify himself* with B even when their interests are not joined, if he assumes that they are, or is persuaded to believe so. (*Rhetoric* 21)

I have argued elsewhere that this explanation produces a specific relationship among "the body," "identification," and "consubstantiality," whose rhetorical limit is disclosed only when Burke's "Definition of Man" makes *man* refer to *all* of humankind (Norton). Burke's "Definition" unwittingly evacuates the body of corporeal substance, replacing it with an abstract universal: man, woman, child—their bodies are all interchangeable. Hence, Burke's shift of the master term for rhetoric from *persuasion* to *identification* ignores morphology and culture, holding on to the notion that fundamentally women's bodies can be understood by comparison to men's bodies and require no further theorizing.

Indeed, not only does Burke's theory of identification depend upon nature/culture, his theory of motive depends upon binarism in general. In *A Grammar of Motives*, he writes:

> The mind-body, being-nothing, and action-passion pairs generalize the first major steps usually taken towards the localizing of identity. That is, the principles of merger and division apply to all thought. . . . (418-19)

In *A Rhetoric of Motives*, binarism is crucial to rhetoric because it motivates identification, which is:

> . . . compensatory to division. If men were not apart from one another, there would be no need for the rhetorician to proclaim their unity. If *men were wholly and truly of one substance*, absolute communication would be of man's very essence. (22, italics added)

While Burke grants that "men" are not "wholly and truly of one substance," he never takes up the implications of differently sexed bodies for his theory of identification. Yet, is it not so that if men and women were *not* apart from one another, there would be no need for Kenneth Burke (rhetoric) to proclaim their unity under the rubric of "Man"?

Rhetorical studies does not avoid interrogating binary logic for the sake of its investment in Burke alone, however. For well over two millenia, rhetoric has secured its institutional identity by inscribing its values *in* that logic. Aristotle sets the institutional rhetorical project in motion by calling rhetoric "the counterpart of dialectic." From the outset, whatever Aristotle's intention, *counterpart* has been construed by philosophers and rhetoricians alike as an opposition: Philosophy theorizes the conditions of truth and the universal, and rhetoric distinguishes itself by accounting for the contingency of "opinion" in everyday discursive practice.

The primary operation of binary logic forces an either/or choice, demanding that one element in each pair be valued over the other. In Western philosophy the "proper" side always turns out to be the one allied to rationality—culture, reason, mind, etc.—and rhetoric accepted not only philosophy's framing of the world in binaries but also the valued element in each pair as well. Subsequently, rhetoric has often sought to demonstrate an intellectual seriousness of purpose on a par with philosophy's by explicitly marking how it too values the "proper" side of each pair (McKerrow). The one exception, of course, is in the theory/practice split where rhetoric necessarily comes down on the side of practice, so it has been the fate of the field to be perpetually caught in an attempt to explain how rhetorical "practice" measures up to "philosophical" theory. This desire to "measure up" is the source of a perennial intradisciplinary theory-versus-practice conflict, perhaps never more plaintively expressed than by Barnet Baskerville's title, "Must We All Be Rhetorical Critics?"

Prior to Edwin Black's keynote address at this conference, it was my intention to turn here to examples demonstrating that binary logic has become so naturalized that rhetoricians have never interrogated its status as a *rhetorical strategy*. Not even Aristotle. That, indeed, its hold on the discipline is so powerful that even rhetoric's keenest intellects are caught up in its demand. I had also intended to turn to Janet Atwill's inquiry into rhetorical's institutional status where the force of her argument suggests that binary logic may be necessary to a certain disciplinary identity for rhetoric.

That was *before* Black's address and his insistence on the *necessity* of a public/private distinction for rhetorical studies. Given the argument I make here, I feel compelled as a rhetorician to at least attempt, in however a limited fashion, to openly resist the seduction of Black's masterful attempt to reinscribe binarism into *my* disciplinary future. This gesture is necessary because for real women working in the academy (but not *only* for them), binarism has been a material disaster: "culture," "reason," "mind," "action," "theory," "energy," "public," always trump their opposites, and since to the victor goes the spoils, they always are appropriated by the domain inhabited by the "masculine."

Black's performance is extraordinary. In the first part of his address, he foregrounds the *rhetoricity* of his argument, magisterially styling his castigation of Richard McKeon's "abstractness" as an inside joke. Just how well he gauges his audience is measured by the roar of laughter when he finally asks, big-eyed and in pear-shaped (bari)tones: "Don't you think an essay on rhetoric would have an example in it *somewhere?*" As he moves through an argument about the necessity of rhetoric maintaining a distinction between "public" and "private," however, the register shifts: The foregrounding of rhetoricity recedes, joviality dissolves, and Black moves into a sermonic mode, turning for *his* example to The Parable of Ted Kaczynski, the alleged Unabomber. By now the story of Kaczynski's withdrawal into hermitical life is a commonplace, and Black retells it, drawing The Moral: "To reject the public life where one's ideas are put into conversation with others in favor of the private life where one disengages from the discourse of others"—that way, he intones, is The Road to Hell: to violence and the failure of rhetoric.

In an age of job anxiety and downsizing, the audience can hardly miss the point of Black's observation that one of Kaczynski's targets was a rhetorician of sorts: Rejection of the public/private distinction means the death of rhetoric(ians). Indeed, he declares, rhetoric "entails a public person regulating a private person," and a society in which the distinction disappears "would have no room in it for rhetoric." He pronounces: "that rhetoric *requires* this distinction is an observation, not an argument for or against *anything*. It's simply that it's a requisite for the existence of the discipline." He pauses (every good rhetor provides a "sense of an ending"), and then enjoins his audience: "Let us occupy ourselves with phe-nom-e-na."

The brilliance of that final gesture must be given its due, for it returns the audience to his earlier comedic excoriation of McKeon but with a difference. Now the audience is thinking about the rhetorical necessity of examples, for it has just seen a first-rate enactment of the claim. What the audience is *not* supposed to notice is how *it* has just been constructed. It is not supposed to be thinking about how the public/private distinction has operated in practice, not as a tension held within each citizen but as an alibi that historically has excluded women from public life—women who often wanted nothing more than to escape the enforced silence of the "private" status to which their female sex destined them, to escape from a *phenomenon* that is the effect of a naturalization.

And that returns me to Luce Irigaray, sexual difference, and her project to uncover the gesture that sets Western discourse in motion. Her analysis of the male and female imaginary, notes Margaret Whitford, corresponds to "the Pythagorean tables of opposites, described by Aristotle in the *Metaphysics*"

(*Irigaray* 59). Whitford cites Genevieve Lloyd's comments about the table, where

> . . . femaleness was explictly linked with the unbounded—the vague, the indeterminate—as against the bounded—the precise and clearly determined. . . . formlessness—the unlimited, irregular or disorderly . . . were seen as bad or inferior. . . . "Male," like the other terms on its side of the table was construed as superior to its opposite; and the basis for this superiority was its association with the Pythagorean contrast between form and formlessness. (Qtd. in Whitford, *Luce Irigaray* 60)

Irigaray's analysis marks three principles of Western rationality: the "principle of identity (also expressed in terms of quantity or ownership)" and

> the principle of non-contradiction (in which ambiguity, ambivalence, or multivalence have been reduced to a minimum); and binarism (e.g., nature/reason . . .)—as though everything had to be one thing or another." (Whitford, *Luce Irigaray* 59)

Binarism's function is nothing less than helping shore up the coherence that produces rationalism. And it does so by keeping "woman" on the inferior side of the ledger with "nature," "emotion," "private," etc., and hence, on the side of formlessness and the inchoate (which by definition are *outside* the symbolic order), so that "man" can secure for himself the unitary identity available only to those inhabiting the world of The Same.

In the most recent Irigaray translation, she reiterates:

> Between man and woman, there really is otherness: biological, morphological, relational. To be able to have a child constitutes a difference, but also being born a girl or a boy of a woman, who is of the same or the other gender as oneself, as well as to be or to appear corporeally with differing properties and qualities. (61)

Nevertheless, she says, "The ingathering (*recueillement*) of spirit's [sic] into the self has yet to occur, in that man has not yet moved on from a pure and simple intuition—namely that he represents human kind" (39), and her critique of identification resonates for rhetoric:

> Some of our prosperous or naive contemporaries, women and men, would like to wipe out this difference [between men and women] by resorting to monosexuality, to the unisex and to what is called

identification: even if I am bodily a man or woman, I can identify
with, and so be, the other sex. This new opium of the people
annihilates the other in the illusion of a reduction to identity,
equality and sameness, especially between man and woman, the
ultimate anchorage of real alterity. (61-62)

For Irigaray, reducing bodies to the Same, permitting sexual *in*difference to
masquerade as liberal egalitarianism, confusing the specificity of identity with
the fantasy of identification, is the opening for the brutalization of the other.

In rhetorical studies that brutalization takes its most pernicious form in the
continuation of "man as the measure of all things." Rhetoric students are
disciplined by methods naming one critical perspective after another: neo-
Aristotelian, dramaturgical, epistemic, deconstructive, Marxist, psychoanalytic,
ideological, feminist, but nowhere is "masculinism" identified as "one"
perspective among "many." It is the *one* value that authorizes perspective itself,
determining what counts as scholarship, who counts as scholar, reducing the
rest to rubble. Hence, it turns out that rhetoric indeed has a proper (speaking)
subject, a body with whom women are expected to identify, a content women
must learn.

The task is by no means impossible: Some of the best "men" *I* know are
walking around in female bodies. But the trap is double. On the one hand, in
the end no matter how much she identifies with masculinism, no matter how
big a man she strives to be (disciplinarily speaking), no matter how sharp she
"talks the talk," no matter now straight she "walks the walk," at the end of the
day, she's still not a man—*but she's not a woman either.* And she is without
reserves to invest in discovering what a "woman" might be. Moreover, she has
been complicit in an institutionally sanctioned program to turn her into the
worst kind of sophist: Simply by issuing coherent arguments in public from a
female body, she already has made "the weaker argument appear the stronger";
she probably has taken positions that are not her own but to which her
institutional interests are linked, and her discourse has often been at odds with
her actual emotions. And worst of all, she has not been a rhetorician: Her
actions have been neither timely for her development as "woman" nor
appropriate to either her sexual specificity or to her real status in the discipline.
(Indeed, if Black has his way, her status will be even more problematized.) On
the other hand, if she does not do *precisely* these things, the woman-scholar
finds no home in the academy.

Now, after thinking more about Black's address, I am struck by the way in
which its logic deafens the speaker as well as the audience. Black is so intent
on making Kaczynksi's rejection-of-the-public-in-favor-of-the-private an
exemplar (hence, turning him into a "woman") that he misses completely this
fact: *Kaczynski finally was caught because he insisted on the publication of the*

Unabomber Manifesto. Kaczynski languishes in jail because he insisted on putting his discourse in "conversation with others." Is the *real* moral in this parable that if women insist on entering the public domain, it will get them in trouble with "the law"?

Irigaray argues that if relations between men and women are to change, intellectuals must take seriously corporeality and sexual differentiation of bodies; they must begin a conversation about how discourse constructs those relations. Of these tasks Black has convinced me that the last will be the most difficult for rhetorical studies, for its most prominent scholars have never taken the history of their own theory production to be a proper object of study. It is not now, nor has it ever been, in their interest to do so. And given the history of Black's oracular insistence that binarism is a given, I do not immediately get a picture of men clamoring to change that, especially once the most profound consequence of accepting sexual difference becomes clear. Such an identity, says Irigaray, "rules out all forms of totality as well as the self-substituting subject" (106). To give up being a god for a limited human existence, to accept the body of the other as a threshhold that cannot be violated, not even discursively, will require a new ethics for rhetoric, an ethics of sexual difference. I urge Professor Black to take seriously his own exhortation and "occupy" *himself* with the real, rhetorical "phenomenon" of his own discursive strategy, a strategy that guarantees an institutional identity for rhetoric at the expense of the perpetuation of women's suffering under the regime of the binary that he takes to be so empirically "given."

Works Cited

Atwill, Janet. "Instituting the Art of Rhetoric: Theory, Practice, and Productive Knowledge in Interpretations of Aristotle's Rhetoric." *Rethinking the History of Rhetoric: Multidisciplinary Essays on the Rhetorical Tradition.* Ed. Takis Poulakos. Boulder: Westview, 1993. 91-117.

Baskerville, Barnet. "Must We All Be 'Rhetorical Critics'?" *Quarterly Journal of Speech* 63 (1977): 107-16.

Burke, Kenneth. *Grammar of Motives.* Berkeley: U of California P, 1969.

——. *Rhetoric of Motives.* Berkeley: U of California P, 1969.

Campbell, Karlyn K. "Proactive Strategies to Address the Devaluing of Women and Their Work." Panel. Eightieth Annual Meeting of the Speech Communication Association. New Orleans, 1994.

Irigaray, Luce. *I Love to You: Sketch of a Possible Felicity in History.* Trans. Alison Martin. New York: Routledge, 1996.

McKerrow, Raymie. "Critical Rhetoric: Theory and Praxis." *Communication Monographs* 56 (1989): 91-111.

Norton, Janice. "Rhetorical Criticism as Ethical Action: *Cherchez la Femme.*" *Southern Communication Journal* 61 (1995): 29-45.

Whitford, Margaret, ed. *The Irigaray Reader.* Oxford: Blackwell, 1991.

——. *Luce Irigaray: Philosophy in the Feminine.* London: Routledge, 1991.

ULRIKE ZINN JAECKEL

University of Chicago at Illinois

Hecklers and the Communication Triangle

In the traditionally accepted version of the origins of rhetoric in Greece, rhetoric emerged in the fifth century BCE as the art of public speaking when Sicilian aristocrats argued before the courts in order to regain the estates confiscated by their dethroned tyrant. All three species of rhetoric laid out by Aristotle—deliberative, judicial, and epideictic—involve public speaking. As public speaking, rhetoric deals with a special case of divided roles in communication: the single speaker addressing a group of listeners. Depending on the situation and the customs of the culture involved, civility requires the audience to hear the speaker out by remaining silent during the speech or by limiting themselves to short manifestations of approval or disapproval; anything more may be regarded as unseemly interruption if not heckling.[1] This pattern assumes the existence of a rhetorical situation as it has been described by Lloyd Bitzer: An exigence presents itself, an audience capable of mediating change is at hand, constraints—enabling as well as hampering—are in place, and a speaker authorized by a legitimate office seizes the occasion to mend the exigence by giving a speech. The audience may not be induced to think or act as the speaker wishes; but by its attendance and willingness to listen, it demonstrates its recognition of the speaker's authority and its concern for the exigence. To use Ellen Rooney's phrase, it is "available to be persuaded" (5). Clearly, the relationship between speaker and audience in situations of public speaking is asymmetrical: The one holds forth; the many hold still. Under normal circumstances, this is not a problem because speech sound can be received by many ears at once. If a crowd of listeners holds still, each one can hear what the speaker says.[2]

Public speaking thus does not correspond to the ideal type of the speaking situation depicted in the communication triangle as used, for example, by James Kinneavy to represent the relationship among speaker, audience, and reality (19). The symmetric design of an isosceles triangle[3] makes visible the assumptions in models of rhetoric as conversation or dialogue that take as their prototype a group of two equals: one speaker (encoder) and one listener (decoder) who cooperate in making meaning and constructing reality. Speaking as encoding and listening as decoding seem to correspond to each other without a remainder: Speaker and listener occupy the same status and have equal power. Moreover, the question how they come together is not asked. The triangle shows them already joined in a rhetorical situation, and this is the assumption rhetorical theory traditionally has made when addressing the relationship between speakers and audiences: It has taken for granted that audiences are available to speakers.

Citing Nevin Laib, Louise Wetherbee Phelps points out that there is a less irenic and more contentious "territorial" model of rhetoric that takes into account potentially conflicting "interests" and political agendas of interlocutors (155). In such a model, equality between speaker and listener is not automatically assumed but may be at issue. One manifestation of contentiousness in rhetoric is heckling. Hecklers refuse to listen in situations of public speaking, thus violating the silent rule that calls for the audience to hold still while one speaker holds forth. By probing the function of heckling, we can complicate our understanding of the roles of speakers and listeners not only in public speaking but in other manifestations of the communication process as well, a change that will be visible in a redrawn triangle.

A comprehensive study of heckling, understood as vocal and otherwise noisy behavior that interrupts or stops a public speech, would doubtless reveal a multitude of intentions, types, techniques, and consequences of this method of disputing a speaker's authority. Heckling can be spontaneous or premeditated. Its purpose may be to gain a voice or to shout the speaker down. It may range from occasional interruptions to an uproar that shuts down the proceedings at hand, and it may turn into violence. The perpetrators may be members of the intended audience or outsiders who "crash" the meeting. What interests me here is the function of heckling as a deliberate violation of the rules that govern public speaking.[4] A few examples will illustrate what is at stake.

An early instance of heckling occurs in the second book of the *Iliad*. In the hope of provoking a renewed fighting spirit, Agamemnon uses the feint of telling an assembly of the Achaeans to sail home. But his reverse psychology backfires, and the men eagerly and noisily prepare to launch the ships. Odysseus, having possessed himself of the *skeptron*, the staff signaling authority, instead drives them back to the place of assembly and bids them sit still and listen to the speeches of the rulers (2.200). When everybody else is finally quiet, the common soldier Thersites heckles and berates the king, Agamemnon, for his mishandling of the distribution of spoils, reiterating—as I. F. Stone points out—complaints uttered by the aristocratic and heroic Achilles in Book One. Thersites advocates returning home, the course of action Agamemnon has just pretended to propose. That is, Thersites defines the exigence differently than Agamemnon—"we've been here too long," not "we must take Troy." He does express the sentiments of a large part of the army and expresses them eloquently, but he garners no support and receives a bloodying blow with the *skeptron* from Odysseus (*Iliad* 2.84-277). In his revisionist reading of this episode, Stone celebrates Thersites' action as "the first attempt of the common man to exercise freedom of speech" (35). To be sure, Thersites violates the expectations associated with his low social status. Thomas Conley, who opens his *Rhetoric in the European Tradition* with a discussion of this episode, points out that "the tension that appears here is the tension between being right and having the social right to participate in public discussion" (2). For, ironically, Thersites' speech has the effect that Agamemnon intended: It incites the Achaeans to continue fighting. Instead of listening quietly, Thersites asserts power—without authority; and since the rest of the army has been brought back in line by Odysseus, they do not support him but laugh at him for being punished. Thersites has broken the rule of civility that binds him to the listening role in the assembly: He "bleat[s] on, defaming the Lord Marshal Agamemnon" (II.254-55).

An isolated heckler can be silenced; a whole group of them is more difficult to manage. In *The Bonfire of the Vanities,* Tom Wolfe depicts a scene in which hecklers gain the upper hand and prevent an officially authorized speaker from delivering his remarks. Thwarted in his attempt to hold a town hall meeting in Harlem, the mayor of New York is shunted off the stage by his bodyguards, leaving reports of a riot in his wake. In the racially torn big city, the trust between citizens and elected officials has been lost. The mayor's exigence is to gain approval for his policies, whereas the inhabitants of Harlem are dissatisfied with what is being done for their part of the city. Heckling is an audience reaction that politicians in the USA encounter with some regularity; but usually the hecklers obey the injunction to stop their shouts, or else they are removed by the police. Here, contrary to the mayor's expectations, the audience consists not of "civic-minded people" (his supporters) but of "Bacon's people," the followers of a charismatic Harlem preacher with his own political agenda (5). If the rest of the audience is more sympathetic to the hecklers than to the officially authorized speaker, the latter has little chance to regain the upper hand.

The assembly of the Achaeans and the New York City town hall meeting are highly scripted occasions with narrowly prescribed roles for the participants. Featured as speakers are the legitimate leaders of the groups to be addressed. The audience is in place, but the expectation that it will limit itself to the listening role is violated. The hecklers are dissatisfied with their leaders because they feel that their concerns are not being addressed. In Bitzer's terms they do not agree with the definition of the exigence.[5] Often a public speech is the only occasion when citizens, workers, or other audiences meet a leader face to face. If the leader is seen as unapproachable and as unwilling to listen to the grievances of the led, heckling may be the only means of reminding the leader that his or her authority is revocable. By heckling, the audience members show "disbelief," one of the "powers of the weak" identified by Elizabeth Janeway in her book of that title. As she points out, "what the powerful need is the consent of the governed to their actions as proper, acceptable, free of blame; and this consent can be granted only *by the governed*, the other member of the power relationship" and only if the governed perceive that their rulers make "an ordered, competent use of power that supplies them with a reasonably safe and stable environment" (111, emphasis in original). Thersites acts in isolation, without the support of the other common soldiers; thus he can be silenced by punishment. "Bacon's people" act in accord with one another and succeed in driving the mayor off the stage. In both cases heckling is done by persons of low status and has the function of expressing dissatisfaction with the way leaders conduct the affairs of the governed and thus of disputing established authority.

However, heckling is not limited to those of low social status. It can also have the function of preventing the establishment of new authority by new speakers, often in new institutions, as is shown in accounts of disturbances at Woman's Rights and other reformist conventions in the nineteenth century. Women who left the "domestic sphere" and attempted to engage in public speaking were accused of ruining the "female character" (Flexner 46; Hoffert 8). Protests against women orators were quite common. For example, at the World's Temperance Convention held in New York City in 1853, "ministers and gentlemen who were themselves delegates and participants in the convention" created disturbances when female delegates attempted to speak and demanded full participation in the proceedings (Hoffert 93). In other cases outsiders congregated where women were scheduled to speak and made their displeasure known vociferously, even violently. When Angelina Grimké gave an abolitionist speech in newly dedicated Pennsylvania Hall in 1838, a mob assembled outside, shouted disapproval, and threw rocks through the windows; two days later, they burned down the hall (Campbell, *Man* 25-32). At the evening sessions of the two-day National Woman's Rights Convention in New York in 1853, a group of "men about town" systematically hissed, yelled, and stamped their feet, making it impossible for the audience to hear the speakers who tried to talk over the ruckus. The convention ended in "complete chaos" (Hoffert 93-94). These outsiders rejected not only the speakers but also the institutional framework (organizations for Woman's Rights) that they were trying to build.

In these examples it is not established authority that is being disputed by hecklers but the attempt to establish authority in the first place. The social status of these hecklers is not easy to assess, but at least the clergymen at the Temperance meeting are of higher social status than the featured female speakers. It would be a mistake to associate heckling with low social status, as if all occasions of public speaking featured persons of high social status addressing audiences of low social status. Rather, it is the subordinate role of listeners that hecklers are protesting. Hecklers speak instead of listening, thereby challenging the separation of speaking and listening roles in public speaking.

Yet most occasions of public speaking proceed without incident. What makes it possible for one person to speak while many listen? As Bourdieu has pointed out, the speaker is backed by the delegated power of the institution that authorizes him or her to act as its spokesperson (*Language* 111)[6]; and in the last analysis, it is the audience that accords authority to the speaker through its acceptance of the speaker's and its own institutionalized roles (116). Moreover, occasions of public speaking are highly ritualized, with scheduled time, location, seating arrangements, order of entrance of the participants, introductions of the speaker(s), and—most important—the polite posture of the audience being the preconditions for a successful deployment of the speaker's rhetorical skill. Often, too, an occasion of public speaking (for example, an annual stockholders' or church business meeting) is largely ceremonial, with the decisions to be made having been negotiated in advance so that the audience can only confirm them. This elaborate apparatus normally assures that one individual is able to maintain ascendancy over an audience of many and to demonstrate the power implicit in the speaking role. For, notwithstanding the equality suggested by the rhetorical triangle, speaking is more powerful than listening.

It is physiologically more powerful. In his daring article, "A Hoot in the Dark: The Evolution of General Rhetoric," George A. Kennedy calls rhetoric "a form of energy" that can be found not only in humans but also in animals (especially birds), and he proclaims as one of his eight "theses" that "the function of rhetoric is the survival of the fittest" (4, 10). That is, he postulates a biological basis for rhetoric. And he sees rhetoric as a vital component in power struggles. Victor Vitanza, who confesses that he cannot decide if Kennedy wrote this article "seriously or farcically with beak in cheek" nevertheless concludes that "for Kennedy now, rhetoric is almost identical with Nietzsche's 'will to power'" ("Editor's Preface" x). Instead of laughing off Kennedy's article as essentialist and positivist, we can at least adopt Vitanza's stance of undecidability and explore the article's implications for the speaking and the listening roles.

As Kennedy puts it, "rhetorical assertion conveys energy and can spark reaction in another energy source" (3). Just as linguists describe speaking as *sending* and listening as *receiving* a message, so Kennedy presents these activities as *action* and *reaction*. Such metaphors suggest that speaking comes first. Moreover, although listening is not a passive state but an activity (as Kennedy makes abundantly clear), whatever amount of energy it uses or produces, it does not manifest itself in large-muscle movements but requires a relatively still posture, whereas speaking is visible as physical action, as the expenditure or production of bodily energy, and thus creates the impression of dominance (which is why, among the canons of rhetoric, Kennedy assigns primacy to *actio*, or delivery [12]). The point is that *at the moment of speaking*, the speaker is in the ascendancy; the listener submits. At that moment the relationship between speaker and listener is physically and physiologically asymmetrical, that is, unequal. Thus, one way to assert and maintain power is to "prolong" that moment, to monopolize the speaker role.

Nevin Laib, who calls rhetoric "the art of claiming, controlling, and defending property and status," makes a similar point when he writes that "reading and listening are, at least superficially, regarded as submissive behaviors" and "speaking and writing are aggressive behaviors" (582-84). But even if it sounds improbable that speaking requires more energy than listening or that speaking is aggressive and listening submissive, the fact remains that the ear cannot sort out speech sounds if there is too much noise (of whatever kind), especially when that noise consists of one's own speaking.[7] Listening requires refraining from speaking because otherwise the speaker cannot be heard, especially in public speaking when a single voice has to reach many ears. When all speak at once, there is no communication.

Equality between speaker and listener would be possible only as "equal time," as turn-taking. In the simplest model of communication between equals, each participant would exchange a turn at listening for another turn at speaking. Such equal turn-taking is rare. As expressed in Kenneth Burke's metaphor of the "human barnyard," competition for speaking roles is fierce, and certain individuals and groups develop ways of increasing their own right to speak and others' obligation to listen (xvii).[8] Although the ideal type of the communicative situation calls for turn-taking, often the listeners' chances to speak are deferred indefinitely.

Far from being the prototypical instantiation of rhetoric, public speaking is a special case that only "works" due to its ritualization and institutional backing: The assembled individuals voluntarily or involuntarily defer their chance to speak in order to listen to a single speaker. By violating it, hecklers make us aware of the silent contract that binds the audience to the listening role, a contract necessitated by the physical power of the audience to shout the speaker down. Even one-to-one communication could not proceed without this contract.

If it is true, then, that there is a basic asymmetry between the acts of speaking and listening that can only be compensated for through turn-taking, this inequality needs to be expressed in the diagram used to present the communication process schematically. Although the triangle remains a useful figure for this purpose, it should be redrawn as a scalene, an irregular triangle, to show the asymmetrical relationship between speaker and listener. A scalene triangle would also make visible that the listener views the "reality" under discussion from a different angle and a different distance than the speaker.

Yet the triangle is no more than a snapshot. It arrests a moment in an ongoing process. To stay with the geometrical metaphor, the triangle marks points on the inner surface of a sphere that is constantly rolling along. Gregory Clark calls a rhetorical statement a "claim to power"—only a claim. And he explains: "What is claimed is transformed into something real only when it is actualized in the authorizing response of the people it addresses"—the listeners, who need to become speakers to respond, turning the speaker into a listener waiting for a validating response (59).

With this tumble of the communication sphere, we should now examine what hecklers also are sabotaging: the power of listening.

Notes

[1] In a call-and-response model, the demarcation between response and heckling may be more difficult to draw.

[2] Originally, the number of listeners was limited by the acoustics of the locale and the volume of the speaker's voice. I am leaving aside the role of modern technology in extending the reach of the human voice.

[3] Kinneavy names the sources for the drawing on page 58. (I won't speculate on the meaning of the fact that the two sides of the drawing on page 19 vary by a few millimeters; they are of equal length in the rest of the book.)

[4] I am excluding heckling in public gatherings that do not primarily involve public speaking, such as sports events or musical performances (opera, concerts).

[5] Carolyn Miller argues that the exigence is not simply discovered but must be defined and negotiated and that there may be more than one exigence ("Genre as Social Action" 30). Karlyn Kohrs Campbell also points out that there may be conflicting exigences for women speakers ("The Rhetoric of Women's Liberation: An Oxymoron" 85).

[6] Bourdieu is talking about "ritual discourse" uttered, for example, by representatives of the clergy or of academia, not about speakers who lack institutional backing (113). But his discussion provides an understanding for what it is that makes it difficult for subordinate groups to gain a public voice.

[7] Research measuring the energy expended in speaking and listening could be done to verify this hypothesis. The amounts may not only vary but overlap. For example, in a conversation a listener not only listens but also plans what to say at the next turn. That kind of listening is probably more active than listening to a public speech where the hearer has no chance of respondimg.

[8] Graddol and Swann provide an overview of linguistic research on turn-taking in conversation, especially between two speakers. One feature studied is interruptions. Although interruptions may be due to lack of competence or dialectal differences in judging the moment for turn-taking, often they are used by the speaker with higher status to regain the floor. (Adults tend to interrupt children; men, women; higher-status males, other males [77, 79].) Another feature is length of turn. See Crawford on man's taking "more than a 'fair share' of talk time" (42).

Works Cited

Bitzer, Lloyd. "The Rhetorical Situation." *Philosophy and Rhetoric* 1 (1968): 1-14.

Bourdieu, Pierre. *Language and Symbolic Power*. Ed. and Intro. John B. Thompson. Trans. Gino Raymond and Matthew Adamson. Cambridge, MA: Harvard UP, 1991.

Burke, Kenneth. *A Grammar of Motives*. 1945. Berkeley: U of California P, 1969.

Campbell, Karlyn Kohrs. *Man Cannot Speak for Her: A Critical Study of Early Feminist Rhetoric*. Vol. 1. New York: Greenwood, 1989. 2 vols.

——. "The Rhetoric of Women's Liberation: An Oxymoron." *Quarterly Journal of Speech* 59 (1973): 74-86.

Clark, Gregory. *Dialogue, Dialectic, and Conversation: A Social Perspective on the Function of Writing*. Carbondale: Southern Illinois UP, 1990.

Conley, Thomas M. *Rhetoric in the European Tradition*. Chicago: U of Chicago P, 1990.

Crawford, Mary. *Talking Difference: On Gender and Language*. London: Sage, 1995.

Flexner, Eleanor. *Century of Struggle: The Woman's Rights Movement in the United States*. Rev. ed. Cambridge: Belknap of Harvard UP, 1975.

Graddol, David, and Joan Swann. *Gender Voices*. London: Blackwell, 1989.

Hoffert, Sylvia D. *When Hens Crow: The Woman's Rights Movement in Antebellum America*. Bloomington: Indiana UP, 1995.

Homer. *The Iliad*. Trans. Robert Fitzgerald. Garden City, NY: Anchor/Doubleday, 1975.

Janeway, Elizabeth. *Powers of the Weak*. New York: Knopf, 1980.

Kennedy, George A. "A Hoot in the Dark: The Evolution of General Rhetoric." *Philosophy and Rhetoric* 25 (1992): 1-21.

Kinneavy, James. *A Theory of Discourse*. 1971. New York: Norton, 1980.

Laib, Nevin K. "Territoriality in Rhetoric." *College English* 47 (1985): 579-93.

Miller, Carolyn R. "Genre as Social Action." *Genre and the New Rhetoric*. Ed. Aviva Freedman and Peter Medway. London: Taylor, 1994. 23-42.

Phelps, Louise Wetherbee. "Audience and Authorship: The Disappearing Boundary." *A Sense of Audience in Written Communication*. Ed. Gesa Kirsch and Duane H. Roen. Newbury Park: Sage, 1990. 153-74.

Rooney, Ellen. *Seductive Reasoning: Pluralism as the Problematic of Contemporary Literary Theory*. Ithaca: Cornell UP, 1989.

Stone, I. F. *The Trial of Socrates*. New York: Doubleday, 1989.

Vitanza, Victor J. "Editor's Preface, Dedication, and Acknowledgments." *Writing Histories of Rhetoric*. Ed. Victor J. Vitanza. Carbondale: Southern Illinois UP, 1994. vii-xii.

Wolfe, Tom. *The Bonfire of the Vanities*. New York: Farrar, 1987.

GREGORY CLARK

Brigham Young University

Road Guides and Travelers' Tales on the Lincoln Highway

In any community there is much we could call "public discourse" that does not address, directly at least, matters of policy and politics. Particularly if the community is a national one, the discourse that constitutes and sustains its identity in the minds of the individuals who compose it is a broad and diverse category. This category is especially expansive and unwieldy in communities where print is prevalent, where access to published documents is ready and cheap, and where general literacy is the rule. In the archives of such communities, an historian of rhetoric finds rich resources for an inquiry into how people use their popular and pragmatic discourse, consciously or not, to negotiate and shape the shared sense of individuality within collectivity that constitutes national identity.

This essay is part of a project examining a category of that discourse that has not been treated as rhetorically significant: texts about travel in America, written for Americans by Americans. Texts in this category were widely read because of their utility for travelers and because of the interest they held for people who wanted to imagine themselves traveling. In this essay I am exploring the rhetorical function of one particular tradition within this category: the published discourse of automobile travel that developed during the first two decades of the twentieth century. I find inherent in the texts of this discourse rhetorical elements that seem to have contributed to that transformation of American national identity that resulted in what we call the "modern," and to do so in ways that might enable us to understand better characteristics of the national identity inherited from the culture at the beginning of this century that as the century comes to an end of the century, Americans might want to rethink.

Jack Selzer defines modernism in the United States as a "controversy or conversation—more a series of semiotic responses and counter-responses to the aesthetic, economic, and social tensions of the first half of the twentieth-century" (3). My purpose in this paper is to explore one interesting and perhaps unexpected source of those tensions—the advent of cross-country travel by automobile, and the popular public discourse that responded to it. I do so in order to examine the extent to which the American highway, populated by American motorists, emerged early in this century to function there as a sign for a transformed notion of national community—a sign in response to which concepts of citizenship changed. My method is to locate in the publications surrounding the development of early autotravel in the United States changes in the images of national community and of citizenship within it that can be considered "modern." I do this within the frame provided by Liah Greenfeld's assertion in a perceptive study of nationalism that the idea of nation itself "forms the constitutive element of modernity" (18).

The Lincoln Highway

Automobiles, initially at least, were not a way of life in America because Americans began to acquire autos before there were roads to drive them on. Before World War I there was no connecting system of roads a motorist could follow to cross most counties, much less a state or the nation. The official history of the first transcontinental road system, the Lincoln Highway, recounts an experience of Henry B. Joy, one of its founders and president of the Packard Motor Company, that exemplifies the situation and what it signified in the national culture.

> Once, plodding through a test trip, he asked the Packard distributer in Omaha for directions to the road West.
> "There isn't any," was the answer.
> "Then how do I go," asked Mr. Joy.
> "Follow me and I'll show you."
> They drove westward until they came to a wire fence.
> "Just take down the fence and drive on and when you come to the next fence, take that down and go on again."
> "A little farther," said Mr. Joy, "and there were no fences, no fields, nothing but two ruts across the prairie."
> But some distance farther there were plenty of ruts, deep-grass-grown ones, marked by rotted bits of broken wagons, rusted tires and occasional relics of a grimmer sort, momentoes of the thousands who had struggled westward on the Overland Route in 1849 and '50, breaking trail for the railroad, pioneering the highway of today. (8)

That trail had been broken decisively by 1850. By 1900 it had been made fast and smooth by rail, and cities and towns across the young nation were connected together by trains. But in 1900 roads were exclusively local, branching in all directions from station centers to connect to the homes, businesses, and farms of the vicinity to the train. The promoters of the Lincoln Highway boosters estimated that in 1910 there were two million miles of roads in the United States all "unrelated, unconnected" and "practically unimproved," and "nobody knew or cared where any road went except that which led to his home: and rarely did a farmer close to town know the farther terminus of the route that passed his front gate" (3-4). Yet the numbers of automobiles on those roads was increasing relentlessly, and motorists were insisting increasingly on driving them well beyond the city limits instead of taking the train.

Recognizing in this situation both a national need and a business opportunity, a group of early automobile industrialists conceived a plan for an improved and maintained transcontinental highway for autotravel and promoted it as a memorial to the great national unifier, Abraham Lincoln. As one of its historians puts it,

> The Lincoln Highway was an expression of the national desire to bind the country from east to west. It captured the American imagination . . . in the same fashion as the great westward migration on the Oregon and California trails, the pony express, and the transcontinental railroad had half a century earlier. (Hokanson xvi)

Indeed, when its founders put their plan into funding competition with the Lincoln Memorial then being proposed in Washington, DC, Henry B. Joy proclaimed that Lincoln should be memorialized for "the good of all the people in good roads. Let good roads be built in the name of Lincoln" (Hokanson 9).

"Good roads" began the new way of life in America. By 1915 the route was at least marked if not yet the "continuous improved highway" from Atlantic to Pacific that the Lincoln Highway Association envisioned. It began in Times Square, continued south to Philadelphia and then west across Pennsylvania, northern Ohio, and Indiana. Bypassing Chicago, it crossed Iowa and Nebraska, southern Wyoming and northern Utah, north-central Nevada and Donner Pass to end in San Francisco—roughly the route now traced by I-80. In 1915, improved or not, the Lincoln Highway was a prominent cultural reality. A million Fords had been built and bought; the first official guide to the highway was in print; Emily Post was writing a description of the route, commissioned by *Colliers* to drive to California and report her experience. The Panama-Pacific Exhibition in San Francisco, opened to inaugurate the Canal and modern America, had attracted ten thousand automobiles crossing the continent from east to west on the Lincoln Highway (23, 75).

In 1919, after the United States had won its first motorized war, the Army Transcontinental Motor Convoy crossed the country on the Lincoln Highway, ostensibly to test the reliability of its new vehicles but, more practically importantly, to celebrate its victory by parading through Philadelphia (the cradle of the nation) and Tippett, Nevada (population 10), alike. By 1926 the public need for a nationally designated and maintained road system was clear, and a Congressional initiative replaced the promoters' routes and their patriotic names with a numbered system of federal highways. US 40 and US 66 gradually replaced the Lincoln Highway in the American imagination. By 1956 what the Lincoln Highway Association had started, Dwight Eisenhower began to complete with his proposal for the national interstate highway system, a concept that came naturally to a President who, as a young veteran of World War I, had crossed the continent with the victorious military convoy that had made prominent and public use of the Lincoln Highway.

In a culture or a community, what we call "a new way of life" expresses a complex of attitudes, born of experiences that as they become generally shared, reshape individual identity within it. In the early decades of this century, a new complex of attitudes, born of experiences made possible by the conjunction of automobiles and a transcontinental system of highways for their owners to travel was expressed in the published discourse of autotravel in ways that shaped what was becoming "modern" America. A representative voice of that discourse, at once self-consciously modern and self-consciously American, dominates the 1924 *Complete Official Road Guide of the Lincoln Highway*. This voice, assuring readers that "the dweller of the East" who first "makes the transcontinental tour over the Lincoln Highway," will experience "an uplifting of the soul" by which "Self becomes smaller and smaller as we realize the immensity of things in traversing this country" (23).

This modern American travels America independently to establish an immediate and personal sense of national identity. And this is an instance of the modern version of the American individualism that had worried Tocqueville. Modern Americans tend to have no faith in the possibility of reform through structured social change, and so base their inherited vision of a community of equals upon a persistent belief in the "transformation of individuals" (Q. Anderson 4). Consequently, inherent in the national identity of the individual American is the desire "to become capable of a dazzlingly complete imaginative grasp of the world" (1). Americans who motored across America on the Lincoln Highway were instructed by the discourse of that experience to use it to construct their "own" imaginative understanding of the nation of which each aspired to be a wholly representative part.

Imagining America

If the idea of a nation "forms the constitutive element of modernity," understanding modern America requires us to understand how the idea of an American nation has, in this modern century, been developed and maintained in the imaginations of its citizens. Americans have always imagined themselves beginning the world over again, doing so individually, for the most part, by attempting to make the national community over, at least imaginatively, in the image of themselves. Here is how that happens.

Benedict Anderson argues that the primary characteristic of modern nationalism and the discourse that establishes and supports it is that it is inherently imagined. Despite the complexity of the actual collectivity that exists within national boundaries, moderns *imagine* there a political community as a "deep, horizontal comradeship" that is both "limited and sovereign" (6-7). These imagined communities are prompted into existence in the consciousness of their citizens by the discourse through which they share, compare, and coordinate what they each believe themselves collectively to be. This is a public discourse that provides them with conceptual resources that support the formation of individual identities within the context of what Anderson calls the "experience of simultaneity" (145).

In the early twentieth century, road guides and travel writing by and for motorists contributed to this experience of simultaneity in important ways. These texts, popular and widely used, functioned rhetorically as a kind of "civic education" for individuals, the primary function of which was the "inculcation of patriotism" (Todorov 180) by prompting readers to establish themselves participants in what Michael Warner calls the "national imaginary" (170).

By the early 1920s, this national imaginary was coherent and commonplace in books and periodicals for autotravelers that both prompted their desire for autotravel and defined for them that experience. For example, this statement from a 1924 issue of the magazine *Motor Camper and Tourist* on the cultural benefits of autotravel: "By ruining sectionalism, it is transforming the provincial-minded man into a national-minded one. Therefore it must aid Americanization and the nationalization of the people at large." Indeed, the statement continues: "The automobile is making more patriots for American than all the silver-tongued orators in the land" (qtd. in Belasco 93). In the twenties autotravel became a rhetorical process so prominent in the culture that it was extended in published discourse of the nation to address readers well beyond those who were actually traveling the road. The editors of *The Nation* began in 1922 a comprehensive series of essays titled "These United States" with this introduction: "The United States 'is' said to be now one vast and almost uniform republic. What riches of variety remain among its federated commonwealths? What distinctive colors of life among its many sections and climates and attitudes?" (qtd. in Borus 27-28). The articles that followed, one on each state written by a prominent native son or daughter, answered these questions by developing a distinct portrait of each with historical and sensory details that simulate the experience of a leisurely trip in an open car. And that experience, as shaped by the popular discourse of autotravel, functioned to broaden and transform the identities of individual travelers (whether actual or vicarious), by enabling them to imagine themselves as recognizing and representing the national community they have crossed, one at once coherent and diverse.

The introduction to one popular narrative of a trip across the Lincoln Highway illustrates the response that this discourse recommended, an individual response that universally experienced, would constitute in America collective progress. Frederic Van de Water begins his 1927 book, *The Family Flivvers to Frisco*, in nationalist terms that describe this individualist transformation: For "Three dusty and sun-baked humans who drove a disreputable Ford from the Atlantic to the Pacific. . . . 'America' no longer is an abstract noun, or a familiar map of patchwork, or a flag, or a great domed building in Washington. It is something clearer and dearer and, we think, higher. It is the road we traveled" (8-9).

Traveling the American Landscape

So what are the elements of the new way of life that prompted an image of America as a road—as, say, the Lincoln Highway—and of citizens as travelers along it? More specifically, what new resources for individual national identity were afforded by a popular public discourse that presents the experience of traveling a transcontinental highway by automobile as a sign for national community?

In his history of the Lincoln Highway, Drake Hokanson describes the 1920s as a transformative time when "the motorcar became a part of everyone's world as it wrought more change on the fabric of American life than any single device, idea, or institution before or since" (105). This "fabric" that automobiles and highways so dramatically changed he defines as the "cultural and natural landscape" of the nation (134). *Landscape*, as a concept, functions as a sign for land—as an expression of a personal perception and experience of place. Integral to the new modern way of American life that this discourse of autotravel describes is a shared sense of collective identity that derives from the individual experience of witnessing a national landscape. What the Lincoln Highway did—what trails, routes, and highways do—is present to the travelers who follow them a landscape sequence they then can read as a natural and cultural narrative to signify a place, or a nation.

If national community is imagined in terms of the common experiences of those individuals who constitute it and if those individuals each draw upon conceptual resources of a shared national imaginary in the process of shaping themselves into an identity as citizens, Jackson's description of the perception of a shared landscape afforded them by the experience of autotravel might suggest to them a fluid kind of identity within community, one that requires individuals, in his terms, "to be on the move . . ." (26-27).

The "modern" America expressed in the early discourse of autotravel has this fluidity—this transience. This is a quality that Stephen Greenblatt identifies as inherent in travel writing, a genre that tends to "present the world not in stately and harmonious order but in a succession of brief encounters, random experiences, isolated anecdotes of the unanticipated" (2). And so the experience of travel itself. But not all travel is alike. The experience of autotravel in the twenties is quite different from the experience of autotravel now, at least on I-80 or I-5. And increasingly, for Americans, traveling is an experience of airports and flight that enables little perception of landscape at all. Still, the discourse of autotravel in America in the early twentieth century suggests to me that since then, in some important ways, the American national identity has been transformed—since then, if not since long before, been located conceptually on the road.

In 1950, the year I was born, George R. Stewart followed the federal route that replaced the old Lincoln Highway to photograph and write the book he published three years later as *US 40: Cross-Section of the United States of America.* Here Stewart offered a classification of American highways that still, I think, is valid and that I can use to clarify the point I am making here. He identified "dominating" highways—"parkways" he called them—as separated, isolated, and autonomous landscapes that prompt the people who travel them to identify themselves as fully apart from the inhabitants of the country they cross. He identified "dominated" highways where the distractions and complications of local traffic eclipse any more expansive identity in route and its travelers alike. And he identified "equal" highways, each experienced by the motorists who travel it as "an intimate and integral part of the countryside through which it is passing" (22-23).

That "equal highway," populated by travelers, seems to me to be a reliable sign for national community. For most of its length, US 40, the route that overwrote the Lincoln Highway, was an "equal highway" where, as a traveler "accepting the commonplace along with the spectacular, seeing people and the country too, taking the good with the bad, and the beautiful with the ugly, you gain a balanced impression of the United States of America" (300). Such a highway is a place. It is, as Hokanson writes of the Lincoln, "a three-dimensional thing with length, breadth, and depth of history" (41). As such, it can be read as a partial and limited but functionally representative landscape, both natural and cultural, for an nation. Such a landscape, articulated rhetorically in road guides and travelers' tales of the first decades of this modern century, and experienced by those who followed the roads or read the tales, presented Americans with a new version of citizenship that had the potential, at least, to school them in an image of collectivity that could accommodate rapid and radical change.

Works Cited

Anderson, Benedict. *Imagined Communities: Reflections on the Origin and Spread of Nationalism.* Rev. ed. London: Verso, 1991.

Anderson, Quentin. *Making Americans: An Essay on Individualism and Money.* New York: Harcourt, 1992.

Belasco, Warren James. *Americans on the Road: From Autocamp to Motel, 1910-1945.* Cambridge: MIT P, 1979.

Borus, Daniel, ed. *These United States: Portraits of America from the 1920's.* Ithaca: Cornell UP, 1992.

Greenfeld, Liah. *Nationalism.* Cambridge: Harvard UP, 1992.

Hokanson, Drake. *The Lincoln Highway: Main Street across America.* Iowa City: U of Iowa P, 1988.

The Lincoln Highway Association. *The Complete Official Road Guide of the Lincoln Highway.* 5th ed. Detroit, 1924.

——. *The Lincoln Highway: The Story of a Crusade that Made Transportation History.* New York: Dodd, 1935.

Rockland, Michael Aaron. *Homes on Wheels.* New Brunswick: Rutgers UP, 1980.

Selzer, Jack. *Conversing with the Moderns: Kenneth Burke, 1915-1931.* Milwaukee: U of Wisconsin P, 1997.

Stewart, George R. *US 40: Cross-Section of the United States of America.* Boston: Houghton, 1953.

Todorov, Tzevetan. *On Human Diversity.* Cambridge: Harvard UP, 1993.

Van de Water, Frederic. *The Family Flivvers to Frisco.* New York: Appleton, 1927.

Warner, Michael. *The Letters of the Republic.* Cambridge: Harvard UP, 1990.

VAN E. HILLARD

Duke University

Entering the Rhetorical City:
The Metropolitan Prospect of Rhetoric

It has become commonplace in contemporary discussions of rhetoric and the teaching of writing to rely upon the metaphor of *community* to represent the public ground upon which rhetorical interactions take place. The concept of community (as in "interpretive community" or "community of discourse") often is delineated by a recognition of common purpose, common attitude, common language, and common referential frames—all of which substantiate an intricate and sometimes invisible network of shared assumptions, beliefs, and ideology. It is, of course, extremely useful to identify communities that share interpretive sensibilities; such recognition permits us to situate knowledge production and to determine the contextual boundaries that control and constrain the production of new meanings and alternate worldviews. Myriad references to discourse communities have provided powerful ways to link rhetorical projects to the sociology of knowledge and have permitted reevaluations of collectivity, collaboration, dialogue, and dialectic that would have been difficult, perhaps even impossible, without access to the epistemologic framework that the term *community* provides. Even more, the notion of discourse communities has prompted important discussions of inclusion, exclusion, membership, power, and privilege. It is extremely empowering, for instance, for my students to learn that they hold places in a variety of discourse communities and that they can engage productively in the disagreements arising both within and between these communities.

But however useful in selective contexts, the term *community* has certain limitations when applied to public discursive practices. First, the term suggests that assent is shaped and reshaped by direct, and in many instances face-to-face, encounters between the community's members. As Raymond Williams reminds us, the immediacy and interpersonal nature of community encounters has been set in opposition to the putatively remote, impersonal interactions among members of the public—the distinction, clarified by Ferdinand Tönnies, between *gemeinschaft* and *gesellschaft*. Second, its rootedness in commonality lends community a utopic and positive valence. Williams speaks of it as that "warmly persuasive word . . . that unlike all other terms of social organization (state, nation, society, etc.) . . . seems never to be used unfavourably, and never to be given any positive opposing or distinguishing term" (76). When discord within communities arises, there is a sense in which it is managed or contained within initial bounds of self-definition. Disagreement is understood as productive or corrective in nature. As Richard Sennett has put this:

> "Community" is a deceptive social term . . . the idea of a community is not interchangeable with the idea of a social group; a community is a particular kind of social group in which men believe they *share* something together. The feeling of community is fraternal, it involves something more than the recognition that men need each other materially. The bond of community is one of sensing common identity, a pleasure in recognizing "us" and "who we are." (*Disorder* 31)

Community tends, then, not only to be localized but to be purified as well—dependent upon an image of town, village, or perhaps suburb. Tending toward such idealization, the concept of community has an uncertain geography and rather limited recognizability. However ironic, it may well be that its very indeterminacy is what finally gives community its powerful presence among us: Community can easily be solicited to supplement the difficult rhetorical functions that such concepts as "public" or "polis" or "civic" formerly embraced.

Both to complicate and to ameliorate the rush to community, we may profitably reenter the space of the city, and begin to build (or rebuild) upon the armature of strong publics and publicity that contemporary urban spaces may provide. Since antiquity, the city has provided an aggressively rhetorical space, an environment that sustains the circulation of diverse and competing discourses and, in its material form of neighborhoods, quarters, enclaves, and other architectures, permits varied publicities. Moreover, entrance into and through the city typically involves more than geographic traverse; negotiating the urban involves subtle and overt acts of differentiation, a range of identifications and role-takings, the expectation of routine, accident, and surprise, and a facility with recontextualization as interpretive practice. Supremely scenic in the Burkean sense, the city, both as built-form and as lived-experience, yields a different public than does community because, as Thomas Farrell has recently suggested, it includes a "conscious awareness of each other's placement in the symbolic landscape of prospective thought and decision" (283). In other words, the city, as an instrument of public life, presents "the model in which diversity and complexity of persons, interests, and tastes become available as social experience" (Sennett, *Fall* 340).

Recently, the urban turn has been made by Susan Miller who, in an essay exploring the interpersonal interests that motivate collaborative writing in the composition classroom, proposes "a new logic of 'collaboration' in which the city, not 'community,' becomes a root metaphor for what actually occurs, what is learned, and what may result" from collective writing and argument (285). Miller names her alternative model for collaborative writing the "new discourse city," a term that stands to modify or to move beyond the prevailing identification of the scene of communicative interaction as "community," a representation that Miller finds both unnecessarily bucolic and unfairly delimiting in its tendency toward the goals of univocality and its maintenance of shared systems of belief. As corrective to the fossilized model of "discourse community," Miller's new discourse city "would celebrate four qualities of urban societies: It would allow for differentiation without exclusion; appreciate *variety*; encourage *erotic* attraction to novel, strange, and surprising encounters; and *value publicity* in public spaces . . . where people stand and sit together, interact or mingle or simply witness one another without becoming a unified community of 'shared final ends'" (299). The urban qualities Miller suggests—inclusive differentiation, respect for the plural and various, attraction to the novelty of strangeness and surprise, and the valorization of strong publicity—may also be found, in sustained and more developed form, in the work of Richard Sennett, the social historian upon whose examination of rhetorical life in the city much of my argument rests.

In a dozen volumes on the history, sociology, and cultural geography of city spaces, Sennett relentlessly explores the dialectic of how "society produces space and space reproduces society" (Cresswell 12). Working against the prevalence of both romanticizations and demonizations of the city and its inhabitants, Sennett aims to convince us that "the jungle of the city, its vastness and loneliness, has a positive human value," that its densities and disorder, once adequately embraced, can help us to recuperate the civic as it rejuvenates our roles as rhetorical persons.

Perhaps Sennett's harshest critique of the arhetoricality of contemporary suburban and community-driven cultures comes in *The Fall of Public Man*, Sennett's attempt to create a "theory of expression in public," a response to his key question: "Is there . . . a difference in the expression appropriate for public relations and that appropriate for intimate relations?" (6). Sennett's chief differentiation between the classical *res publica* and the contemporary American public sphere lies in the modern valorization of intimacy and familiarity over ritualized civil distance and acceptance of strangeness. In contemporary politics we notice this as the fierce opposition between suburban families and urban others. As Sennett reminds us,

> A *res publica* stands in general for those bonds of association and
> mutual commitment which exist between people who are not joined
> together by family or intimate association; it is the bond of a crowd,
> of a "people," of a polity, rather than the bonds of family or friends.

> As in Roman times, participation in the *res publica* is most often a
> matter of going along, and the forums of this public life, like the
> city, are in a state of decay. (*Fall* 4)

For Sennett, the contemporary public is robbed of its rhetoricalness by the twin
thieves of authenticity and privatized individualism: "Manners and ritual
interchanges with strangers are looked on as at best formal and dry, at worst as
phony. The stranger himself is a threatening figure, and few people can take
pleasure in that world of strangers, the cosmopolitan city" (*Fall* 3). In other
words, "Community becomes a weapon against society, whose great vice is now
seen to be its impersonality" (*Fall* 339).

    Public culture is overthrown by the ideology of intimacy, a debilitating
mindset that suggests "social relationships of all kinds are real, believable, and
authentic the closer they approach the inner psychological concerns of each
person," a pernicious humanitarianism spirit, where "warmth is our god" (*Fall*
261). The cosmopolitan person does not, by definition, feel warmth toward
fellow city strangers. Instead, "A cosmopolite, in the French usage recorded in
1738, is a man who moves comfortably in diversity; he is comfortable in
situations which have no links or parallel to that which is familiar to him" (*Fall*
17). By the eighteenth century, public civil behavior was most often configured
in terms of the *theatrum mundi*, a mode of public behavior dependent upon the
deployment of social roles, constructed personae, and the enactment of
elaborate analogies between stage and street. Sennett goes so far as to suggest
that the city was a social space produced by role encountering role, stranger to
stranger as it were: "Belief in the theater . . . like belief in a stranger, is a
matter of taking the immediate encounter as the limit of knowable reality. In
both, external knowledge on the part of the audience is not involved—in the
city by necessity, in the theater by fiat" (*Fall* 40). Public behavior, then,
involves first "action at a distance from the self, from its immediate history,
circumstances, and needs; second, this action involves the experiencing of
diversity" (*Fall* 87). Freed from the compulsion to authentic interaction, the
space of the city is a space given to play, to acting, and to the exercise of the
imagination. The city has the potential to disencumber the self, identifications
with strangers stimulating an empathy that lies at the heart of civil action. In
Sennett's terms the imagination carries a social as well as a psychologic
function:

> The creation of a public geography has . . . a great deal to do with
> imagination as a social phenomenon. When a baby can distinguish
> the me from the not-me, he has taken a first and most important
> step in enriching his symbol-making powers: no longer must every
> symbol be a projection of the baby's own needs onto the world. The

creation of a sense of public space is the adult social parallel to this psychological distinction in infancy, with parallel results; the symbol-making capacity of a society becomes much richer, because the imagination of what is real, and therefore believable, is not tied down to a verification of what is routinely felt by the self. Because an urban society which has a public geography has also certain powers of imagination, the devolution of the public and the rise of the intimate has a profound effect on the modalities of imagination which prevail in that society. (*Fall* 41)

Elsewhere, Sennett locates the encounter with strangeness and alterity as at the very core of full civic participation. For him, the city is best understood as a environment of transformative disorder and potent conflict—a geography of disagreement and conflicting significations. Sennett locates the historical enactment of a lived "equilibrium of disorder" in an imaginary tour down Chicago's Halstead Street in 1910, a ghetto street that embodies the spatialization of disorder, diversity, and difference:

The street was twenty-two miles long, and for the most of it filled with teeming population. Were we to start at its northern end and move south, we would be conscious that it was filled with "foreigners," but at every place with different kinds of foreigners, all mixed together. A native might tell us that a certain few blocks were Greek or Polish or Irish, but were one actually to look at particular houses or apartment buildings, one would find the ethnic groups jumbled together. . . . The functioning of all these groups . . . . would appear hopelessly tangled to modern observers. For the apartments would be mixed in with stores, the streets themselves crowded with vendors and brokers of all kinds; even factories . . . would be intermixed with bars, brothels, synagogues, churches, and apartment buildings. (*Disorder* 54)

Here, survival depended directly upon the facility to position and to reposition oneself in relation to shifting contexts of allegiance, affiliation, and association:

What was contained in this life on Halstead Street could be called a multiplicity of "contact points" by which these desperately poor people entered into social relations with the city. They *had* to make this diversity in their lives, for no one of the institutions in which they lived was capable of self-support. The family depended on political "favors," the escape valve of coffee shops and bars, the inculcation of discipline of the *shuls* and churches. . . . The

> multiplicity of contact points often took the individuals of the city
> outside their ethnic "subcultures" that supposedly were snugly
> encasing them. Polish people who belonged to steel unions often
> came into conflict with Polish people who had joined the police.
> This multiplicity of contact points meant that loyalties became
> crossed in complex forms. (*Disorder* 56)

It is relatively easy to envision the city (or the village, town, or suburb for that matter) as a social geography punctuated by encounter; the mere intersection of streets predicts contact. But Sennett's contact points aren't intersectional; they are interstitial. They require a mode of interaction that exists somewhere between or beyond the previous, more stable, more familiar positions of the interlocutors' categories of knowledge and belief. In Sennett's vision the city's density of potential contact points is directly proportional to the quality of civic life that its residents may obtain. Postindustrialism, combined with a Protestant ethic that "denies the outside a reality in itself," has given America its suburban landscapes of gridded neutrality, so that the

> American "individual," rather than being an adventurer, is in
> reality most often a man or woman whose circle of reality is drawn
> no larger than family and friends. The individual has little interest,
> indeed, little energy, outside that circle. The American individual is
> a passive person, and monotonous space is what a society of passive
> individuals builds for itself. A bland environment assures people
> that nothing disturbing or demanding is happening 'out there.' You
> build neutrality in order to legitimate withdrawal. (*Conscience* 65)

The antiseptic environment depends on the invisibility of its ineffectual public. In Sennett's conceit the eye cannot exercise its conscience.

Now, if we are to enter the rhetorical city, we must work to make the invisible visible. This will involve the arts of close observation, accompanied by deliberate inquiry into appearances and the casting and recasting of rhetorical propositions—the method of investigation that as Thomas Farrell points out, gives us access to the interstices between the stability of phenomena and the "shifting way in which they appear" (27). Potential contact points in the city invite us to reckon with ambiguity, with irony, and with the insistent texture of specificity itself.

> Appearances come to us as configurations, as ensembles of objects,
> habitats, paths, tools, tasks, icons, and more or less recognizable
> characters that engage and reassure us with their own emergent
> familiarity. For the most part, most of the time, most of us are at

home in the world of appearances. The stability of the familiar and the persistence of the recognizable lend a solidity to one another. Yet it is in their very particularity that appearance can begin to seem ambiguous or even equivocal and incomplete. When we have some stake, or interest, in the array of things around us . . . we are not likely to be concerned with an underlying cause or a larger, more inclusive general opinion. For the particularity of things has become a provocation. We cannot leave well enough alone (Farrell 27).

The city has long demanded of us a rhetoric of visibility—beyond appearances. For the city to become visible, we may embrace an attitude of seeing, one that is characterized by a constituent discursive movement from particularity to specificity, a critical examination motivated by conscience and by the desire to propose new knowledge. In the space of the city, recognition also involves a reckoning—with history, with ideology, and with the ontologic status of our common places. If we are patient and appropriately curious, the city's contact points will yield what Benjamin once termed the "dialectic image," an interpretive moment whereby the familiar is made comfortably strange and the strange is made irresistibly familiar. Such promise the rhetorical city holds.

Works Cited

Cresswell, Tim. *In Place/Out of Place: Geography, Ideology, and Transgression*. Minneapolis: U of Minnesota P, 1996.

Farrell, Thomas B. *Norms of Rhetorical Culture*. New Haven: Yale UP, 1993.

Miller, Susan. "New Discourse City: An Alternative Model for Collaboration." *Writing With: New Directions in Collaborative Teaching, Learning, and Research*. Ed. Sally Barr Reagan, Thomas Fox, and David Bleich. Albany: State U of New York P, 1994. 284-99.

Sennett, Richard. *The Conscience of the Eye: The Design and Social Life of Cities*. New York: Norton, 1990.

——. *The Fall of Public Man*. New York: Norton, 1974.

——. *The Uses of Disorder: Personal Identity and City Life*. New York: Norton, 1970.

Williams, Raymond. *Keywords: A Vocabulary of Culture and Society*. New York: Oxford UP, 1981.

DIANNE L. JUBY

University of Oklahoma

Memory Arts, Electronic *Topoi*, and Dynamic Databases

In *The Book of Memory*, Mary Carruthers offers a connection between the classical art of memory and computer memory: "What I find most interesting about the similarities between ancient and modern memory design is not that the ancients anticipated modern artificial memories (for they did not) but that human beings, faced with the problem of designing a memory (whether their own or a machine's), should repeat many of the same solutions" (296 n.51). Neo-Luddites naturally take offense at comparisons of computer memory and human memory. Roszak, for instance, after suggesting that the analogy has as little meaning as comparing a saw's teeth to human teeth, expresses his distaste for the commonplace notion that computer memory is superior because it "remembers so much more," and idealizes natural memory as "the invisible psychic adhesive that holds our identity together from moment to moment" that "flows not only through the mind, but through the emotions, the senses, the body" (96-97). True enough. But Roszak avoids the ancient distinction between natural and artificial memory. If we restrain ourselves from romanticizing the human/machine relationship long enough to recall that the ancient memory art was a literate technology, as are computers and databases, the issue becomes not one of anthropomorphizing comparisons of quantity and quality, but of effective, practical *access* to stored memories when they are needed for our performance in rhetorical situations.[1]

In this paper I focus on the cross-disciplinary intersection to which Corbett alludes: Theorists in information retrieval who argue that the "teeming storehouses of knowledge," today manifested in the proliferation of electronic databases and the World Wide Web, can be made more accessible by turning to rhetorical theory and recovering the *topoi*. Whether referring to mentally visualized architectural niches holding vividly memorable images or to the more abstract places where dialectical and rhetorical arguments reside, *topoi* since classical times have held the promise of rhetorical power and have had an essential connection with memory. Aristotle invokes the art of memory toward the end of the *Topics* as a means of "mak[ing] a man readier in reasoning, because he has his premises classified before his mind's eye" (163b30).[2] At present, database search programs do not offer this powerful topical *technê* to user-rhetors. The information retrieval theorists that I discuss in this paper have turned to rhetoric and the possibility of electronic *topoi* to enhance searching power. They have a special interest in the searcher who transgresses disciplinary boundaries, seeking arguments from discourse realms in which she is not an expert. Can we, as database searchers and World-Wide-Web users, find the arguments we seek in this teeming electronic cultural memory, a realm whose vast diversity situates us all as nonexperts?

Exigencies of Information Retrieval

According to David Blair, Information Retrieval (IR) has the central task of understanding the relationship between the representation of documents and the effective retrieval of those documents. IR is an eminently rhetorical discipline, given that it juggles three elements: the needs of variously situated end-users (searchers), texts, and representations of those texts (subject descriptors) assigned by indexers who are more or less familiar with the disciplinary exigencies surrounding the production of articles.[3] Claiming that the most pervasive characteristic of searching is the "indeterminacy inherent in the representation of documents," Blair contradicts traditional IR researchers who consider this indeterminacy to be a "minor irritant" and who assume that a "perfectly rational" representation of documents is attainable. Instead, he argues that these problems of representation are "not just due to sloppiness or irrationality, but are products of much more fundamental linguistic processes" (23). Subject descriptors pretend to represent the "intellectual content" of a text, what it is "about."[4] Indexer consistency studies show that subject descriptor "representations" of documents are never as unproblematic as this theory of representation might suppose. Presenting what would seem a persuasive case even to his positivistic IR colleagues, Blair cites Wittgenstein: "We don't start from certain words, but from certain occasions or activities." Blair argues for the improvement of search capability through the enhancement of contextual (as opposed to "representational-of-content") information. Also drawing on Austin and Searle, Blair argues that documents are always embedded in a network of speech acts that can provide contextual cues for retrieval (156-57, 194-212). In other words, current search programs offer little for the wide-ranging user in terms of constructing queries that account for disciplinary paradigm shifts or theoretical stances. We can search, sometimes even successfully, for semantic representations of what a document is "about," but not for what it argues.

The purely serendipitous online retrieval of the two key articles I discuss in this paper reflects these access problems. Like classical rhetors who searched the mnemonic and rhetorical/dialectical *topoi* for the arguments they needed to win their cases, I too was looking for arguments—arguments about the still undeveloped state of information retrieval in the emerging field of rhetoric/composition. Without a database of our own (the *CCCC Bibliography* is not online), we as electronic researchers rely largely on ERIC and MLA databases with their problematic classification systems based on social-science and literary categories, respectively. My search (of information science databases through DIALOG) using keywords and Boolean operators produced articles that argued a very different relation between my terms: that information retrieval needed to turn to rhetorical theory not to *index* its written products but to provide a *resource* for conceptual strategies to improve database searching in all disciplines. IR theorists have found formal logic and language-as-representation as problematic for their purposes as we have for ours. Two information theorists, Kircz and Sillince (Dutch and British, respectively), turn to rhetoric for help, specifically to argumentation theory inspired by Perelman and Olbrechts-Tyteca, to suggest a dynamic program of searchable *topoi* for electronic databases. Kircz and Sillince are, in essence, calling for the electronic adaptation of the ancient dialectical/rhetorical *topoi* to develop an arguer search program. They might agree with Cicero that "if we wish to track down some argument we ought to know the places or topics," and their recommendations for new directions in IR could provide cyberspace searchers with an electronic means "for inventing arguments so that we might come upon them by a rational system without wandering about" (*Topica* II 7; I 2). They might modify Aristotle's definition of rhetoric for IR to read "the ability to find the available means of effective document retrieval in each particular, situated case."

Topoi: **Possibilities in Database Futures**

Kircz, basing his proposal on an analysis of scientific articles, begins with the linguistic and rhetorical challenges facing IR: The indexing of the content of scientific articles "digs deep into the problems of meaning and understanding" (354). According to Sillince, Kircz's article "uses rhetoric as the motif for the first time in the information retrieval literature" (394).[5] Whereas Blair turned to Wittgenstein and to speech-act theory to contextualize documents, Kircz begins by analyzing the argumentational structure of scientific articles, citing Bazerman, Latour, and Woolgar as a start in the needed direction but calling for more analyses of scientific articles along the lines of Perelman and Olbrechts-Tyteca's. (He apparently is not aware of Prelli's study of scientific argument as informal reasoning in terms of problem-solving and evaluative *topoi*, which would seem exceptionally relevant to his purpose.) The "reductionist practice" of identifying articles solely by subject descriptors is not useful for searchers who are interested in "the reasoning of why and how something has been done"; therefore, he proposes "that a new net has to be spanned over the document, this time not a set of semantic equivalents, but an argumentational or rhetorical network" (355). He recommends the development of a full-text search program using hypertext links of "argumentational entities." These "entities" include experimental constraints, experimental assumptions, data handling methods, theoretical assumptions, etc., and would allow expert browsers and nonexpert searchers to find arguments based on the structure of the article rather than on specific, semantically indexed content.

Sillince begins from the same premise as Blair and Kircz: IR currently works from the assumption that "knowledge can be adequately represented as a semantic network," that "information is value-free, that there is only one way of interpreting it, and that it is unidimensional in only consisting of 'facts' rather than possessing the attributes of intention, goal, activity, theory, evidence, and so on" (387, 388).[6] Existing search capabilities could be greatly enhanced, he argues, through the addition of a radically different indexing approach based on an analogy with rhetorical reasoning. Calling on Perelman and Olbrechts-Tyteca for their "vast typology and catalogue of rhetorical arguments," he develops a list of argument types from which he then derives relations for an argumentation grammar of "content-free rhetorical markers."

Writing to an IR audience, both Kircz and Sillince demonstrate at length what is obvious to students of rhetoric: Scientific and academic articles are arguments, arguments that we corroborate, refute, enhance, develop, and rhetorically engage as we invent and put forward our own claims. Indeed, for his own argument that argumentation could offer an improved indexing method, Sillince marshals support from empirical cognitive studies that reject formal deductive logic in favor of informal reasoning as the basis of human memory function. He finds parallels with the indexing problem in the popular cognitive science concept that human memory represents meaning by coding information as propositions, and in argumentation's concern "with gaining influence over others as well as with gaining control over one's own reasoning tasks." These various links in his argument would not be retrievable with current indexing methods. He offers sample queries that could search for such a link, based on his proposed argumentation grammar: "(**understanding** successful memorisation) *is_means_to* (**goal** of **inventing** new indexing **method**)"; or (indexing **problem**) *analogous_to* (problem of how to successfully memorise)." The italicized term is a relational entity recognizable by the program grammar; bold words are terms in the grammar, appearing as menu choices or icons, for which the user would substitute her keyword; the program would search for instances of "indexing" and "successful memorisation" that have been indexed as "problem" (390-91, 394).

Sillince's relational entities, developed, remember, from argument types gleaned from Perelman and Olbrechts-Tyteca, include *topoi* such as *implies, enables, causes, justifies, earlier_than, similar_to, different_from, means _to_end, good_compared_with_bad, is_good_for, is_goal, is_observable, not_worth_change_to, acceptable_by_stages_to, taken_to_logical_limit_is*, and *is_prestigious*, among the several dozen he suggests. Although it is not my purpose here to enter into the elaborate discussions of exactly what the *topoi* were, it seems clear that Sillince's argumentation grammar reflects both dialectical *topoi* (according to Ochs's definition of *topoi* in Aristotle's *Topics* as "formal patterns of relationships existing between classes of terms") as well as the enthymematic *topoi*, "an amalgam of miscellaneous molds into which rhetorical arguments usually are cast," of the *Rhetoric* (Ochs 200).

As rhetors in search of an argument, expert browsers and nonexpert searchers create what Sillince calls a "multidimensional prototype," which I call "positing a dynamic relation between search terms." For instance, Sillince offers this example: "criticisms that Boolean or best match search require too much user foreknowledge" as a query prototype. In contrast, his translation of this query into "Boolean" seems a parody: "'criticism' and ('Boolean' or 'best match') and 'too much user knowledge'" (392). Obviously, what current search approaches cannot encode is this dynamic relation between terms, the propositional nature of the argument sought. We are not seeking "criticism *and*" but "criticism *of*"; and the Boolean construction likewise obscures the relation between the second and third terms; there is no chance of an argument here, but a static set of terms to be haphazardly matched semantically. There are no relationships between terms; there are no verbal connections to put the terms into action. As Ochs concludes, "a dialectical topic is a relational principle enabling a person to locate and analyze the ways in which a specific predicate may be attributed to a subject" (200). Sillince's program would enable a searcher to locate "the ways in which a specific predicate *has been* attributed to a subject" in various retrieved documents. Ochs argues that relationships, not terms, are essential in classifying arguments; Sillince argues that relationships, not terms, are essential in searching for arguments.

Forty years ago Grimaldi lamented that the *topoi* "have lost the vital, dynamic character given to them by Aristotle, a character extremely fruitful for intelligent, mature discussion of the innumerable significant problems which face man" (176). Carruthers reminds us that "The proof of a good memory lies not in the simple retention even of large amounts of material; rather, it is the ability to move it about instantly, directly, and securely that is admired" (19). Although Sillince admits that his approach "does little more than scrape the surface of modern argumentation theory," I would argue that the essential, radical thrust of his proposal lies in its recognition of the need to put electronic searching in motion (392). He advocates the cyber-equivalent of the dynamic aspect of the *topoi* that gets lost as they become inert headings or even subject categories that pretend to catalogue "all knowledge" in a static encyclopedic format. If we are to think of databases as the technological manifestation of large portions of our cultural and disciplinary memories, then access to that memory, I think Sillince suggests, must be put in motion, in the same way that classical rhetors created their own memory *technê* not as a static storage device or as a simple, linear scheme for the recollection of points in a speech, but as a dynamic access system allowing them to move intellectually within the *paideia*, serving their practical reasoning needs. Perhaps with such an advance in IR methods, the neo-Luddite apprehension over the "cult of information" would fade, and we would become artful users of a vast memory system organized by productively accessible, dynamic *topoi*.

Dialectic Databases and Undisciplined Arguers

Kircz and Sillince, and IR theorists in general, display an acute awareness of the disciplinary situatedness and particular positionalities of readers (searchers). I would therefore like to conclude by returning to Kircz's and Sillince's interest in the nonexpert searcher, the "ignorant (but interested) reader." Kircz maintains that "informed readers" (someone in the same field as he or she is searching) are fairly well served by existing indexing and search techniques because they know what they are looking for and are familiar with authors' names, research, and theoretical stances. The "partially informed reader," less well served by these techniques, "is someone who is starting up in a field, or is just generally interested in adjacent fields to his or her own." However, Kircz is most interested in "the uninformed readers, those who want to learn something new" (357). Although all of his categories refer to scientists, I suggest that they are also applicable across the disciplines. Sillince's argumentational syntax searching might bridge disciplines by making accessible, and searchable, various disciplines' preferred *topoi*. The *topoi* of electronic databases blur the boundaries of writer, reader, and searcher: The database or Web user is an inquirer, a searcher, inventing his or her own arguments, but is also a reader of recalled arguments. Inquirer, reader, and writer become points in a process rather than discrete, static entities; the *topoi* link writers with available arguments at different places on a continuum of production, at points of intersection where inquirer, reader, and writer functions meet.

Searching, inventing, and arguing across disciplines require a more dialectical notion of audience/arguer. At this writing we are in the midst of an electronic storm generated by the Alan Sokal/*Social Text* affair. The spate of virulent condemnations of discipline-hopping Sokal's stunt prompted from both sides amply demonstrates the potential volatility of transdisciplinary excursions. Whatever turns our analyses of the hoax may have taken by the time this reaches print cannot be foreseen, but I think the possibility of electronic *topoi* has something to teach us about disciplinary transgressions, always an issue in rhetorical studies. Sokal, it is essential to recall, claims that many of us working in science studies (whether cultural studies, sociology, or rhetoric) don't know how to argue. Pollitt writes in *The Nation,* "Indeed, the comedy of the Sokal incident is that it suggests that even the postmodernists don't really understand one another's writing and make their way through the text by moving from one familiar name or notion to the next like a frog jumping across a murky pond by way of lily pads."[7] The kind of argument-searching Sillince proposes could offer less hostile means for exploring other disciplines' argument practices, other disciplines' preferred *topoi.* The expansion of databases and documents from specialized disciplines available "freely" on the World Wide Web can either increase the divisiveness, exclusivity, and mean-spiritedness that seems to be perpetrated by notions of interpretive or discourse communities, or it can force us out of those comfortable communities and into a cosmopolis of multidisciplinarity. Electronically searchable *topoi* can make our complex differences more accessible, less threatening, and mutually enriching.

Notes

1 Although in service of oral rhetoric as well as writing, ancient memory was habitually compared to a written surface, and the process of storage and retrieval to writing and reading, by its explicators. For a discussion of ancient memory as a literate technology, see Carruthers Chapter 1, especially pp. 28-32.

2 See Sorabji for a complete discussion of memory in Aristotle.

3 Helen Tibbo offers a book-length treatment of the complexities of indexing in a discipline (history) that reflects a variety of epistemological positions and research methods. Although no similar assessment of rhetoric and composition exists, many parallels are evident.

4 See Maron and Weinberg for more traditional IR reevaluations of these problems.

5 Sillince has published a slightly revised version of this article in *Online Review,* a less technical forum. All of my citations are from his *Journal of Documentation* article.

6 See Bolter, 185, for another critique of the semantic net problem.

7 Of course, this is essentially how Bruno Latour describes scientific argumentation—except for the important difference that scientist-frogs work very hard to tie all those lily pads together and tow them around.

Works Cited

Aristotle. *Topics.* Trans. W. A. Pickard-Cambridge. *The Complete Works of Aristotle.* Vol. 1. Ed. Jonathan Barnes. Princeton: Princeton UP, 1984.

Blair, D[avid] C. *Language and Representation in Information Retrieval.* Amsterdam: Elsevier Science, 1990.

Bolter, Jay David. *Writing Space: The Computer, Hypertext, and the History of Writing.* Hillsdale, NJ: Erlbaum, 1991.

Carruthers, Mary J. *The Book of Memory: A Study of Memory in Medieval Culture.* Cambridge: Cambridge UP, 1990.

Cicero. *Topica.* Trans. H. M. Hubbell. Loeb Classical Library. Cambridge: Harvard UP, 1949.

Corbett, Edward P. J. "The *Topoi* Revisited." *Rhetoric and Praxis: The Contribution of Classical Rhetoric to Practical Reasoning.* Ed. Jean Dietz Moss. Washington, DC: Catholic U of America P, 1986. 43-57.

Grimaldi, William M. A. "The Aristotelian Topics." *Aristotle: The Classical Heritage of Rhetoric.* Ed. Keith V. Erickson. Metuchen, NJ: Scarecrow, 1974. 176-93.

Kircz, Joost G. "Rhetorical Structure of Scientific Articles: The Case for Argumentational Analysis in Information Retrieval." *Journal of Documentation* 47 (1991): 354-72.

Latour, Bruno. *Science in Action*. Cambridge: Harvard UP, 1987.

Maron, M. E. "On Indexing, Retrieval and the Meaning of About." *Journal of the American Society for Information Science* 28 (1977): 38-43.

Ochs, Donovan J. "Aristotle's Concept of Formal Topics." *Aristotle: The Classical Heritage of Rhetoric*. Ed. Keith V. Erickson. Metuchen, NJ: Scarecrow, 1974. 194-204.

Ong, Walter J. *Rhetoric, Romance, and Technology: Studies in the Interaction of Expression and Culture*. Ithaca: Cornell UP, 1971.

Perelman, Chaïm, and Lucie Olbrechts-Tyteca. *The New Rhetoric: A Treatise on Argumentation* [1958]. Trans. John Wilkinson and Purcell Weaver. Notre Dame: U of Notre Dame P, 1969.

Pollitt, Katha. "Pomolotov Cocktail." The Nation. URL: http://www.thenation.com/issue 960610/0610poll.html (24 May 1996).

Prelli, Lawrence J. *A Rhetoric of Science: Inventing Scientific Discourse*. Columbia: U of South Carolina P, 1989.

Roszak, Theodore. *The Cult of Information: A Neo-Luddite Treatise on High-tech, Artificial Intelligence, and the True Art of Thinking*. Berkeley: U of California P, 1994.

Sillince, J. A. A. "Argumentation-Based Indexing for Information Retrieval from Learned Articles." *Journal of Documentation* 48 (1992): 387-405.

——. "Literature Searching with Unclear Objectives: A New Approach using Argumentation." *Online Review* 16 (1992): 391-409.

Sorabji, Richard. *Aristotle on Memory*. Providence: Brown UP, 1972.

Tibbo, Helen R. *Abstracting, Information Retrieval and the Humanities: Providing Access to Historical Literature*. Chicago: American Library Association, 1993.

Weinberg, Bella Haas. "Why Indexing Fails the Researcher." *The Indexer* 16 (1988): 3-6.

WINIFRED BRYAN HORNER

Texas Christian University

Kneupper Memorial Address: **An Allegory**

When I started teaching at the University of Missouri, a student remarked to a fellow instructor who repeated the comment to me—"That lady you were with yesterday—she looks as though she has really been there." And that was thirty years ago. Today I feel as though I have been there and back—through the mine field of the academic world as a linguist, a rhetoric/comp specialist, and a woman. Before I started teaching at the U of MO, I had sold several articles to the *Saturday Evening Post*, lived on a farm, raised a huge garden, stripped a tobacco crop, castrated baby pigs, raised orphan lambs, been happily married (most of the time), and had four children. During my academic career, I have been an adjunct (at Missouri we were called "others"), a part-timer, an instructor, supervisor of freshman composition, an assistant, associate, and full professor, an endowed chair-holder, a foremother, and lastly a distinguished emerita tutor. I am now an emerita everything. You name it and I was it. Through it all I have had one abiding interest—rhetoric and a continuing fascination with ways in which we use language and are used by language. So I speak with some authority because I have indeed "been there" and back. Today I want to tell you a story.

Those of us who have been around for awhile remember an article by William Riley Parker (titled "Where Do English Departments Come from?") that appeared in *College English* in February 1967. The part of that article that I have never forgotten was the allegory that he used. I can't seem to forget it. When I reread the article, I was amazed to discover that that allegory was only one paragraph, but it stays in my mind. Let me remind you of how it went. Parker tells us that English was born one hundred years ago—that was in 1967—so it would be roughly 1867. Its mother, the eldest daughter of Rhetoric, was Oratory, or what we now call speech. Its father was Philology, or what we now call linguistics. Their "marriage," he suggested, was shortlived, so English is therefore the child of a broken home. This unhappy fact accounts, perhaps, for its early feeling of independence and its later bitterness toward both parents. "I date the break with the mother, however," he continues, "not from the disgraceful affair she had with Elocution, but rather from the founding of the Speech Association of America in 1914, which brought the creation of many speech departments." English teachers, Parker concludes, absorbed in what they considered more important business, were neglecting speech by 1914 and losing all vital concern with linguistics in 1924. Here he drops his allegory.

Today I should like to take that allegory into the second half of the twentieth century when English grew up and became a mother. She was indeed independent and never found anyone that she thought was good enough to marry, but she became a single mother many times over. There were the two older children—Old English, who spent a lot of time with his cousins in Germany, and Middle English, who had a speech impediment diagnosed as Medieval Latin—Renaissance, called "Renny" for short, and American Literature, who was much younger and considered something of an upstart. Finally, there was Composition, a late child born when the mother was approaching menopause. He was never considered quite right. Several children had left home early. Linguistics, a half-brother to English, never felt part of the family and early ran away and set up house with Anthropology and thrived. For a long time, Speech, another half-brother, had lived with English; but after his association with Elocution, English just couldn't accept him, so he soon moved out. Speech later broke up with Elocution but in the sixties had a happy relationship with Rhetoric and a large and successful family. Composition was a happy child, much beloved by his rich uncle, Administration, but despised by his mother and forced to live in the basement. The whole family disapproved of his friends, especially Pedagogy. They thought Peddy should go live with Education on the other side of the academic railroad tracks, according to English. Old English and Middle English were the oldest, and they were snobbish—they didn't really want to be associated with the rest of the family.

Renny was a happy child, and American Lit grew up to be the largest of the children and had many friends. Around 1970 Composition struck up an acquaintance with Rhetoric, who was not getting along very well with Speech. Rhetoric was quite elderly and had let herself go. Speech was into other things and thought that Rhetoric was too old-fashioned. She had also lost her figure and needed a face-lift. Well, Composition thought Rhetoric was beautiful—he loved each one of her wrinkles and wanted to know more about them. And Rhetoric thought Composition was cheerful and sweet, but innocent. Well, the result was that Speech lost interest in Rhetoric, and Rhetoric took up with Composition on the rebound. Edwin Black and Lloyd Bitzer begged Rhetoric not to leave them. Composition took her into his basement room and they got along just fine. Composition's big brothers had never even heard of Rhetoric, but since she could speak Medieval Latin, Middle English thought she was probably okay. English was surprised to learn that Rhetoric came from a fine old family, numbering Aristotle and Plato among her ancestors. She was also extremely well connected with relatives in classics and philosophy. But these cousins thought Rhetoric had died some time ago and were surprised to see that she was still alive. Well, Composition and Rhetoric were married, and instead of a hyphenated last name, they used a slash and became Rhetoric/ Composition.

Now they began to join some cults. There was the 4Cs that Composition had been attending for a number of years. Now he dragged Rhetoric along, but Rhetoric was often excluded from the festivities. Rhetoric continued her association with the Rhetoric Society, but here Composition began to feel unwelcome. They attended the ISHR, but the Europeans still felt that Rhetoric had died in the eighteenth century and thought that she must be a ghost. And Composition—well, they felt that he was just an American upstart—something that *their* students might run around with in high school, but their university students were much too sophisticated for Composition. Rhetoric/Comp also felt that they should join the MLA mostly so that they could have their name in the directory and so they could get out of the basement room, which was cold and damp in December and was bothering Rhetoric's arthritis. Also, Rhetoric didn't understand why all the nice young people were sitting on the floor in the hallways in their good suits and why the senior scholars all had hair growing out of their ears. Composition explained that it had something to do with what was inside their heads. By this time Rhetoric was beginning to wonder about the marriage anyway. Composition wasn't so sweet anymore, but he turned out to have a lot of money thanks to his rich Uncle Administration. They also had several new journals to call their own now—Theresa Enos's *Rhetoric Review*, *JAC*, *CCC*, Victor's *PRE-TEXT*, the *Composition Chronicle*, *Rhetorica*, *Rhetorik*. They had become a media favorite.

After Rhetoric and Composition were married, they too had some children—there was the Writing Center, Writing across the Curriculum ("WAC" for short), WPA, and ESL—they were big on initials. But by this time Rhetoric and Composition were having their personal problems. Rhetoric didn't feel that she was always welcome at Composition's conferences, and Composition felt that Rhetoric was inclined to be snobbish about his friends, especially WPA and Tech Writing. Also, he was becoming very aware of Rhetoric's age. She wasn't really very feminine anymore. People were beginning to wonder if this marriage would last, but Comp and Rhet decided to stay together for the children's sake, and then they wrote to Dear Abby who told them to ask themselves if they would be better off with or without each other, so they decided to stick with it.

So in 1996 they took a trip together to Tucson to the RSA conference—sort of a second honeymoon. That was a great event for them—they had drinks with Speech, who had changed his name to Communications and who by this time had broken off completely with Elocution, who was languishing in a nursing home somewhere. But the latest news was that Elocution had had an emergency call from the Dole headquarters and had moved to Washington. The Comp/Rhetorics had a great time getting reacquainted with their cousins—Philosophy, who was as old as Rhetoric; Classics, who was even older; and even a cousin they hadn't met before—Folklore. It was a great family reunion—nobody was snobbish. Rhetoric and Classics and Philosophy discussed their arthritis; Speech and English discussed their common friend and mentor, Rhetoric; and Composition, of course, bought all the drinks—thanks to his rich uncle. The Doubletree Hotel lobby resonated with different languages. Hui Wu and Mary Garrett were speaking Chinese. Jan Swearingen and Dick Fulkerson were speaking Texan; Kathleen Welch and Jim Kinneavy were speaking Latin. Linda Ferreira-Buckley, Lynee Gaillet, and Win Horner were getting rowdy. They had had a little too much Scotch. But the latest gossip was that Rhetoric had been hanging out with Cheryl Glenn, Andrea Lunsford, and Catherine Hobbs and had become a feminist.

I don't want to pursue this allegory any further, but I do want to conclude with some caveats about the prospect of rhetoric. Knowing full well from the history rhetoric's inclination to get taken over, absorbed, raped, prostituted, hypothesized, and abandoned, I hope that rhetoric with all its age can keep its identity. I remember that when I proposed a division on rhetoric for the MLA, the board looked confused (as they truly are) and brushed it aside with the comment, "Well, isn't it all rhetoric?" Well, it isn't "all rhetoric" because when it's "all rhetoric," rhetoric becomes nothing. Critical theory may serve as one side of the coin, but let's not forget the generative, creative side—that finally informs us in teaching our students. And that is the final point I want to make: Let's never forget our connection with the classroom. Literature scholars delegated freshman comp to graduate students as fast as they could, and we are in danger of doing the same. Because we are involved with Aristotle, Plato, and Augustine, our English department colleagues afford those of us in the history of rhetoric some small respect that they sometimes deny to composition researchers. We need to remember our roots and our theoretical kinfolks. When we fail to meet in the bar and exchange stories with our cousins, we have lost something very important. Let's not forget in going forward into the future where we came from. I don't know how this soap opera allegory will continue in the next century. Just tune in to 2000 on your radio dial, or check RSA's home page on the Web, or better yet drop by the bar at the next RSA conference. We'll all be there.

MARVIN DIOGENES

University of Arizona

The Rhetoric Blues

The historical links between rhythm and blues and rhetoric are well known. The following landmarks from the rock 'n' roll 'n' rhetoric tradition, based on work by Chuck Berry and Elvis Presley, were performed at the conference's opening reception by Arizona's own English Department "Composition Blues Band": Barry Briggs, guitar; Larry Burkett, guitar; Clyde Moneyhun, guitar; John Warnock, bass; Marvin Diogenes, lyrics and vocals.

Rhetor B. Goode

Before the modern era, five hundred BC
They overthrew a tyrant down in Sicily
The people there contested every point they could
Taught by a sophist boy called Rhetor B. Goode
He never ever learned to read or write so well
But he could argue both sides as persuasive as hell

Go, go,
Go, Rhetor, go, go, go
Go, Rhetor, go, go, go
Go, Rhetor, go, go, go
Go, Rhetor, go, go, go
Rhetor B. Goode

When Rhetor got no tenure down at Syracuse
He went peripatetic, yes, he got real loose
Wearin' out his sandals ramblin' Athens way
The Greeks all gathered 'round to hear that Rhetor play
He said, "I'll teach you practical philosophy,
and the thing about the truth is its contingency"

Go, go . . .

Rhetor was a speaker of such wizardry
Made the best appear the worser for a modest fee
His potent words had power close to absolute
Don't ask about his ethics, boy, the point is moot
When Plato had a problem with that oversight
Begged him, "Rhetor be good tonight"

Go, go . . .

Rhetoric Hotel

Ever since my Plato left me
I found a new place to dwell
Among doubts and probabilities
in the Rhetoric Hotel

I'm so uncertain
I'm so uncertain, baby
I'm so uncertain I could cry

I said to Aristotle
"Please get me back on track"
He handed me some lecture notes
"Read these and you'll get the knack"

It's just a *technê*
It's just a *technê*, baby
It's just a *technê*, don't you cry

A guy dressed in a toga
Said his name was Cicero
He said, "Everything about everything
is all you need to know"

Along came old Quintilian
instituting oratory
He said, "Be a good guy all your life,
dare to be hortatory"

Knowledge and virtue
Knowledge and virtue, sonny
Knowledge and virtue show the way

In search of illumination
I went to Lunsford and Ede
How much collaboration
can two people really need?

I read the hotel bible
by Herzberg and Bizzell
It may not be inclusive
But the royalties are swell

It's not the gospel
It's not the gospel, baby
It's not the gospel, just a try

In the continental ballroom
Cheek to cheek with Derrida
He suavely whispered in my ear
"viva la *differánce*"

We're under deconstruction
No faith left in the word
It's terminal dysfunction
when all meaning's been deferred

I'm so uncertain
I'm so uncertain, always
I'm so uncertain, I could cry

Adjunct Blues

One was my BA
Masters made two
Finally got past ABD
My PhD is through
Now don't you
give me those adjunct blues

Cause I did everything
Lay off of those adjunct blues

Took all the classes
Read all the books
Listed the sources
Cited the shnooks
Wrote a dissertation
insightful and true
Then I wrote it all again
when you said to make it new

Now don't you
give me those adjunct blues
I did everything
Lay off of those adjunct blues

Got me a *vita*
Long as my arm
Letters testifyin'
to my scholarly charm
Sent out my *vita*
from Quebec to Peru
No one wants to hire me
My loans are coming due

Now don't you . . .

I'd work in the city
Breathe in the smog
Wouldn't mind the country
Sleep in a log
I'd serve on committees
With a heavy teaching load
I'd swallow all my theory
Heck, I'd even teach the modes

Now don't you . . .

Rhetoric Society Blues

Went down to Arizona
to a conference called RSA
I wanted a little fun in the sun
But I'm in panels all of the day

I got the Rhetoric Society blues
Each new title makes me squirm
I got the Rhetoric Society blues
Won't someone please define these terms

I've heard calls for counternarratives
Historiographies revisionist
Undermine the old imperatives
It's our duty to be derisionist

I've heard some earnest speakers
valorize liminal transgression
If order is so stultifyin'
Why do we sit still for these sessions

I got the Rhetoric Society blues
All this jargon makes me sweat
I got the Rhetoric Society blues
Are we speaking English yet?

I've heard about the centrality
of rhetorical analysis
If I hear about one more strategy
I'll get rhetorical paralysis

It's not enough to just understand
You're an old dog without some new tricks
Interpretation is old-fashioned and bland
You need radical hermeneutics

I got the Rhetoric Society blues
I can't figure out this deal
I got the Rhetoric Society blues
I ain't got no appeal

Knowledge is never simple
It's situated, disciplinary
Wherever it is you think you are
Turn around to face the contrary

I've heard about the future
in which all text will be hyper
In this hailstorm of verbiage
I'll need hyper windshield wipers

I got the Rhetoric Society blues
My headache is recursive
I got the Rhetoric Society blues
Inner peace is so e-lursive

I went to every session
I noted every word
Heteroglossic polyphony
I think that's what I heard
Nothing left to be foundational
Just blanks for us to fill in
We're living under erasure
in this carnivalesque cotillion

I got the Rhetoric Society blues
A pathetic way to feel
I got the Rhetoric Society blues
I ain't got no appeal
I got the Rhetoric Society blues
I ain't got no appeal

CAROLYN R. MILLER
North Carolina State University

Epilogue: On Divisions and Diversity in Rhetoric

When Richard Enos suggested that the twenty-fifth anniversary of the 1971 publication of *The Prospect of Rhetoric* would make an interesting program theme for the 1996 Rhetoric Society of America conference, I seized on the idea with gratitude. Not only did it answer a huge question for me as program planner, but it was exactly the kind of answer I wanted. For that book raised fundamental questions about rhetoric that I thought should be raised again, and it raised them in a way that I thought would be particularly beneficial for RSA.

As we discovered at the conference, *The Prospect of Rhetoric* serves as a generational marker. For those of the generation that participated in the two conferences leading to the book, it was a disciplinary coming-of-age: It put rhetoric on the national academic map. For the generation that came of age immediately afterwards, it marked the division of the old from the new. And for those in subsequent academic generations, it became an increasingly dusty library volume, now out of print.

Nevertheless, the aims addressed by the essays in the volume are again timely ones for rhetoric and rhetoricians: "to outline and amplify a theory of rhetoric suitable to twentieth-century concepts and needs." It's a goal worth taking up twenty-five years later as we contemplate the twenty-first century. For one thing, so much about rhetorical practice and available conceptual resources have changed since 1971 that the same outlines and amplifications of theory do not satisfy now. For another, our exigence for theorizing is quite different: Rhetoric is a prominent player on the national intellectual scene, as it wasn't twenty-five years ago. In part because of the reorientation and rethinking represented by *Prospect*, rhetoric is of interest to historians, anthropologists, political theorists, sociologists, literary scholars, and philosophers— intellectuals engaged in understanding the constructed nature of human thought and society. This broad and lively interest in rhetoric makes the aims of *Prospect* relevant again.

But rhetoric today is a house divided. Perhaps the most salient fact of rhetoric's academic existence in the United States is its division by institutional and educational history into two departmental homes, communication and English. There are lively and active communities of inquiry and criticism in both departmental locations, and too few scholars who are familiar with both. To be sure, both communities draw on common intellectual resources: the classics, of course, and the subsequent rhetorical tradition at least through the eighteenth century; many contemporary thinkers, such as Kenneth Burke, Chaïm Perelman, Stephen Toulmin, and many postmodernists; as well as aspects of the more empirical traditions of linguistics and psychology. And rhetoricians in the two departments also have in common the fact that they are usually a minority faction, often a disfavored one.

In spite of these common experiences, departments of communication and English, as twentieth-century artifacts, are separate and distinct operational units in most institutions of higher education—they train and hire different people, teach different courses and students, fight different institutional battles. Rhetoric in English has taken shape in dialectic with literary studies, whereas in communication the dialectic has been with empirical communication research. These two different shaping tensions have produced different debates, concepts, and bodies of work in rhetorical studies.

Rhetoricians in the two departments also have quite different connections with rhetorical pedagogy. In English departments rhetoric has drawn inspiration and motivation from the challenge of teaching writing, first at the basic level and more recently at advanced levels; in many English departments, in fact, rhetoric is synonymous with composition. Research and scholarship have drawn their issues and materials from classrooms and students. In communication departments, however, the introductory courses in public speaking and interpersonal communication have not played the focal role that the composition course has in English, and rhetoricians turn not to the student novice but to the expert practitioner in the world of public affairs or popular culture for their paradigm examples and objects of study.

Many at the RSA conference in Tucson remarked at the dramatically changed gender composition of the field in the past twenty-five years, but we should also note the change in the departmental affiliations of those who are rhetoricians. Only three of the forty scholars involved in the *Prospect* project were from English, whereas today the proportion of rhetoricians from English and communication may have tilted in the opposite direction, with continuing educational emphasis on the teaching of writing and the development of new doctoral programs in rhetoric and composition under the aegis of English departments. Not surprisingly, because it was published by the Speech Communication Association, *Prospect* has played a stronger role in disciplinary development in communication departments than in English. And this was another reason I was eager to feature it at the conference, as a way of reemphasizing the role of communication departments and of encouraging a readjustment of RSA membership.

Diversity can surely be a source of disciplinary vigor for rhetoric, but we should wonder whether rhetoric can be a discipline—and whether it can play an effective role in the academy or in intellectual life—if it is divided into two primary contingents that barely speak to each other. It is my hope for the Rhetoric Society of America that it should serve as the one organization where rhetoricians from all academic departments can work together and learn from each other, not only those from English and communication but also scholars from philosophy, history, and classics, as well. I think the Tucson conference proved that can happen.

In helping to select the papers for this volume, I hoped that we could create a collection that would represent the conference as an event in the history of RSA—who are the members now? what are their interests and styles? how does their work taken together create a picture of rhetorical studies in 1996? The picture created by the conference as a whole is instructive. In organizing the accepted papers into panels, I found that they fell into several fairly distinct areas, which I used to structure the program itself. There were 14 panels on rhetorical history, 11 on the conference theme, 10 on rhetorical theory and postmodernism, 9 on rhetorical criticism and public discourse, 9 on rhetoric and gender, 8 on rhetorical education, 7 on community and diversity, 7 on rhetoric of disciplines and professions, 5 on rhetorical media, and 3 roundtables on professional issues. Although it was impossible to represent the full scope of this work here, we have attempted to preserve this diversity, given the papers actually submitted for the volume. In addition, I was eager to have the volume emphasize the conference theme, by featuring papers that provided reflections on the 1971 *Prospect of Rhetoric* and speculations on the 1996 prospect of rhetoric. I think we have produced a volume with this scope and focus, as well as with good representation from rhetoricians in both communication and English.

As long as the academy retains its current form, the Speech Communication Association, the Conference on College Composition and Communication, and the Modern Language Association will serve continuing needs of rhetoricians affiliated with communication and English departments. The RSA and its journal, the *Rhetoric Society Quarterly*, can play an important role in helping rhetoric achieve some metadepartmental identity; it can turn division and difference into productive diversity. If rhetoric is the master art, it is not to be contained by one department or one scholarly association. But if it is to operate in the world of academic and disciplinary affairs, it should not allow itself to be fragmented into powerlessness.

Index

A

Abbott, Don Paul, 136
Aesthetics of rhetoric, 68
Agency, 38-40
Allen, Paula Gunn, 134
American Indian, 123
Anishinabe, 125, 126, 127, 129
Anthropology, 85, 86
Anzaldúa, Gloria, 134
Applied Linguistics, 84
Archival research, 8
Argument, 60, 63
Argumentational syntax
    searching, 194
Arnold, Carroll, 16, 17
Audience, 165-72
Aune, James, 70
Australian Structural Functional
    Linguistic School, 84
Automobile Travel, 10, 173
Aztlan, 135, 136

B

Bazerman, Charles, 6
Becker, Samuel, 38, 71
Benson, Tom, 70
Bernstein, Richard J., 95
Biesecker, Barbara, 59, 60, 101,
    103
Binarism, 158, 159, 161, 163
Binary logic, 10, 157, 159
Bitzer, Lloyd, 1, 3, 4, 11, 44, 45

Bizzell, Patricia, 4, 6
Black, Edwin, 1, 3, 4, 5, 7, 10, 69
Black, Max, 141
Black power movement, 44
Blair, Carole, 4, 191
Blair, David, 190
Boolean, 191, 193
Booth, Wayne, 21-23, 39, 83,
    91, 151
Britton, James, 150
Brockriede, Wayne, 83
Bryant, Donald C., 15
Burke, Kenneth, 19, 61, 78, 79,
    142, 146, 158, 159

C

Campbell, Karlyn Kohrs, 60,
    102, 157
Ceccarelli, Leah, 6
Charland, Maurice, 80
Chicano, 44, 135, 137
Chinese rhetoric, 43, 115-19
Clark, Gregory, 10, 171
Cole, Thomas, 53
Communication technologies, 46,
    83
Communication triangle, 165
Community, 5-7, 9, 11, 39, 44-
    46, 47, 80, 92, 181-84
    discourse, 153-56, 181-83
    national, 174, 177-79
Comparative rhetoric, 5, 8
Condit, Celeste, 80